RUTHLESSLY CARING

RUTHLESSLY CARING

AND OTHER PARADOXICAL MINDSETS LEADERS NEED TO BE FUTURE-FIT

BY AMY WALTERS COHEN

WILEY

This edition first published 2023

Registered Offices

John Wiley & Sons Ltd, The Atrium, Southern Gate, Chichester, West Sussex, PO19 8SQ, UK

John Wiley & Sons, Inc., 111 River Street, Hoboken, NJ 07030, USA

Editorial Office
The Atrium, Southern Gate, Chichester, West Sussex, PO19 8SQ, UK

For details of our global editorial offices, customer services, and more information about Wiley products visit us at www.wiley.com.

Wiley also publishes its books in a variety of electronic formats and by print-on-demand. Some content that appears in standard print versions of this book may not be available in other formats.

Library of Congress Cataloging-in-Publication Data

Names: Walters, Amy, author.
Title: Ruthlessly caring : and other paradoxical mindsets leaders need to be future-fit / by Amy Walters.
Description: First edition. | Hoboken, NJ : Wiley, 2023. | Includes index.
Identifiers: LCCN 2022056917 (print) | LCCN 2022056918 (ebook) | ISBN 9781394177172 (cloth) | ISBN 9781394187058 (adobe pdf) | ISBN 9781394187041 (epub)
Subjects: LCSH: Leadership—Forecasting. | Management—Technological innovations.
Classification: LCC HD57.7 .W355 2023 (print) | LCC HD57.7 (ebook) | DDC 658.4/092—dc23/eng/20221202
LC record available at https://lccn.loc.gov/2022056917
LC ebook record available at https://lccn.loc.gov/2022056918

Cover Design: Wiley

Set in 12.5/15pt Minion Pro by Straive, Chennai, India

SKY10039713_120822

To my family and friends, for all your love, laughter, and support.

CONTENTS

ACKNOWLEDGEMENTS

Many thanks go to all those who helped and encouraged me in the writing of this book.

With special thanks to Dominic Mahony, Kate Bamford, and Thomas Hacker.

PREFACE

This book will not make leadership easy, but it will help you evolve and expand your thinking. Consequently, if you are looking for a simple paint-by-numbers guide to leadership, this is not it.

Leading a business is hard and involves grappling with numerous conflicting demands, tackling unprecedented challenges, and making tough decisions. Especially in today's environment, where megatrends such as advancing technology, climate change, rising inequality, and hyper-connection via social media are converging, across all industries, leaders are finding themselves operating on shifting sands. Required to carve out success in a landscape that is constantly changing and highly complex.

This book tackles the reality of senior leadership and explores the mindsets and skills that determine high performance in today's context.

Specifically, whilst the title highlights the 'ruthlessly caring' mindset, there are in fact five paradoxical mindsets leaders need to thrive in today's business landscape:

1. ruthlessly caring
2. ambitiously appreciative
3. politically virtuous

4. confidently humble
5. responsibly daring.

These mindsets originated from interviews with award-winning leaders from around the world, who had been recognised for their future-thinking, innovation, and disruption. Following this, two years of research was carried out to dig deep into what underpins each mindset and how to develop it. This research also explored the nature of paradoxes and leadership identity.

While being heavily based in research (with evolutionary, occupational and neuropsychology woven in throughout), the book (hopefully!) avoids being overly academic, theoretical, or jargony. It aims to be practical and action orientated, synthesising what is most useful to know and staying focused on the 'what' and 'how' – what you need to do differently and how to do it.

In the spirit of staying practical, alongside the insights from research, there are numerous 'leader-to-leader' stories throughout the book. These were gathered via first-hand interviews and aim to bring key concepts and ideas to life with real-world examples. Each leader interviewed was candid in their advice and support, and it is hoped this will help others in senior leadership positions feel they are not alone, as well as spark fresh conversations and idea-sharing across leadership groups and networks. Essentially, these 'leader-to-leader' stories offer up practical wisdom – top tips and 'lessons learnt the hard way' – providing something of a learning fast-track, by enabling you to draw on a greater bank of experiences, maximising your own ability to exercise judgement and wisdom at critical moments.

It is worth emphasising that no leader mentioned in the book is being held up as perfect. None of the leaders interviewed in the initial research had perfectly mastered all five paradoxical mindsets. Not all the leaders cited as examples in text via second-hand sources have a 'perfect-10' track record of behaviour or performance. Similarly, the leaders interviewed for the 'leader-to-leader' stories would be the first to say there are still areas they are working on and are keen to develop. This is not a catalogue of leaders who are perfect and over-the-finish-line of development. It is a collation of leaders who have different strengths and development areas and who are on their own journey with it. This book is therefore not about helping you on a quest to be perfect – it aims to help you on a quest to keep developing, unlearning, and relearning, so you can adapt effectively to the context you are in and the challenges you will face, now and in the years to come.

Finally, whilst many people in the corporate world talk about 'future-proofing' – this book instead refers to leaders becoming 'future-fit'. The notion of 'future-proof' suggests building up a protective shield against the future. It suggests installing something fixed and durable against all elements, whatever comes. This is an unhelpful mindset to have. The future is not something to be guarded against, tomorrow will come, circumstances will change, and events can be influenced. The last thing leaders need is to be 'proofed' against the future. What they need is to be fit and well-matched to the context they are in and adaptable to changing conditions.

Other key points to flag to you as a reader:

- **This book is best nibbled and digested slowly (after Chapters 1 and 2, go straight for the chapters that appeal the most).** Like a buffet of evidence and brain food, there's a lot in here and it will be hard to digest in one go. Read Chapters 1 and 2. But then, after that, do not feel the need to work through Chapters 3–7 diligently in a linear way. Go straight to the mindset which looks most appealing to you. Tuck in. Digest. Come back later to explore something else.

- **Read the last chapter.** Implementing these paradoxes into your day-to-day world requires identity-level change. The final chapter discusses identity in detail so do not miss it out. Understanding how to expand your identity is critical if you want to embrace all five paradoxical mindsets and enhance your leadership performance.
- **Be critical. Feel free to violently disagree or agree, add in your own ideas and thinking** – these are ideas based on interviews with leaders and research into the topics of megatrends, paradoxes, identity, and each of the mindsets. Not all concepts are new (that would be bizarre and worrying), it is an evidence-based proposal that aims to add to existing knowledge and ideas. It can and should be challenged, discussed, added to, reviewed; it is a contribution to what is known about leadership, not a conclusion. It is a synthesis and proposal to spark further thoughts and prompt an evolution in leadership practice.

CHAPTER 1

MEGATRENDS THAT ARE RESHAPING THE WORLD

Your assumptions are your windows on the world. Scrub them off every once in a while, or the light won't come in.

—Isaac Asimov, writer and professor of biochemistry

There are certain periods and moments throughout history where significant change and trends have occurred, yet leaders failed to respond to them prior to their impact – often caught out by continuing to think and operate in outdated ways.

Take World War I, for example – the course of events had started to be shaped over 160 years earlier, as the first Industrial Revolution got underway.

In response to the need to find efficient ways to scale production, British manufacturers invented game-changing technologies, such as steam locomotives for army transport, ironclad steam-powered warships, and cast-iron cannons. Enabled by advancements in metal-shaping precision, the United States, Germany, and France brought in the first machine guns and rapid-fire rifles.

These technological changes disrupted the business-as-usual routines in militaries across the world. However, many leaders failed to shift their thinking and approach and were slow to respond even when the stark new reality of war was brutally apparent. The French army, for example, was still using the same drill formations and colourful uniforms as they had been 100 years previously, but now they were sending their troops to face machine guns in those bright blue coats, red trousers, and plumed helmets: a tragic case of leaders failing to adapt to the times they were in.[1,2]

History is also littered with examples of business leaders who failed to evolve their thinking and keep pace with the trends occurring. Take America's so-called 'retail apocalypse' as an example. In 2017, the overall disposable income in America rose along with an increase in consumer spending, and yet many prominent retailers found themselves in trouble. By April 2017, already the number of bankruptcies had nearly surpassed the entire total of the previous year.[3]

Whilst the media's use of the term 'apocalypse' was not without controversy, there is no doubt that many retailers were (and continue to be) hit hard by a fast-changing landscape.[4] The rise in online shopping, shifts towards experiential consumer spending (i.e., restaurants and travel over material possessions), and an oversupply of malls changed the game for brick-and-mortar retail stores. But, many leaders missed the defining issue of the day: shopper experience.[5] They did not realise they needed to switch from a transaction mindset focused on, 'how do we sell more stuff?' to a value-creation mindset exploring, 'how do we create value beyond the transaction?'[6] This mismatch between context and thinking led to several years of industry devastation, and in 2019, American retail store closures due to bankruptcy reached a new record high.

Why is this relevant to you? Because the business rulebook is being rewritten. The context in which senior leaders are operating has fundamentally altered, and a significant recalibration of thinking is required.

Of course, there have always been turning-point moments where specific industries were disrupted, with leaders forced to evolve their approach or risk going under. But what is different today is the scale, speed, and complexity of the change occurring in the business world. At least 12 megatrends are interacting and redefining 'the way the business world works', as a whole, not piece by piece. Every industry is being disrupted as numerous trends converge.

Alongside these trends, company life expectancy is shrinking, with sustained high performance becoming ever more elusive. Specifically, there is a long-term trend of declining corporate longevity, with the average lifespan of a company on the Standard and Poor's 500 Index (S&P 500) currently at 20 years, having reduced from 36 years in 1980, and forecast to shorten further to 16 years throughout the 2020s.[7] Credit Suisse reviewed the reasons for company removal from the S&P 500 Index, between 2000 and 2016, and found 52% of these removals were a result of merger and acquisition activity and 32% were due to business failure.[8] Consequently, while some of this shortened performance lifespan can be accounted for by M&A activity, a third cannot. It is also clear that younger companies are outperforming long-standing companies, indicating that leaders are finding it increasingly difficult to sustain high performance in the long term and keep well-established organisations successful.

To sustain high performance in today's megatrends environment, leaders must challenge their entrenched assumptions and embrace new ways of thinking. As survey results show, 60% of C-suite leaders report that these mega trends require them to think and act differently,[9] with 79% of C-suite leaders agreeing that senior leaders throughout their organisation will need to adopt a different set of mindsets for their business to succeed in the future.

The key message here is that leaders cannot tackle new challenges with old thinking and outdated approaches: the game has changed. A new form of leadership will be required to take on the scale, speed, and complexity of changes occurring. A fundamental shift in thinking and decision-making is called for.

Before we dig into how leadership thinking needs to evolve to match the context that leaders are facing, let us first explore the drivers of change: the megatrends.

The Megatrends Shaping the Current and Future Leadership Context

Megatrends are major patterns or directions of development that occur at a global scale. They are the driving forces that define the world today and shape the world of tomorrow. They permeate all sectors and impact all types of organisations.

As shown in Figure 1.1, reports and forecasting data from businesses, governments, and think tanks collectively show how at least 12 megatrends are shaping the current and future landscape. Therefore if you wish to be aligned with the times you are in, lead in a way that is 'future-fit', and safeguard the future of your organisation, these are the global trends you need to be aware of and actively consider.

Let us look at each megatrend in more detail:

Technological Changes

- **Advances in technology and biological science.**

  Technology is advancing in multiple directions at great speed.[10] For years, there has been rapid innovation and progress across many areas of technology; for example, in physical technology (e.g., with autonomous vehicles, drones, 4D printing, and robotics) and digital technology (e.g., with the Internet of Things, edge computing, 5G, digital twins,

Advances in technology and biological science	Aging populations and multigenerational workforces	Big data and the rise of the behavioural economy	Climate change and scarcity of resources
Evolving workforce and customer expectations	Global skills gap and competition for talent	Growing numbers of disruptive start-ups	Hyper-connectivity through social media
Increasing and high levels of inequality	Rising geopolitical tensions	Shifting economic powers	Urbanisation

Figure 1.1 The 12 megatrends shaping the current and future leadership context.

digital platforms, digitally extended realities, blockchain, and distributed ledgers).

Similarly, in fields like material technology, 2D materials (namely, graphene and borophene) have sparked huge excitement and investment over recent years. Specifically, these new monoatomic materials are super-strong, flexible, have extraordinary heat conductance, and conduct electricity a thousand times better than copper. They have the potential to fully charge an electric car in minutes, unlock clean drinking water for millions, improve health testing, and create a new generation of electronics.[11,12]

Meanwhile, already artificial intelligence is all around us in various forms, and, with the advances in quantum computing, 5G connectivity, and precision sensors, much progress is anticipated in the next decade around human augmentation (where technology enhances our human capabilities, either permanently or temporarily).[13]

Significant advancements are also being made in the field of biological science, with the past decade seeing a growing wave of innovation in synthetic biology and microbiology. For example, microbiome advances ('microbiomes' being the communities of bacteria, fungi, viruses, and their genes that naturally live on and in our bodies) are expected to influence innovation of nearly every industry, with microbiome applications unlocking a wealth of new products, services, and operational approaches to tackling key challenges like climate disruption, chronic diseases, and urban pollution.[13] As Steve Jobs put it, 'the biggest innovations in the 21st century will be at the intersection of biology and technology. A new era is beginning.'[14]

Leadership implications: The pace of technological advancement is hard to comprehend. The impact of all the innovation occurring in different sectors is nearly impossible to anticipate. What is clear is that no organisation is exempt: leaders must stay alert to change and drive ongoing transformation to survive and stay relevant. Whether it is staying ahead of the market and harnessing new technologies or keeping up with market disruptions and protecting their business against the emerging risks that technologies present, no business is immune.

It is also critical for leaders to remember that, even though technological advancements are driving change, investing in the right technologies is only part of the challenge. People (i.e., human emotions, responses, and behaviours) remain the determining factor in whether a transformation is successful.[15]

- **Big data and the rise of the behavioural economy.**

Like the size of the solar system, the exponential growth of data is difficult to get your head around. Every year, over 94 zettabytes of data is created, captured, copied, and consumed.[16] Every day, 319.6 billion emails are sent and over 28 petabytes of data is generated by wearable devices.[17,18] Every minute, close to 42 million WhatsApp messages are exchanged.[19] And, this is just a snapshot. The amount of data in existence is skyrocketing and it has frequently been said that the world's most valuable resource is no longer oil but data. But it is the insight into human behaviour that holds real value.

By harvesting and analysing the wealth of data generated about our lives, organisations can now understand and shape behaviour like never before, using increasingly precise and sophisticated tactics of persuasion. There is increasing awareness that if something is free or low-cost, as a user, you and your data are the product they are selling. But it still does not stop us entering our details or clicking 'accept all' when asked to 'allow cookies'. As a megatrend report published by EY stated:[13] 'we unwittingly reveal more about our desires and fears to search engines than to our families or friends. Our phones and social media platforms have more data about our behaviours, preferences, and states of mind than we may realize'.

Leadership implications. While the advancement of behavioural economics (the study of the factors influencing human decision-making) can be a force for good, with governments and organisations using the insight positively to help people lead healthier lives and make more planet-friendly choices, the potential to exploit data is also very real. As we enter an era where the datasphere is growing and behavioural insight is the most valuable commodity, both individuals and leaders will need to tread carefully.

- **Hyper-connectivity through social media.**

Current figures show 58.4% of the world's population now uses social media,[20] with the average user spending 2 hours 26 minutes on social networks per day.[21] While the percentage of the population using social media is steadily increasing (by an average of 10.1% year-on-year), the time spent appears to have plateaued (averaging 2 hours 22 minutes for the past five years).[20]

Social media is still predominantly about connecting with friends, family, and communities across the world; however, for a while now, these platforms have not just been a place to connect but a key source of news. For example, a survey by Pew Research Centre showed how 48% of adults in America get their news from social media 'often' or 'sometimes'.[22]

Similarly in the United Kingdom, reports from Ofcom show how, while TV is still the most-used platform for news, 49% of adults also use social media as a key news source.[23]

News via social media is unquestionably quick and easy, but there is a catch. A study by the Massachusetts Institute of Technology (MIT) revealed how false news spreads more rapidly on social media than real news – by a considerable margin.[24] The MIT researchers analysed data sets from the social network Twitter and found that false news stories are 70% more likely than true news stories to be retweeted. Furthermore, it takes true stories six times longer to reach 1,500 people as it does for false stories to reach the same number of people.

Combine this with the fact 'deepfakes' are getting harder and harder to spot, as AI algorithms are able to fabricate increasingly realistic audio, video, and text-based content – content depicting events that never happened and showing people doing and saying things they never did or said. This exemplifies the notion that we are now in a 'Post-Truth' era, where facts are less influential in shaping public opinion than appeals to emotion and personal belief. 'Alternative facts' can be created, with almost anything 'becoming true' and spreading rapidly through social media – whether it is correct or not.

Leadership implications. At a societal level, the impact of hyper-connectivity through social media is a very mixed bag of blessings and concerns. On the one hand, this connectivity helps us as a society to learn, fight crime, help others in our community, and raise awareness of important issues. But it also amplifies inequalities, keeps us addicted to our phones, leaves us vulnerable to misinformation, polarises views, and has been correlated with increased depression and suicidal behaviour.[13,25,26]

At a leadership level, social media also has power to both destroy and build a brand (or career). The fact that images, news, and information (including misinformation and disinformation) can spread like wildfire through social media, reaching a global audience in seconds, means leaders and their organisations are more exposed than ever.[27] One fake story, one photo, one lapse in judgment – and profits can slump dramatically overnight, with calls for resignations being made. In today's hyper-connected age, the reputational risk is huge and the option of being able to 'brush a bad decision under the carpet' is no more.

Demographic Changes

- **Ageing populations and multigenerational workforces.**

The age structure of our society is steadily shifting. In 1950, the median age was a sprightly 23 (i.e., half of the population was younger than 23, half was older). Today, the median age is 30 and by the end of the century, it has been forecast to have risen to 42.[28] Factors such as wars and epidemics will continue to cause fluctuations, but as a species, we tend to live longer.

Young people are also having fewer children, with global fertility rates gradually declining.[29]

Increasing life expectancy mixed with declining birth rates means many countries now have an ageing population, with a growing number of citizens over the age of 65 and a gradually shrinking number of people in the traditional working-age pool (i.e., aged between 25 and 64 years). For example, projections indicate that by 2050, one in every four persons in Europe and Northern America could be aged 65 years or over.[29]

Leadership implications. Amongst the implications of this for healthcare systems, urban planning, and the 'grey pound' market, this shift in demographics also means the workforce is more age-diverse than ever before. For the first time in human history, many organisations already have five different generations working side by side. Workforce demands and career patterns are changing, and talent attraction, development, and retention strategies will need to keep pace.

- **Global skills gap and competition for talent.**

  Global talent shortages are the highest they have been in over a decade, with 75% of employers reporting difficultly in filling roles (rising from 31% reporting difficulty in 2010).[30] By 2030, studies have predicted that there will be a global talent shortage of more than 85 million people (roughly equivalent to the population of Germany).[31]

  Aside from the human cost, in terms of unemployment levels remaining high while workforce participation stagnates, such shortages impair productivity and hamstring businesses from innovating and evolving in the way they need in order to stay effective and relevant. Financially, it is also likely to cost nations trillions of dollars in unrealised annual revenues.[31]

  What is going on is a growing mismatch between the types of skills employers need and number of individuals with these skills in the talent pool; demand is outstripping supply. Part of the reason for this is shifting demographics, with low birth rates and ageing populations shrinking the size of the working-age talent pool in many countries. However, the main cause is the pace of change being driven by the application and integration of new technologies (such as AI, machine learning, robotics, and automation).

These advancements are changing the nature of work and creating a highly dynamic skills landscape, with many roles becoming obsolete and many more new roles and skills becoming needed.[32] As statistics show, 1 in 3 jobs are likely to change radically as individual tasks are automated and adoption of technology increases.[33] Furthermore, 40% of HR leaders report that they cannot devise skill development solutions fast enough to meet evolving skill needs.[34]

Leadership implications. Across all sectors, effective talent management is quickly becoming a number one priority for senior leaders.[34] Specifically, leaders are having to review how they can identify the critical 'hard' and 'soft' skills they need, optimise the talent already in the business (via upskilling, reskilling, rotations, and redeployments), acquire and outsource talent as necessary, enhance their employee experience, and create a culture of continuous learning within their organisation.

Environmental Changes

- **Climate change and scarcity of resources.**

Climate change is already affecting every region on Earth in multiple ways, causing intense droughts, heatwaves, water scarcity, wildfires, coastal flooding, catastrophic storms, food insecurity, and declining biodiversity. Climate-driven change is also happening much faster than initially thought, with satellite data showing how the Himalayan glaciers that supply water to 800 million people in South Asia are melting twice as fast as previous estimates suggested,[35] and that 300 million people worldwide (not 120 million as first thought) will be subject to coastal flooding by 2050 due to sea-level rise.[36]

To put climate change in context, throughout history, changes in Earth's orbit around the sun (referred to as

Milankovitch cycles) have shifted greenhouse gas concentrations and caused global temperatures to fluctuate between ice ages (low CO_2) and interglacials (high CO_2). But before the Industrial Revolution, atmospheric concentrations of CO_2 during these interglacial CO_2 highs had not exceeded 300 parts per million (ppm). Today, global CO_2 concentrations are well above 400 ppm, having risen rapidly over the past few centuries and in recent decades.[37] Global temperatures have, in turn, increased to 0.87°C (rising from −0.52°C in 1904). This 1.28°C temperature shift may not sound like a lot, but it is steep in planetary terms and enough to disrupt natural systems significantly.

The influence of human activity is undisputed, and scientists have flagged that a global temperature rise of 1.5°C (above the pre-industrial level of -0.52°C) is the indicator point at which climate impacts will become increasingly harmful for humans and other species on the planet. There is now a 50:50 chance of the annual global temperature temporarily reaching that point for at least one of the next five years.[38]

Theoretically, it is still possible to limit the global warming increase to 1.5°C, but realistically that target is now out of reach (without unprecedented, drastic, and immediate action). In line with the Paris Agreement, leaders and nations need to pursue all efforts to restrict warming to below 2°C. Several tipping points may be triggered in a range of 1.5 to <2°C global warming (such as the collapse of the Greenland and West Antarctic ice sheets and die-off of low-latitude coral reefs), but more are likely at 2–3°C of warming.[39]

However, implementing all the climate and energy policies currently in place will not be enough; they put us on track for warming of 2.5–2.9°C by 2100.[37] While the timelines seem long, it is action now that is critical, as various tipping points will lead to cascading and irreversible consequences.[40] There are options available in every sector that can reduce emissions between 40–70% by 2050, but immediate and audacious action is needed now to keep the below 2°C threshold within reach.[41]Specifically, reducing greenhouse gas emissions requires particular focus on two fundamental areas: decarbonisation of energy systems and reducing emissions from food production and food waste.[37]

This challenge is compounded by the fact that the global population is still increasing, and it is estimated to grow to around 8.5 billion by 2030 and reach 9.7 billion in 2050.[29] That is an extra 2 billion people (or, put another way, another India and China) and as populations and economies grow, demand for natural resources (including energy, food, and water) will continue to increase. Pair this trend, not only with climate change but the fact that we are already using 70% more resources than the Earth can replenish each year, and it can be clearly seen that we are heading towards an 'ecological credit crunch'.[42]

Leadership implications. Awareness of these issues is not new and progress is being made, but it is not happening fast enough or at the scale required to prevent the most severe effects from being unleashed. Actions from individuals, organisations, and governments can still make a difference to the future. But business leaders must lead the way, delivering on pledges to decarbonise their business models and entire value chains (where possible aiming to be carbon-negative, not just carbon-neutral) and taking bold, targeted action to drive the immense change needed to tackle the climate crisis and resource scarcity challenges.

- **Urbanisation.**

  By 2030, it is estimated that 60% of the world's population will be living in cities.[43] The increase in urban living is forecast to be heavily concentrated in India, China, and Nigeria, but across the world, there will be a rise in the number and power of 'megacities' (i.e., cities with more than 10 million inhabitants),[44] with reports showing how some cities already outpower countries in terms of GDP.[45]

  During the COVID-19 pandemic, the trend of urbanisation stalled somewhat, with many fleeing city life in favour of more remote locations. However, reports from the United Nations indicate this city exodus was only a temporary stalling, with the global urban population still on track to grow by another 2.2 billion people in the next 30 years.[46]

  On the one hand, urban growth brings investment wealth, employment, and education opportunities, but it also presents numerous challenges around housing, sanitation, energy demand, air pollution, overcrowding, urban poverty, and traffic congestion. Consequently, there is a strong drive towards sustainable urbanisation – i.e., urban design and planning, which does not exacerbate inequalities but instead enables economic opportunities for all, reduces greenhouse gas emissions, protects people's well-being, and ensures urbanisation occurs in harmony with rural development.[46,47]

  Leadership implications. Urbanisation not only has implications for business leaders in terms of office location and design but presents numerous opportunities for those organisations that can respond to the requirements of sustainable urbanisation.

There are also implications of this trend for leaders to consider around people's well-being. Many research studies document the benefits of nature on well-being,[48] with specific benefits including enhanced social interactions,[49] improved manageability of life tasks,[50] better memory and attention,[51] as well as increased imagination and creativity.[52] However, with rapid urbanisation, never will so many people be so far removed from the natural world. To enhance well-being and performance, leaders may therefore increasingly need to consider how they can help their workforce reap the benefits that connection to nature provides.

Economic Shifts

- **Shifting economic powers.**

The world's economic centre has long been drifting across from North America and Europe over to Asia. By 2030, reports forecast that China will have overtaken the United States as the world's largest economy (on all accounts, including GDP, population size, technological investment, and military spending); however, how long China will sustain this economic lead is a matter of intense debate.[53]

By 2040, the economic power of E7 (China, India, Indonesia, Brazil, Russia, Mexico, and Turkey) could be double the size of that of G7 (the United States, the United Kingdom, France, Germany, Japan, Canada, and Italy), from being the same size in 2015 and half the size in 1995,[54] with fast-ageing economic heavyweights gradually losing ground on the global GDP table to countries with younger populations (**Note: the 'E7' is not actually a forum or alliance, like the G7, but merely an economic concept*).

Vietnam and the Philippines are also expected to experience the greatest improvement in their GDP rankings. Vietnam, for example, was one of only a few countries to post GDP growth in 2020 when the pandemic hit, with growth slowing to 2.58%

in 2021 (due to the emergence of the Delta variant) but then rebounding to above 5.5% in 2022.[55]

Meanwhile, Africa is a continent set to become a larger player in the future global economy, with the combination of technological connectivity, global trade, and continued growth in working-age population creating the potential to supercharge productivity and leapfrog traditional models of linear growth.[56]

Leadership implications. To effectively navigate this gradually shifting balance in the global economy, business leaders will need to pay even closer attention to trade patterns, policies, and shifting global value chains. Multinational organisations will also face a new breed of competitors from emerging countries looking to establish their place on the global stage.

- **Growing numbers of disruptive start-ups.**

With advances in technology lowering traditional barriers to market entry, flood gates have opened in terms of start-ups being able to quickly enter and disrupt well-established industries. Often without 'owning' or 'providing' very much in the traditional sense, it is possible for start-ups to leverage technology, connect suppliers directly with consumers, and fundamentally change consumer behaviour (for example, in payments, transportation, delivery, and health).

A few years back, this sparked the emergence of the so-called 'unicorn companies': privately owned start-up companies valued at or over $1 billion. Venture capitalist Aileen Lee coined the term 'unicorn' to represent the statistical rarity of such successful ventures, and these companies were hailed as impressive outliers.[57] Today, however, 'unicorns' are no longer rare but plentiful. Research shows that at the start of 2016, there were 165 unicorns, and by mid-2021, there were 743, an increase of 350% in 5.6 years.[58] Current figures show there are over 1,100 'unicorn' companies, mostly in China and the United States but with an increasing number emerging in India. Now there are also 'decacorn companies', private start-ups valued at or over $10 billion, and even a few 'hectocorns', start-ups valued at over $100 billion.

Leadership implications. Whether from start-ups, supply chains, or geopolitical tension, disruption is commonplace in today's business landscape, with 87% of board members reporting market disruptions to have become increasingly frequent and 83% reporting disruptions to have become increasingly impactful.[59] Pressure is mounting on leaders to keep successfully transforming their business and do so continuously in the face of disruption; the ability to reinvent and innovate becoming ever more important. Organisations cannot afford to wait for others to disrupt them, they must disrupt themselves. To keep continuously transforming in this way, leaders need to ensure their workforce is highly adaptable and skilled at embracing and implementing change, and, that their organisation's culture encourages continuous learning, improvement, and experimentation. In addition, leaders and individuals throughout the organisation will need to should be hyper-vigilant to the changes, threats, and opportunities arising in the market.

Societal Changes

- **Increasing and high levels of inequality.**

Over the past two decades, global inequalities between countries have declined, but income inequality within most countries has increased, with the income gap between the top 10% and bottom 50% of individuals within countries almost doubling across that time frame. Specifically, the latest World Inequality Report[60] highlights how the richest 10% of the global population currently take home 52% of the income, whilst the poorer half of the global population earn just 8%.

This gap widens even further when you look at wealth (i.e., the valuable assets and items owned over and above income). In terms of wealth, 50% of the global population owns just 2% of the global total, while the richest 10% owns 76% of all wealth, with the very top 1% owning 38% of total wealth.[61]

Many existing inequalities were also exacerbated by the COVID-19 pandemic; for example, research in the UK highlighted how the pandemic disproportionately impacted those with less money, fewer resources, lower levels of qualifications, women, and people from minoritised racial and ethnic groups.[61,62,63]

Similarly, when it comes to climate change, the most vulnerable communities in society will be hit first and worst by its effects (despite having done the least to cause the damage). Social media, whilst sometimes a force for good in terms of raising awareness, also exacerbates inequality tensions by providing a platform for the very wealthy to promote their lavish lifestyles. Unsurprisingly, frustration is bubbling at the unfairness within current economic and social systems which, in various ways, operate on the premise that 'the more you have, the more I give you'.[64]

However, despite high and increasing levels of inequality being a persistent challenge in nearly all countries, it is getting harder and harder for governments to tackle issues (such as economic inequality) because while private wealth has risen, public wealth has sunk (in most cases to negative or close to zero).[60] Businesses leaders consequently have a critical role to play in forging new systems.

Leadership implications. Organisations must step up to tackle all forms of inequality, with leaders identifying and addressing the systemic barriers and helping to create a more equitable system for low-income groups and marginalised communities.

Amongst other actions, this includes making life-enhancing products and services affordable and accessible to all, providing opportunities for decent employment, driving progress and tangible action in relation to diversity and belonging, distributing value more equitably throughout supply chains, and broadening participation in governance and ownership.[65]

- **Evolving workforce and customer expectations.**

  Expectations on business and business leaders are shifting substantially in numerous ways. For example, when it comes to customer service, trends like advancing technology and hyper-connectivity have led people to expect an immediate 'always-on' service, with 83% of customers expecting to interact with someone immediately when they contact a company.[66]

  Furthermore, given the amount of data available and number of AI algorithms often working in the background, consumers and employees alike are expecting an increasingly streamlined and personalised experience. For example, 71% of consumers expect companies to deliver personalised interactions, and 67% get frustrated when this does not happen;[67] similarly, employees want development experiences that are tailored for them, with over 75% of learners valuing personalised course recommendations that are based on their own career goals and specific skills gaps.[68]

  There has also been a dramatic shift since the pandemic in terms of employee expectations around flexible working, with 80% of employees wanting to work at least two days remotely per week and 85% of people who are currently on a hybrid work model wanting to continue with this model in future.[69,70]

  Swelling awareness around global challenges (such as climate change) also means both consumers and employees are expecting more from organisations and their leaders in terms of positive social action and sustainability. Specifically:

- 86% of people expect CEOs to publicly speak out on societal challenges[62]
- 66% agree CEOs should take the lead on change rather than wait for governments to impose change on them[62]
- 74% of customers say a company's sustainability practices matter more now than a year ago[71]
- 67% of people have a strong expectation that their employer has a greater purpose and will provide a job that has a meaningful impact on society (with 25% stating they just would never work for a company that does not offer this greater purpose and societal impact).[57]

Recent survey findings also show how this expectation on businesses to be purpose-led is only increasing, with 84% of employees reporting it to be 'very important' or 'important' for them to work for an organisation that positively impacts society.[72]

Leadership implications: To thrive in the twenty-first century, leaders must stay tuned in and keep pace with the multiple ways in which workforce and customer expectations are evolving. Alongside refreshing solutions and services, leaders need to keep their employee value proposition and organisation culture aligned to the times. In particular, purpose and sustainability are the lenses through which a business is increasingly judged; people are demanding greater responsibility from the organisations they work for, buy from, and invest in. Consequently, to sustain business performance long term, it is vital that leaders recognise and embrace this expanded mandate.

Political Changes

- **Rising geopolitical tensions.**

At a point in history when shared global challenges require urgent collaborative action, tensions between world powers are intensifying and society is more fragmented than ever. Russia's invasion into Ukraine, for example, represented the largest, most dangerous military mobilisation in Europe since WWII, resulting in immense and catastrophic damage, with a risk of further intentional or accidental escalation between NATO and Russia.[73]

Meanwhile, in what has been dubbed the 'Technomic Cold War' (a potent blend of technology and economics), the United States and China are competing to be the dominant superpower in next-generation technologies, such as AI, quantum computing, 5G networks, big data, and advanced weaponry.[13] This 'tech race' has so far resulted in a bitter trade war, with hundreds of billions of dollars' worth of tariffs imposed on one another's goods.[74] Alongside tariffs, governments are also increasingly using corporate blacklists, cyberattacks, and weaponising disinformation (i.e., using data and social media to manipulate the behaviour of the masses), with the lines between business and politics becoming increasingly blurred.[75]

Underneath these tensions, populism is fuelling protectionism. Growing economic inequality is driving a global rise in populist politics, i.e., the rise of parties or individuals claiming to represent the people against the 'elites'.[76,77] Populism can be left- or right-wing but tends to share certain characteristics, one of which is nationalism: the assertion of a nation's identity and right to self-governance, with the interests of that nation placed above all others. Whether domestically from political rivals, or externally from other countries and supranational organisations, the notion of 'taking back control' has been reverberating across many countries;[78] a trend that may only amplify as the national-security implications of climate change are felt (such as resource conflicts, food and energy shortages, and forced migrations).

The use of social media is also exacerbating political tensions and societal fragmentation, by polarising views and providing fertile ground for the spread of misinformation.[79,80]

Leadership implications. Zooming out from specific examples and causes, this rising geopolitical tension has numerous macro effects on the global economy. In particular, leaders today must grapple with ongoing supply-chain disruption (with supply chains shifting from being leaner and efficient to more diversified, resilient, and localised),[81] changes in labour markets, varying inflation outlooks, and the stifling impact such levels of geopolitical risk has on innovation.[82]

That's a whistle-stop tour of the megatrends.

It is a lot to take in. The key takeaway point though is that these are not predictions, they are trends that already exist and are gaining momentum. The question is therefore not so much 'what's on the horizon?', but 'are you as a leader ready to face and thrive in this megatrends environment?'

A Washing-Machine Effect: Interactions and Tensions

It is often tempting to compartmentalise megatrends into neat little boxes. Here, for ease of reading, the trends were categorised under the headline buckets of: 'technological', 'demographic', 'environmental', 'economic', 'societal', and 'political'. However, in reality – the megatrends are not neatly compartmentalised at all. They are much messier.

As Figure 1.2 shows, the trends overlap and interact with one another, meaning leaders across all domains are having to face a complex medley of challenges, threats, and opportunities. For many senior leaders, this modern business environment can feel like being in a washing machine; everything is churning around, at speed, in constant motion, with no let-up to breathe and take stock of the surroundings.

And the word 'complex' is not used flippantly. As Margaret Heffernan articulates, the business environment leaders operate in is 'complex' rather than 'complicated'.[83] The useful distinction being that:

- **Complicated situations** are tricky, but essentially linear problems that can be broken down into stages and tackled once enough information is gathered. Eventually, in a complicated

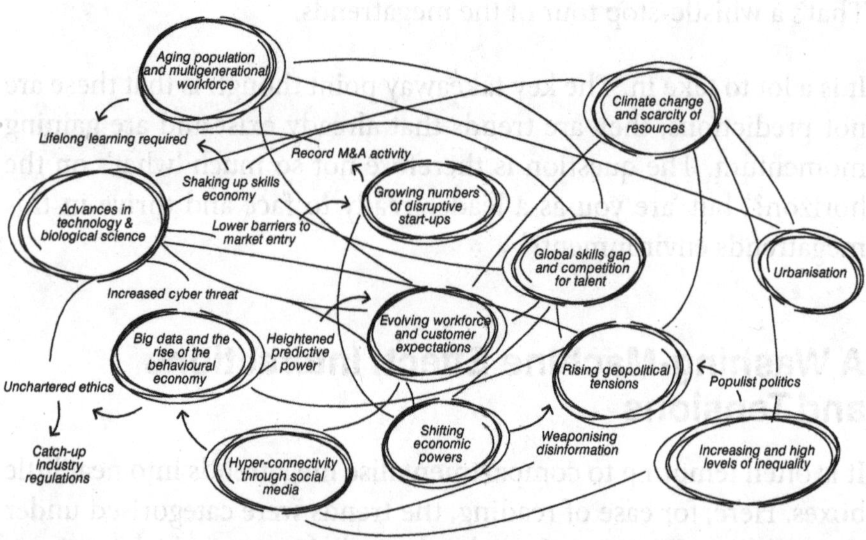

Figure 1.2 The 'washing-machine effect' created by megatrends accelerating and interacting.

situation, a solution or decision can be reached, with aspects of the process automated.

- **Complex situations** contain many multifaceted interdependent factors. These systems are not linear; they are more like a spider's web. Consequently, it is impossible to break the challenge down into stages and tackle it in a sequential way.[84]

The megatrend environment is without doubt in the complex category, and, within such complex systems, paradoxes abound.

Paradoxes Are Endemic in the Megatrend Context

As we will explore further in Chapter 2, a paradox is where 'two seemingly opposite yet independent states need to coexist over time in order for success to occur'.[85] In today's complex 'washing-machine' environment, where many different megatrends are gaining momentum, converging, and interacting, paradoxes are endemic.

Megatrends such as advancing technology, climate change, rising inequality, and hyper-connection via social media are all converging and combining, forcing leaders to address an array of different paradoxes. For example, leaders are required to create long-term value whilst delivering short-term targets, drive change whilst building-in stability, create values-based belonging whilst celebrating difference, and protect well-being whilst delivering high performance.

It is important to clarify that many of the paradoxes that leaders face are not new, it is just that the requirement to navigate all of them effectively has amplified.

There is heightened expectation on and urgency for leaders to get the balance right on many different fronts, with leaders needing to skilfully embrace a complex medley of paradoxes for their organisations to survive, stay relevant, and succeed in the long term.

Becoming Future-Fit: A Paradoxical Environment Calls for a Paradoxical Leader

The basic principles of evolution state that the fittest thrive because they are the best adapted to the environment they are in. From this perspective, the logic underpinning this book is quite simple: a highly complex and paradoxical environment calls for a highly complex and paradoxical leader.

Dealing with tensions and challenges cropping up 'out there' at an organisational level is one thing. But leaders who thrive amidst the megatrends excel in something even more intricate: they embrace and integrate paradoxes within themselves.

These leaders explore the full range of what it means to lead. In fact (without wishing to sound too grandiose), they explore the full spectrum of what it is to be human.

As individuals, we are not straightforward. Our values, behaviour, beliefs, and interactions are full of contradictions and tensions. Whilst a retreat or spell of adventurous travel may promise that we will 'find ourselves', the idea that 'if we dig down deep enough, all will become clear'—is a chimera. We all do and should have complexity within us. Opposites exist within the very core of our personality and identity, creating tensions; however, often we find it easier to reject these tensions than to integrate them. Our brains inherently prefer to have a coherent picture of 'who we are' and a tendency to think in terms of 'either/or' choices, rather than embrace the complexity and possibility of 'both/and' options.

The global leaders who win awards for their future-thinking, innovation, and disruption, understand this.[86] Such future-fit leaders are not perfect, nor are they completely 'integrated' in every way (as integration is a process that never ends) – but they are comfortable operating with beliefs, attitudes, and values that seem contradictory. Intuitively or through experience, future-fit leaders know that to lead and thrive in a modern age, you cannot be one-dimensional. To succeed, you must integrate complexity and paradox into your very being. You must think of yourself in terms of 'both/and'.

Just as paradoxes are not new in the business world, this notion of integrating paradoxes in yourself is not new either. These are age-old aspects of human nature and the requirement to 'be both' is something that senior leaders have probably grappled with (consciously or unconsciously) since the dawn of time. What has changed is the environment leaders are in and what is interesting is that this capacity to integrate paradoxes at a personal level has surfaced as a differentiator for leaders operating in the context of these megatrends.

In the next few chapters, the task of navigating paradoxes is explored in more detail, followed by insight into each of the five paradoxical mindsets, with the final chapter outlining the identity-level work necessary to embrace these mindsets and boost leadership performance. Using knowledge backed by psychology and neuroscience, leader-to-leader stories, tips, advice, and fresh insight – this book aims to offer practical support for those leaders on the quest to become future-fit.

Notes

1. Carlin, D. (2014). *Blueprint for Armageddon II.* Hardcore History 51 Podcast.
2. Mirouze, L. (2006). *The French Army in the First World War – To Battle 1914: Uniforms – Equipment – Armament, Volume 1.* Vienna, Austria: Verlag Militaria.
3. Elder, J. (2017). *Credit Analysis Risk Insight 2017 Retail Bankruptcies Set Record Pace – Which Companies are Most at Risk.* Manhattan, New York: S&P Global Market Intelligence.
4. Peterson, H. (2019). Retailers are filing for bankruptcy at a staggering rate – and these 17 companies could be the next to default. New York, US: *Business Insider.*
5. Rosenblum, P. (2014). Walmart's out of stock problem: only half the story? New Jersey, US: *Forbes Magazine.*
6. Morse, G. (2011). Retail isn't broken. Stores are. An interview with Ron Johnson. *Harvard Business Review.*
7. Statista (2021). *Average Company Lifespan on Standard and Poor's 500 Index from 1965 to 2030, in Years (Rolling-7-Year Average).* Hamburg, Germany: Statista.
8. Credit Suisse (2017). *Corporate Longevity Index Turnover and Corporate Performance.* Zürich, Switzerland: Credit Suisse.
9. Walters, A. (2021). The future of leadership: Developing a new perspective. London, UK: EY.
10. Schwab, K. (2017). *The Fourth Industrial Revolution.* Currency.
11. University of Manchester (2019). Applications of Graphene. *University of Manchester website article.*

12. Joshi, D., Malek, N.I., and Kailasa, S.K. (2022). Borophene as a rising star in materials chemistry: synthesis, properties and applications in analytical science and energy devices. *New Journal of Chemistry* 10: Advance article.

13. EY (2020). Are you reframing your future or is the future reframing you? *EY Megatrends Report.*

14. Isaacson, W. (2021). *Steve Jobs.* Simon & Schuster Paperbacks.

15. Saïd Business School and EY (2022). *The Future of Transformation is Human.* Oxford, UK: University of Oxford.

16. Statista Research Department (2022). Volume of data/information created, captured, copied, and consumed worldwide from 2010 to 2025.

17. Statista (2022). *Number of Sent and Received E-Mails Per Day Worldwide from 2017 to 2025.*

18. Raconteur (2019). *Day in Data. Infographic.*

19. Domo (2020). *Data Never Sleeps 8.0. Research Infographic.*

20. Kepios, Hootsuite, and We Are Social (2022). *Digital 2022 Global Overview Report.*

21. GWI (2022). Social: The biggest social media trends for 2022. *GWI Report.*

22. Pew Research Centre (2021). News Consumption Across Social Media in 2021. *Survey Data.*

23. Ofcom (2021). News Consumption in the UK: 2021. *Ofcom Report.*

24. MIT (2019). Study: On Twitter, false news travels faster than true stories. *MIT.*

25. Tóth, G., Wachs, J., Di Clemente, R., et al. (2021). Inequality is rising where social network segregation interacts with urban topology. *Nature Communications* 12: 1–9.

26. Twenge, J.M. (2020). Increases in depression, self-harm, and suicide among US adolescents after 2012 and links to technology use: possible mechanisms. *Psychiatric Research and Clinical Practice* 2: 19–25.

27. Binham, C. (2019). Companies fear rise of fake news and social media rumours. *Financial Times Article.*

28. United Nations, Department of Economic and Social Affairs, and Population Division (2021). *World Population Prospects 2021; Median Age of Population. Online Edition. Rev. 1.*

29. United Nations (2022). *World Population Prospects 2022: Summary of Results.* New York, US: Department of Economic and Social Affairs Population Division.

30. ManpowerGroup (2022). *Employment Outlook Survey.* NYSE: MAN.

31. Korn Ferry (2018). *Future of Work: The Global Talent Crunch.*

32. World Economic Forum (2020). *Future of Jobs Report 2020.*

33. OECD (2019). *The Future of Work: OECD Employment Outlook 2019.*

34. Gartner (2021). *Top 5 Priorities for HR Leaders in 2022.* Gartner HR Priorities Survey.

35. Maurer, J.M., Schaefer, J.M., Rupper, S., and Corley, A.J.S.A. (2019). Acceleration of ice loss across the Himalayas over the past 40 years. *Science Advances* 5: eaav7266.

36. EY Analysis of CoastalDEM data, Climate Central.

37. Ritchie, H., Roser, M., and Rosado, P. (2020). *Our World in Data CO_2 and Greenhouse Gas Emissions. Our World in Data Article.*

38. United Nations (2022) 50:50 Chance of Global Temperature Temporarily Reaching 1.5°C Threshold in Next 5 Years. *United Nations Climate Change Press Release.*

39. Armstrong McKay, D. I., Staal, A., Abrams, J. F., Winkelmann, R., Sakschewski, B., Loriani, S., et al. (2022). Exceeding 1.5° C global warming could trigger multiple climate tipping points. *Science* 377: eabn7950.

40. Weise, E. (2022). The world is 'perilously close' to irreversible climate change: 5 tipping points keep scientists up at night. *Phys Org Article.*

41. IPCC (2022). *Climate Change 2022: Mitigation of Climate Change: Sixth Assessment Report.*

42. Grooten, M., and Almond, R.E.A. (2018). *Living Planet Report 2018: Aiming Higher.* WWF, Gland, Switzerland.

43. United Nations (2020). Population facts: policies on spatial distribution and urbanization have broad impacts on sustainable development. *Department of Economic and Social Affairs.*

44. United Nations (2018). *2018 Revision of World Urbanization Prospects.*

45. Florida, R. (2017). *The Economic Power of Cities Compared to Nations.* City Lab.

46. UN Habitat (2022). *World Cities Report 2022: Envisaging the Future of Cities.*

47. UN Habitat (2020). *World Cities Report 2020: The Value of Sustainable Urbanization.*

48. White, M.P., Alcock, I., Wheeler, B.W. and Depledge, M.H. (2013). Would you be happier living in a greener urban area? A fixed-effects analysis of panel data. *Psychological Science* 24: 920–928.

49. Jennings, V., and Bamkole, O. (2019). The relationship between social cohesion and urban green space: An avenue for health

promotion. *International Journal of Environmental Research and Public Health* 16: 452.

50. Roe, J., and Aspinall, P. (2011). The restorative benefits of walking in urban and rural settings in adults with good and poor mental health. *Health and Place* 17: 103–113.
51. Stevenson, M.P., Schilhab, T., and Bentsen, P. (2018). Attention restoration theory II: A systematic review to clarify attention processes affected by exposure to natural environments. *Journal of Toxicology and Environmental Health, Part B* 21: 227–268.
52. Williams, K.J., Lee, K.E., Hartig, T., Sargent, L.D., Williams, N.S., and Johnson, K.A. (2018). Conceptualising creativity benefits of nature experience: Attention restoration and mind wandering as complementary processes. *Journal of Environmental Psychology* 59: 36–45.
53. Rajah, R., and Leng, A. (2022). *Revising Down the Rise of China.* Lowy Institute.
54. European Commission (2022). Economic power shifts. *Competence Centre on Foresight, Summary Data.*
55. Uyen, N.D.T. (2022). *Vietnam Sees 2022 Growth Beating Goal as Recovery Powers On.* London, UK: Bloomberg UK.
56. Wolfenden, R. (2022). Boost in intra-continent trade, points to rise in economic fortunes for Africa. *EY Article.*
57. Lee, A. (2013). Welcome to the unicorn club: learning from billion-dollar startups. *TechCrunch Article.*
58. Eckert, V.H. (2022). Living in a world of unicorns. *PwC article.*
59. EY (2021). EY Global Board Risk Survey 2021. *EY Report.*
60. World Inequality Lab (2022). *World Inequality Report 2022.*
61. Elderman (2021). *2021 Elderman Trust Barometer.*

62. Connor, J., Madhavan, S., Mokashi, M., *et al.* (2020). Health risks and outcomes that disproportionately affect women during the Covid-19 pandemic: A review. *Social Science & Medicine* 266: 113364.

63. Lopez, L., Hart, L.H., and Katz, M.H. (2021). Racial and ethnic health disparities related to COVID-19. *JAMA* 325: 719–720.

64. Astrid Zweynert (2016). World's growing inequality is 'ticking time bomb' – Nobel laureate Yunus. *Reuters Article.*

65. Hinde, G., and Cline, M. (2021). What more can businesses do to tackle inequality? *EY Article.*

66. Salesforce (2020). *Fourth Edition State of Service Report: Insights and Trends from Over 2,600 Global Service Trailblazers.*

67. McKinsey and Company (2021). *Next in Personalization 2021 Report.*

68. LinkedIn Learning (2020). *4th Annual 2020 Workplace Learning Report: L&D in a New Decade: Taking the Strategic Long View.*

69. EY (2022). EY 2022 Work Reimagined Survey. *Survey Report.*

70. Condeco (2022). Attitudes to Hybrid Working. The Impact of Hybrid Work on Employees and Employers. *Research Survey Report.*

71. Edelman (2019). Edelman Trust Barometer. *Global Report.*

72. Wilmot, D. (2022). *From Ambition to Action. How to Attain Purpose-Led Transformation.* EY white paper.

73. Black Rock (2022). Geopolitical risk dashboard: July 2022 update. *Black Rock Investment Institute Report.*

74. Colback, L. (2020). How to navigate the US-China trade war. *Financial Times.*

75. Raman, G., AlShebli, B., Waniek, M., et al. (2020). How weaponizing disinformation can bring down a city's power grid. *PloS One* 15: e0236517.

76. Hadiz, V. R., and Chryssogelos, A. (2017). Populism in world politics: a comparative cross-regional perspective. *International Political Science Review* 38: 399–411.

77. Timbro (2019). Authoritarian populism index. *Timbro Report*.

78. Statista Research Department (2020). *Populism in Europe – Statistics & Facts*. Hamburg, Germany: Statista.

79. Margetts, H., John, P., Hale, S., and Yasseri, T. (2015). *Political Turbulence: How Social Media Shape Collective Action*. New Jersey, US: Princeton University Press.

80. de Rosa, A.S., Bocci, E., Bonito, M., and Salvati, M. (2021). Twitter as social media arena for polarised social representations about the (im) migration: the controversial discourse in the Italian and international political frame. *Migration Studies* 9: 1167–1194.

81. Lagarde, C. (2022). *A New Global Map: European Resilience in a Changing World. Keynote Speech by Christine Lagarde, President of the ECB, at the Peterson Institute for International Economics*. Europa, EU: Washington.

82. Astvansh, V., Deng, W., and Habib, A. (2022). When geopolitical risk rises, innovation stalls. *Harvard Business Review*. March 03, 2022.

83. Heffernan, M. (2020). *Uncharted: How to Map the Future*. London, UK: Simon & Schuster UK.

84. Emery, J. (2019). *Leading for Organisational Change: Building Purpose, Motivation and Belonging*. New Jersey, US: John Wiley & Sons.

85. Emerson, B., and Lewis, K. (2019). *Navigating Polarities: Using Both/and Thinking to Lead Transformation*. Paradoxical Press.

86. Walters, A., Moorhouse, A., and Mahony, D. (2021). *Five Leadership Mindset: 5 Leadership Mindsets. The Paradoxical Mindsets Needed in a New Age of Leadership*. London, UK: EY.

CHAPTER 2
THE FIVE PARADOXICAL MINDSETS OF FUTURE-FIT LEADERSHIP

Paradoxical thinking requires that we embrace a view of the world in which opposites are joined, so that we can see the world clearly and see it whole. The result is a world more complex and confusing than the one made simple by 'either/ or' thought – but that simplicity is merely the dullness of death. When we think together we reclaim the life force in the world.

—Parker Palmer, author, teacher, and activist

The Five Mindsets: High-Level Summary

There are five paradoxical mindsets that leaders need to embrace to thrive in today's business landscape. Specifically, performance amidst the megatrends hinges on a leader's ability to think and lead in a way that is:

1. ruthlessly caring
2. ambitiously appreciative
3. politically virtuous
4. confidently humble
5. responsibly daring

To become future-fit, the best leaders will learn to combine all these different mindsets within their approach. As Table 2.1 shows, this means embracing the core tension within each mindset and integrating the whole spectrum of behaviours required.

In the rest of this book, we will explore each of these mindsets in more detail. For each one, unearthing the core tension, why it is an important paradox to embrace in today's business context, top tips for staying in 'the sweet spots', and how to avoid edging off-piste into the extremes as you attempt to follow the best path forward.

But first, let us look at paradoxes more generally, defining what a paradox is and why they are so challenging to navigate.

Table 2.1 The five paradoxical mindsets: core tension and key behaviours.

	Mindset tension	Behaviours
Ruthlessly caring	I make the tough decisions necessary to drive results **and** remain compassionate no matter what	Ruthlessly caring leaders are performance focused and driven to achieve results; they are challenging and willing to make decisions that have a tough human impact. They also deeply care about people, always show compassion, treat others with respect, are highly supportive, provide the feedback people need (but may not want) to hear, and never shy away from the tough emotional conversations.
Ambitiously appreciative	I must be relentless and determined **and** retain a sense of perspective and balance	Ambitiously appreciative leaders are highly driven, never satisfied and in the habit of perpetual striving, and yet retain a sense of perspective and appreciate life outside work. They give 110%, set demanding objectives, deeply value their own and others' wellbeing, celebrate performance as well as attainment, and appreciate the 'moments that matter' outside work.
Politically virtuous	I always try to do the right thing at the first opportunity **and** be politically savvy in the circumstances	Politically virtuous leaders are canny, genuine, and have integrity. They influence others, live their values (i.e., are willing to make a stand for what they believe and lead by example), are transparent with people, and can judge when telling everyone everything would be counter-productive.

(*Continued*)

Table 2.1 (*Continued*)

	Mindset tension	Behaviours
Confidently humble	I inspire others to have confidence in my ability **and** know I cannot achieve ambitious goals on my own	Confidently humble leaders are self-assured, decisive, and driven to learn from others. They know they must be credible in their role and inspire others to have confidence in them (i.e., to believe in their vision, back their decisions, and trust in their overall ability to deliver results). They also know they cannot achieve ambitious goals alone, are willing to be vulnerable, are open about their limitations, surround themselves with experts, are inspired by others, and value everyone's ideas and opinions.
Responsibly daring	I believe everything is worth trying and anything is possible **and** stay accountable for making a difference and safeguarding the business	Responsibly daring leaders set bold, audacious, 'seemingly impossible' goals; they are willing to take risks, and feel responsible for making a difference and safeguarding the business. They are pragmatic visionaries: highly optimistic and, at the same time, realistic about what can and needs to be achieved. They are future-focused, driven to innovate, and continuously striving to transform their business and the world for the better.

What Exactly Is a Paradox?

As Brian Emerson and Kelly Lewis explain in their book *Navigating Polarities*, a paradox is:[1]

> *a situation in which two seemingly opposite yet independent states need to coexist over time in order for success to occur*

The key point to emphasise here is '*seemingly opposite yet independent*'. On the first reading of the five mindsets, the pairs of elements appear contradictory; they seem like opposites, like two opposing ends of the same spectrum (as shown in Figure 2.1). But that is a false interpretation.

In fact, each paradoxical mindset has two distinct but connected elements that need to coexist for high performance to occur. Confidence and humility, for example, are not the two extremes of the same construct (as shown in Figure 2.1). They are two separate constructs that can (and must) coexist. Each element has its own separate continuum (i.e., a confidence continuum and a humility continuum), and there is a 'sweet spot' to be found within both (as shown below in Figure 2.2).

As well as noting that the two constructs within each paradoxical mindset are simultaneously distinct and connected, it is important to clarify three further points about paradoxes upfront:

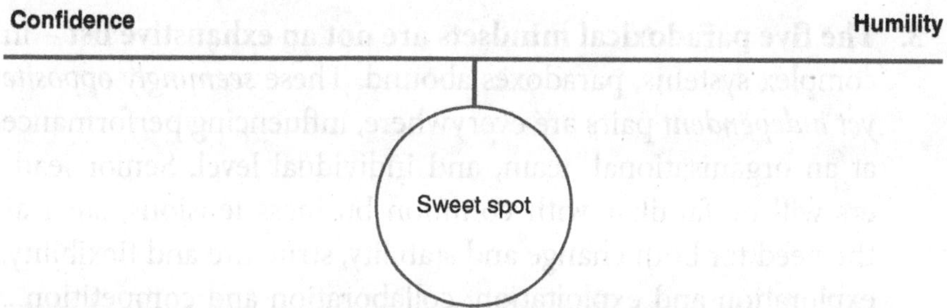

Figure 2.1 A false interpretation of a paradoxical mindset ('confidently humble' example).

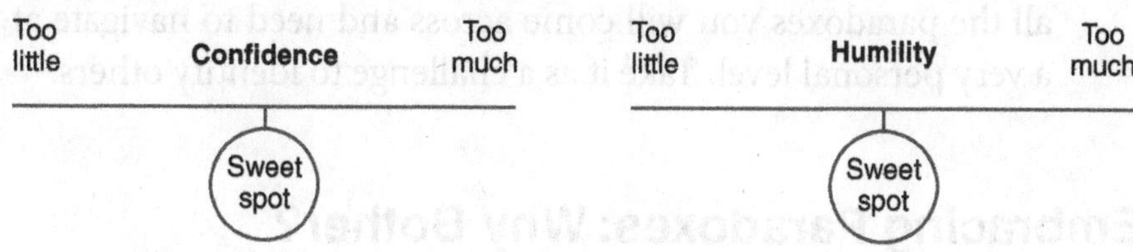

Figure 2.2 Each paradoxical mindset contains two distinct yet connected elements ('confidently humble' example).

1. **You cannot solve them** – paradoxes can never be solved; they can only ever be actively managed. A paradox means you are facing demands that are contradictory but interdependent, constituting a persistent tension over time.[2] Any impression that the paradox has somehow been resolved neatly and no longer requires navigating is therefore an illusion (sorry!). Leaders can become more adept at managing paradoxes, harnessing certain tensions to enhance performance, but the requirement to navigate the paradox will never disappear.
2. **It is not about dialling one side up and the other down at different moments** – it is easy to fall into the trap of thinking managing paradoxes is just about dialling two competing elements up or down at different moments; this is a misunderstanding. The beauty of the paradox is that the two elements are distinct. This means it is not 'either/or' at different moments, but 'both/and' at every moment.
3. **The five paradoxical mindsets are not an exhaustive list** – in complex systems, paradoxes abound. These *seemingly opposite yet independent* pairs are everywhere, influencing performance at an organisational, team, and individual level. Senior leaders will be familiar with common business tensions, such as the need for both change and stability, structure and flexibility, exploration and exploitation, collaboration and competition... However, as a leader, you should also be on the lookout for the paradoxical tensions required from you personally. These five mindsets are a starting point. They are not an exhaustive list of all the paradoxes you will come across and need to navigate at a very personal level. Take it as a challenge to identify others.

Embracing Paradoxes: Why Bother?

The call for leaders to embrace paradoxical thinking is nothing new. For a long time, in research, the ability to embrace paradox has been identified as a source of competitive advantage,[3] with leaders who are able to leverage tensions shown to perform better over time and generate more robust and sustainable solutions to issues.[4–6]

The literature around paradoxes, polarities, dualities, dialectics, wicked problems, or competing tensions (whatever you wish to term it. . .) has been bubbling steadily for decades. In Jim Collins's seminal book *Good to Great*,[7] for example, a key factor required to transform 'a good organisation into a great one' was the CEO's ability to display a paradoxical combination of personal humility and indomitable will. Similarly, researchers Wendy Smith, Marianne Lewis, and Michael Tushman have long claimed that knowing how to handle paradox and operate with a 'both/ and' (rather than 'either/or') mentality is among the top skills needed by leaders in our modern time, articulating how:[8]

> *As business organisations face increasingly unpredictable, complex, and challenging environments, those that have the greatest hope of surviving and contributing to the world will have leaders who embrace strategic paradoxes.*

In the megatrends environment, the requirement for leaders to tackle contradictory demands is intensifying and corresponding interest in how to effectively embrace paradox is surging. For example, as discussed in Chapter 1, leaders are under more pressure than ever to incrementally improve whilst simultaneously radically reinvent, to reach a global network whilst also serving distinct local needs, and to remain profitable whilst positively contributing to climate change and societal issues.

As a leader, embracing paradoxical thinking into your way of being and day-to-day decision-making is no longer a 'nice-to-have' but a necessity. It is a key ingredient if you want to become 'future-fit'.

What Makes Paradoxical Thinking So Difficult?

Embracing paradoxical thinking is tricky to do because it goes against how our brains like to operate. From an evolutionary perspective, the brain likes simplicity; it aims to preserve our resources and ensure our survival through quick solutions and efficient decision-making. Safe or dangerous, friend or foe, fight or flight, right or wrong – 'either/or' thinking is part of the brain's survival mechanism and default mode.

In fact, when we try to hold two seemingly inconsistent beliefs at the same time, we tend to experience a form of psychological discomfort known as 'cognitive dissonance'.[9] This stress or tension occurs because our brain has an inner drive for consistency; we like our attitudes, beliefs, and behaviours to all be in harmony with each other – for things to be straightforward. Clear-cut.

Of course, in some instances 'either/or' thinking is entirely appropriate and necessary. However, when there is a need (and opportunity) to embrace a paradox, this 'either/or' default mode can get in the way, restricting our view of the situation and imposing false boundaries and limits to our choices.

Identity Bucketing: How Leaders Polarise Themselves and Their Approach

With respect to the five mindsets, most problematic of all is our tendency to polarise ourselves. We construct our sense of identity by claiming certain attributes as either 'me' or 'not me', defining ourselves using 'either/or' terms. This 'identity bucketing' helps us understand who we are, what we stand for, and get a sense of belonging to certain groups. By identifying as one or the other, we build up a clear and consistent picture of who we are and how we are different or similar to others, for example stating: 'I'm vegan or I'm vegetarian', 'I'm a big picture person or I'm a details person', 'I'm an introvert or I'm an extrovert', 'I'm a people-person or I'm all about performance'.

This is beyond the brain striving for simplicity and order, it is our need for a clear sense of self. Our drive to have one unified, coherent image of who we are and eliminate any apparent contradictions.

Unfortunately, when it comes to paradoxes, identifying part of who you are by only embracing one specific style or attribute makes it easy to slip into overuse and neglect the behaviours that are different but complementary to performance.

Research shows how leaders who deeply identify with a specific style are often concerned about demonstrating enough of those behaviours and are sensitive to underdoing it.[10] For example, a 'perfectionist' leader who values quality and worries about performing to a high enough standard will often strain excessively to prove themselves. They will also likely have an aversion to leaders who seem to accept average or pragmatically focus on what is necessary to deliver, rather than what is possible. Similarly, a 'diplomatic' leader who deeply values relationships may find themselves being over-accommodating of others or excessively canvassing views. They, in turn, will likely have an aversion to leaders who seem to push ideas through quickly to make things happen.

The risk here is that once you have hooked your identity onto a singular style, your leadership perspective can become very polarised seeing only 'good vs. bad' in differing approaches. Researchers Brian Emerson and Kelly Lewis visualise this as 'operating on the diagonal' (see Figure 2.3) – with, for example, leaders who identify strongly as being 'highly competitive' focusing only on the benefits

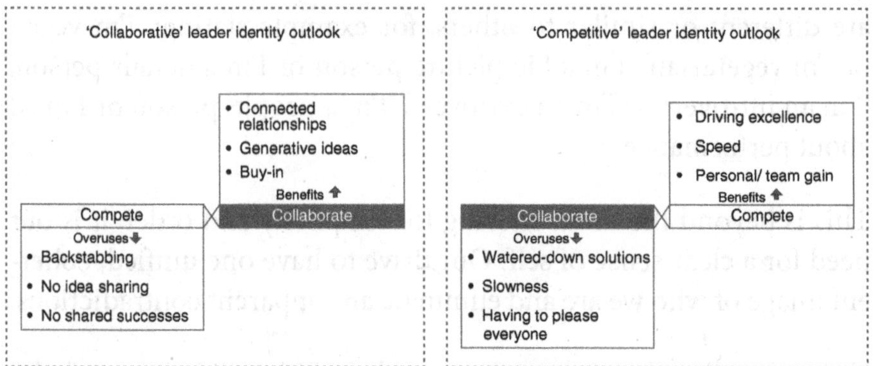

Figure 2.3 How identity bucketing can lead to polarised perceptions.
Source: Adapted with permission from Emerson, B., and Lewis, K. (2019). *Navigating polarities: Using both/and thinking to lead transformation.* Paradoxical Press.

of a competitive mindset and the negatives that come from overusing a more collaborative approach. Similarly, leaders who identify strongly with being 'highly collaborative' may get stuck perceiving only the benefits of collaborating and the negatives of overusing a competitive mindset. From this standpoint, there is no beneficial middle ground to both; there are only good vs. bad, right vs. wrong ways to lead.

Over time, this 'all of one' and 'total rejection of the other' way of operating significantly impairs leadership performance. It blocks leaders from attaining the benefits of both, because vision is tunnelled into only seeing the benefits of one and negatives of the other. What is instead required is a balanced appreciation for the benefits of harnessing, and perils of overusing, both paradoxical elements.

We will explore this idea in more detail throughout this chapter. But, for now, the takeaway message is this: as a leader, it is important not to bucket yourself and your identity into one set dimension. Thank your brain for trying to simplify your life for you and protect your image of who you are, but know that oversubscribing to one style or one specific way of thinking will restrict your performance in the long run.

Paradoxical Thinking: Preferences and Pendulums

Slight or strong, most people will have a preference towards one side of each mindset. One element of each paradox will simply feel more comfortable and natural to embrace, like putting on a comfortable pair of shoes or going for a walk down a familiar path. Embracing one element will also be benefitting you in some way; for example, if you pride yourself on being a 'very caring and approachable' type of leader, you will enjoy being people's 'go-to' and confidant. Similarly, you may fear that if you embrace a more ruthless mindset, you might upset or lose people's trust and friendship.

However, as discussed, it is vital to remember neither element of each paradoxical mindset is inherently better or worse, good or bad. Both elements to each paradoxical mindset have benefits and both need to be embraced for optimal leadership performance. The downsides only arise from under- and over-use.

When you are off-balance (i.e., embracing one side of a paradoxical mindset too strongly) you will find one of two things occurs:

Consequence 1: the benefits of the 'opposite' approach become very appealing – each element of the paradox will bring unique performance benefits. But, if you overindulge and exclusively focus your attention on only one element of the paradox, the benefits will begin to sour. For example, at an organisational level, you may have been focusing on implementing clear processes but now find things are so slow it is difficult for people to get anything done. The temptation at this point is to swing back the other way and make things flexible and innovative. **(N.B.: This pendulum swing is more common when navigating business tensions at the organisational level.)**

Alternatively . . .

Consequence 2: if it is a 'way of being' you deeply value, you will tolerate the impact of overuse – for example, if as a leader you deeply value relationships (e.g., spending time with others, building strong connections, hearing different points of view, helping people out), you will most likely tolerate the downsides of its overuse (e.g., spending too much time doing favours for others, getting bogged down gathering other's opinions, perhaps feeling your own voice does not get heard enough, or your priorities are not respected). You will accept this as the 'price you pay' to get things done, an inherent cost that comes of your style of leadership. **(N.B.: This preference trap is more common when navigating paradoxes at the individual and identity level.)**

In sum, over-embracing one element of a paradox will leave you either: swinging between extremes or stuck (i.e., frustrated with the status quo but making excuses for why you cannot change it).

Pendulum swinging is more likely when managing competing tensions at the organisational level; whereas being 'stuck' is more common when navigating paradoxes at the individual and identity level (such as the five paradoxical mindsets outlined in this book). In the next section, we will focus on how to get 'unstuck' from overidentifying with a preference, but first let us briefly explore those two consequences in more detail.

Consequence 1: The Paradox Pendulum Swing

At the organisational level, there are numerous competing tensions (i.e., paradoxes or polarities) leaders must navigate, such as celebrating differences whilst creating belonging, reducing cost whilst improving quality, defending what works whilst driving change, requiring discipline whilst allowing freedom . . . (the list goes on). A major risk at this organisational level is getting sucked into the 'paradox pendulum swing.' Instead of finding a way to harness both, you find yourself swinging between extremes. Embracing one approach too tightly and exclusively, to the point where the best and only solution appears to be to completely embrace the 'alternative' approach.

In the short-term, this switch in focus provides welcome relief, a breather, some fresh perspective, and unlocks numerous issues. But, in the long-term, the same thing happens again. Perhaps as a leadership team, you have embraced freedom, autonomy, and flexibility so heartily that it is now impossible to track what is happening or collate the data and knowledge you need. So, you focus on embracing processes again. You clamp down, strive for discipline, centralise decision-making, seek to impose order, drive efficiency. . . But then you reach a point where the organisation has become too rigid and stifling again, there is no creativity, innovation, entrepreneurial spirit, and so on. . . back and forth.

This pendulum swing approach may feel like an effective way to manage competing tensions, but navigating paradoxes is not about swinging between overuse and underuse. It is about finding the two 'sweet spots' and unlocking ways to embrace both elements simultaneously. It is a requirement to consistently do the 'both/and', not 'each/sometimes'.

Consequence 2: Stuck in a Preference

As discussed, the pendulum swing is more common for leaders managing tensions at the organisational level. It is rare you will find a C-suite leader who is one day highly collaborative and the next, a very competitive individual, or perhaps continually seems to switch from being relentlessly driven and overly relaxed.

At the individual level, the more common issue you will face is getting stuck: oversubscribing to a certain style or specific way of operating.

To become future-fit and embrace the five paradoxical mindsets, you will need to learn how to get unstuck, to unfreeze yourself, and expand your leadership identity.

Unfreezing Your Leadership Identity: Old Habits and Current Assumptions

By the time you reach the upper echelons of management, you would have formed a go-to leadership style. Certain habits, assumptions, and ways of thinking and behaving as a leader will have set in. Moreover, this go-to approach will be precious to you as it is part of what has got you where you are today and made you successful. It also gives you a clear sense of who you are, how you like to lead, and what you bring to each role that adds value and guarantees results. It's part of your recipe for success.

However, to a degree, your success will have led you to become entrenched. Frozen. Strongly attached to your own winning leadership formula, which has consistently proven itself to work well for you. But such overattachment leaves you exposed, less able to adapt and respond effectively as new situations arise. Increasingly vulnerable in the megatrends landscape.

In the megatrend's context, the key to success hinges on adaptability; it is imperative your approach does not become frozen but continues to flex, evolve, and expand.

The good news is that to become more adaptable and embrace the five paradoxical mindsets, you do not need to 'give up' parts of yourself. You do not have to sacrifice what makes you *you* as a leader. For example, if you pride yourself on your maverick, adventurous, 'can-do' spirit, you do not have to give that up to be more responsible. The requirement here is not to 'ditch-and-switch' but merely to loosen your grip so you can embrace more ways of thinking and operating.

If it helps, think of it like a yoga practice: to become more adaptable, you need to soften and expand your leadership identity. Chapter 8 explores how to expand your identity in more detail, but for now, let us just focus on the first initial step towards embracing the five paradoxical mindsets: building self-awareness.

Building Self-Awareness

To be able to embrace the five mindsets, you first need to understand where you are currently at. You may feel you navigate some of the paradoxes well already, whereas with regard to some others, you might feel more off-balance.

Take a look at each mindset element and roughly rate where you are:

	Too low	Just right	Too high
Ruthless			
Caring			
Confident			
Humble			
Political			
Virtuous			
Ambitious			
Appreciative			
Responsible			
Daring			

This exercise seems straightforward enough, but it may be difficult to do it alone without the help of a skilled coach. For example, if you are a deeply compassionate individual who likes to please others and provide support – you might have a blind spot when rating yourself against 'caring'. In other words, you may have easily ticked caring as 'just right', when in fact, on closer inspection, it may be 'a bit high': a mindset you tend to embrace strongly because it aligns with your preferences and values, so you are willing tolerate or overlook any negative impacts its overuse might be having on your own performance or that of your teams.

Take the time to work through and honestly rate yourself.

Once you have really reflected on all the elements and identified which paradoxical mindset seems most unbalanced and would offer the most performance value to work on, then you can start digging deeper.

The following chapters will help you understand how to stay in the 'sweet spot' of each element and avoid going off-piste (into the overuse and underuse territory) but as a quick starter-for-ten, ask yourself:

If you rated an element 'too high':

- How has embracing this mindset element helped you become successful and stand out in your career?
- What benefits does embracing this mindset give you? What joy does it bring within your leadership role?
- How does this mindset show up day-to-day? (e.g., in your characteristics, habits, tendencies. . .)
- What underpins your belief that this is the best way to lead?
- What are your biggest frustrations at work? And, are there any knock-on effects that you tolerate as 'the price you have to pay' to lead in the way you do?

If you rated an element 'too low':

- What assumptions do you have about leaders who adopt this mindset element strongly?
- What do you fear is at risk if you embrace this mindset element more?
- What about this mindset feels scary or uncomfortable to you?
- On a scale of 1–10, how equipped do you feel to lead more in this way? (10 being very equipped, with all the necessary skills and understanding)

It is important to remember that fear will often be what is holding you back from adopting paradoxical thinking: fear that you will lose part of your leadership identity, fear you will lose what underpins your success, fear you will become what you dislike, fear of the unknown, and fear of judgement from others.

Without digging into these deep-rooted beliefs, assumptions, and fears, you will find it difficult to truly expand how you lead. You will struggle to shake old habits and find yourself reverting to what is comfortable in critical moments – when adaptability would have been a game changer. If you want to get results, you need to put in the hard yards when it comes to self-reflection.

Research and Psychology: Why Is It Hard to Learn About Ourselves

Carl Jung referred to the journey towards understanding ourselves as 'individuation'.[11] A process that requires unconscious habits and tendencies to be surfaced and examined in the light, with self-awareness and self-acceptance ultimately paving the way to personal growth and transformation. At its heart, it is a process of facing up to yourself, of learning to embrace all aspects of who you are and all you are capable of.

However, when it comes to building self-awareness, research shows how strong forces can often blinker us.

Specifically, research shows how people typically have three core motives for gathering self-knowledge:[12]

1. **Desire for truth** – a desire to learn the truth about themselves, whatever it may be

2. **Self-enhancement** – a desire to hear good things and receive favourable information about themselves and their character
3. **Consistency** – a desire to have whatever they already believe about themselves confirmed or verified (even if that information is unflattering)

Unfortunately, as you might expect, research has also shown that whilst people do have a genuine desire to learn the truth about themselves, this tends to be outweighed by their appetite for flattery and, to a lesser extent, their drive to have preconceptions about themselves confirmed.[13]

Consequently, building self-knowledge is not always easy.

Top tip: Notice when your desire to hear good things and have your current beliefs confirmed seems to be dominating the self-awareness process. Instead, be open, be brave, and brace yourself. Dial up your genuine desire to learn and face the truth, whatever it may be.

In the next chapters, we take a close look at each of the five paradoxical mindsets in more detail. Do not feel the need to work diligently through from Chapter 3 to Chapter 7. Go straight to the paradox that sparks your interest and feels most relevant for you to explore to lead more effectively.

Notes

1. Emerson, B., and Lewis, K. (2019). *Navigating Polarities: Using Both/and Thinking to Lead Transformation*. Washington, US: Paradoxical Press.

2. Gaim, M., Clegg, S., and Cunha, M.P.E. (2021). Managing impressions rather than emissions: Volkswagen and the false mastery of paradox. *Organization Studies* 42: 949–970.

3. Heracleous, L., and Wirtz, J. (2014). Singapore Airlines: achieving sustainable advantage through mastering paradox. *The Journal of Applied Behavioral Science* 50: 150–170.

4. Andriopoulos, C., and Lewis, M.W. (2009). Exploitation–exploration tensions and organizational ambidexterity: managing paradoxes of innovation. *Organization Science* 20: 696–717.

5. Smith, W.K., and Lewis, M.W. (2011). Toward a theory of paradox: A dynamic equilibrium model of organizing. *Academy of Management Review* 36: 381–403.

6. Sokol, M.B. (2012). Developing polarity thinking in global leaders: an illustration. *Industrial and Organizational Psychology* 5: 231–233.

7. Collins, J. (2001). *Good to Great*. New York, US: Random House Business Books.

8. Smith, W.K., Lewis, M.W., and Tushman, M.L. (2016). 'Both/and' leadership. *Harvard Business Review* 94: 62–70.

9. Festinger, L. (1962). Cognitive dissonance. *Scientific American* 207: 93–106.

10. Kaiser, R.B., and Overfield, D.V. (2011). Strengths, strengths overused, and lopsided leadership. *Consulting Psychology Journal: Practice and Research* 63: 89.

11. Jung, C.G. (2014). *The Symbolic Life: Miscellaneous Writings*. Oxfordshire, UK: Routledge.

12. Baumeister, R.F. (2010). *The Self*. Oxford, UK: Oxford University Press.

13. Sedikides, C. (1993). Assessment, enhancement, and verification determinants of the self-evaluation process. *Journal of Personality and Social Psychology* 65: 317.

CHAPTER 3
RUTHLESSLY CARING

A true leader has the confidence to stand alone, the courage to make tough decisions, and the compassion to listen to the needs of others.

—Douglas MacArthur, military leader

What Is a 'Ruthlessly Caring' Mindset?

Ruthlessly caring leaders hold the following mindset:

- To achieve performance, they have a responsibility to make tough decisions.
- They must remain compassionate no matter what.
- They must stay connected to people at a personal level, prioritising communication and taking time to talk to people individually in tough moments.
- They must step up to provide support and challenge.

These leaders are therefore both strongly focused on performance and emotionally connected to people in their business. At a personal level, they deeply consider and consciously stay close to the human impact of their business decisions.

In 2020, the COVID-19 pandemic threw the crux of this mindset into sharp relief. Economies shut down and companies were plunged into survival mode, forcing their leaders to make tough decisions whilst calling on them to protect people's health, safety, and livelihood.

During the crisis, so many senior leaders stepped up and showed immense care for people. Michelle Penczak, CEO of Squared Away, for example, was intensely aware of the stress and strain that her employees were under – as parents, military spouses, and as employees. Consequently, she gave all her staff her personal mobile number, making sure they knew she was always available to them and they could give her a call whenever they needed to. Meanwhile, alongside the duty of care, leaders across sectors were under immense pressure to perform and make the tough decisions necessary to ensure business survival. The requirement on leaders to be both ruthless and caring was stark.

A golden thread that runs throughout this book is the idea of embracing your shadow self: the side of yourself you do not like or feel you cannot afford to acknowledge. As a leader, it is much easier to settle your identity in one camp, either 'camp caring' (thinking: 'I'm the type of leader that prioritises my people') or 'camp ruthless' (thinking: 'at the end of the day, it's business, I prioritise performance. If I don't, there is no business, and no one gets paid'). This either/or trap is tempting; it makes things simple. But future-fit leaders do not make this choice – for them, it is not people or performance. It is people and performance.

Leader to Leader

During a management career that has taken him from small-town America to senior roles in retail banking and onto the executive team of a FTSE 250 company, Greg Reed has experienced first-hand the vicissitudes of organisational life. Greg was promoted to UK CEO having helped the company recover from a major setback, but twelve months in, he was faced with yet another challenge. For many years, the growth engine of the Plc group, the main board's attention had been drawn to high-growth opportunities in North America. Consequently, the highly profitable UK company would no longer benefit from growth investment and the business needed to be scaled accordingly.

'Customers had changed and we had to change accordingly. We had grown too fat and for the health of the business,

(*Continued*)

we had to look hard at any role that was not fully customer oriented', he said.

Knowing that this meant redundancies and drawing on his own personal experience of being made redundant without any form of feedback or adequate explanation, Greg committed to do the right thing for the business whilst caring for those people who would lose their jobs. And he started with his top team. 'We had the discussion as a team and acknowledged that we couldn't cut into the management of the business without looking at ourselves, first'. A day or so later, one of his most trusted lieutenants and a personal friend came to Greg and said, 'Given the circumstance, I have to go'. Another top team colleague followed shortly thereafter, despite the pain, and knowing that both executives loved their role and the company, Greg knew it was right, too.

Thereafter, as the consultation period developed, Greg made himself personally available to see any manager at risk should they wish to reach out. 'I saw dozens of people, and with each one I drew on my own experience and how I felt about no one explaining to me why I had to go. In each case, I tried to help each person make sense of the situation and offered to help via my personal network, writing recommendations, etc'.

Throughout this difficult challenge, Greg neither shied away from tough decisions nor disconnected from the personal impact those decisions had.

Before delving into why being ruthlessly caring is so important in a megatrends environment, let us first get clear on what these two terms mean:

Defining Terms:

- **Ruthless** is defined in the dictionary as showing no pity or compassion for others; here we use the term differently to refer to task-focused styles of leadership.[1] Leaders who are performance-focused, driven to achieve results, and willing to make decisions that have a tough human impact.
- **Caring** refers to more benevolent styles of leadership. Leaders who care deeply for those they lead, providing coaching and mentoring, showing genuine concern for people's personal and career development, and who invest time building authentic and lasting relationships.[2]

Why Embracing a 'Ruthlessly Caring' Mindset Matters Amidst the Megatrends

Any leader responsible for a team or organisation through the COVID-19 crisis will have grappled with this paradox. Sleepless nights caused from the inherent tension between: 'How do I keep my business alive? What will it take to remain viable? What actions need to be taken?' and the questions of 'How do I care for my people? How do I keep them safe? How do I protect both their health and livelihood?'

Whilst the challenge of ruthlessly caring was thrust into the spotlight during COVID-19, it is not a challenge that will fade away. Various megatrends are combining to turn the heat up on this mindset. Specifically: shifting workforce and customer expectations, high inequality, advancing technology, and high numbers of disruptive start-ups, are all converging to require leaders who excel in being both ruthless and caring.

Increasing Pressure on Business Leaders to Show You Care

Workforce and customer expectations about leadership and the purpose of business are continuing to change. People no longer judge organisations based on their financial performance, salary, or quality of products alone. Businesses are increasingly judged based on the way they take care of their suppliers, employees, customers, and the impact they have on society.[3] People expect genuine action from business leaders on important issues such as systemic racism and climate change; appearing to do the right thing is not enough, leaders must care, and they must act.

Similarly, capitalist ideals of 'profit at all costs' are fading fast. Whilst leaders during the Industrial Revolution could get away with holding the mindset that 'it's okay to be wasteful in terms of people's energy, motivation, and expertise so long as the business keeps growing', times have long since changed. Global competition for talent is increasing, and Gen Z have been termed 'the purpose-driven generation'; seeking socially responsible, human-centred, and ethical companies to work for. Younger workers are also rejecting hierarchical structures and want to be involved in the way future business is done.[4] They want to be treated as partners, not pawns to be moved around.

Increasing Pressure on Business Leaders to Sustain Performance and Deliver Results

Technology and disruptive start-ups are creating a highly competitive and fast-changing operating context. Company life expectancy is shrinking and sustaining company performance is getting harder and harder to do. Advancing technology has created a highly competitive, fast-changing market, where barriers to entry are low, and so the number of disruptive start-ups across many industries is consequently high. All the while, the digital playing field continues to rapidly shift and evolve.

Change, innovation, efficiency, and the ability to self-disrupt are essential ingredients for organisations wishing to survive and thrive in this twenty-first century environment. And, with that pace of change and level of disruption, comes tough decisions.

All too often senior leaders avoid or delay making tough calls, perhaps wanting to 'be considerate to others', 'avoid a dip in morale', or because they 'want to be seen as fair'.[5] However, in this megatrend's context, there is no buffer zone. Those leaders who fail to make difficult performance decisions in a timely manner will not last long as the wheels of change continue to accelerate around them.

As a business leader, it is your responsibility to keep the organisation nimble and relevant. Part of this, unpleasant though it may be, means walking into the storm: communicating the difficult messages, quickly addressing issues of underperformance, restructuring the business to stay relevant, disrupting the status quo, and having the tough conversations with people.

Leading Ruthlessly: Making Tough Performance-Focused Decisions

Ruthlessness, in our definition, refers to a leader's ability to make the tough decisions necessary to achieve performance. In this section, 'leading ruthlessly' is broken into its two elements: 1) having a performance focus and 2) making tough decisions.

1) Having a Performance Focus

In the context of work, performance can be defined as:

> *How well a job is done and the degree to which goals are successfully achieved.*

A leader's job is to get results. At an executive level, this means doing what needs to be done to help an organisation survive, improve, and keep making a positive difference. Leading ruthlessly is not about perceiving business as a 'dog-eat-dog', 'win-at-all-costs' world but about providing focus, stretch, and discipline so people can do their job well and achieve key objectives. When boiled down, a performance focus involves:[6]

- expecting the best from people
- helping people achieve stretching goals

Done in the right way, expecting the best from people empowers them. It fuels people to take on challenges and draw on their strengths. Whether you realise it or not, what you believe about someone's ability will be transmitted to them, through your manner, tone of voice, energy levels, time spent with them, type of support offered, and the goals you set – it all combines to send a message people pick up on. As a leader, it is your job to have high expectations of those around you, anything less will be doing people a disservice.

Research and Psychology: the Rosenthal Effect

The Rosenthal (aka Pygmalion) effect refers to the psychological phenomenon in which high expectations lead to improved performance.

While many studies have now demonstrated the power of expectations on performance,[7] the effect was first described in 1968. In this landmark experiment, psychologist Robert Rosenthal and principal teacher Lenore Jacobson told a group of teachers at an elementary school that an intelligence test had identified some of the students in their class as 'growth spurters' who were likely to intellectually flourish over the coming year. In fact, the children identified as likely to flourish had been chosen at random. However, when Rosenthal and Jacobsen tested all the students later in the year, it was the students whom teachers had been told to expect to excel and flourish that scored higher and showed the greatest improvement.

This study was the first to show how a leader's expectations of someone's ability may come to serve as a self-fulfilling prophecy. Since then, numerous studies have demonstrated how expectation alters both the behaviour of the individual and the leader.[8] Firstly, because expecting excellence and believing in people's ability lead people to expect and believe more in themselves. Secondly, because high expectations spur the leader on to create a more positive environment and give better support, offering the individual more constructive feedback and challenging assignments.

Alongside expecting the best from people, a performance focus requires clear goal setting. Having high expectations of someone without being crystal clear about what is expected from them is just setting someone up for failure. Goal setting matters no matter what level of leadership you are at, it is just the goals become bigger and more complex. Achieving performance hinges on always working with people to making sure it is crystal clear what outcome needs to be achieved, how success and progress will be measured, and then empowering them to determine what the best tactical approach is to achieve the objective.

To drive high performance, it is important for these goals to be sufficiently ambitious and stretching. As, mentioned earlier, setting easily achievable goals for people does no one any favours. It may feel like a 'confidence builder' but what actually builds people's confidence is a leader who has high expectations of them, sets them ambitious goals, and provides them with both trust and support. It is about transmitting the message: 'this may feel scary, but I know you can do this well' and backing that with a deep, internalised belief in that person's ability to grow and perform.

2) Making Tough Decisions

Leading a business means making lots of tough decisions. People know this and yet still it catches leaders out when they reach the upper echelons of management. In one 10-year longitudinal study of more than 2,700 leaders, 57% of newly appointed executives said that decisions were more complicated and difficult than they had expected.[9]

Sometimes decisions are made difficult because of the impact you know that decision will have on people, for example, deciding to close hundreds of shops, shutting a factory which employs hundreds of people, or making the call to fire a close friend. These choices are always tough, no matter how obviously correct or necessary they may be. Other decisions may be tough because there is no right answer. You are stuck between a rock and a hard place, or the answer may be such an unknown grey area that no matter how much research is done or how many experts are consulted, the answer is still unclear.

The problem is, when facing these tough decisions often a 'no-decision outcome' is the one thing you simply cannot afford. However, as author Ron Carucci explains, leaders frequently end up there, with one of the following rationalisations paralysing their decision-making ability.[9]

Rationale. . .	What is holding this leader back. . .
'I'm being considerate of others'	The thought of disappointing people, negatively impacting morale, or adding to people's stress
'I'm committed to quality and accuracy'	Fear over the long-term implications of being wrong and appearing stupid
'I want to be seen as fair'	Fear of being perceived as uncaring or playing favourites, reluctance to separate people out based on their performance

Unfortunately, despite the seemingly valid justifications, the impact of not making tough choices can be far more damaging. For example, protecting people from bad news can leave them ill-equipped with barely any time to adapt. Depending on the situation, it can also set a dangerous precedent with regards to the decision-making culture of an organisation; with people taking the lesson that mistakes are to be avoided at all costs or that you should try to avoid sharing bad news.

Making tough decisions will never be easy, but there are a few strategies that help:

- **Understand the risk of not deciding** – it is a common bias to overestimate the risk of action and underestimate the risk of inaction. To avoid decision paralysis, it is therefore useful to get clear on the potential consequences of not making the decision within a certain time window.
- **Focus on the integrity of the process (not the potential outcome)** – with some decisions, it can be hard to know how they will turn out. What matters is whether you can look at yourself in the mirror, whatever the outcome, and trust in the integrity of the process upon which that decision was made.
- **Do not seek consensus** – taking different viewpoints into consideration is not the same as seeking consensus. Tough decision-making is a lonely place; one person needs to make the final call. The goal should not be to appease everyone's views on the situation, but to decide on and commit to a clear course of action within a time frame.

The Ruthless Leadership Continuum: How to Stay on Track

As discussed in the previous section, a leader who is in the sweet spot of 'ruthless' will be challenging, focused on performance, and able to make tough decisions: actions, all of which take courage, energy, and commitment.

Under pressure, the temptation here is for leaders to either 'move away' or 'move against'. Moving away is essentially opting for 'the ostrich approach': sticking your head in the sand, letting things be, and avoiding any conflict or tough decision that comes along. Moving against is opting for the 'wolverine strategy': being extremely fierce and aggressive to win big, using all the power at your disposal, and making decisions in solitude.

These two approaches, avoid or attack, are at the extreme ends of the ruthless continuum (see Figure 3.1): but, under pressure, it is surprising how frequently we can slip into such fight or flight responses.

Let us look at the subtle ways you can find yourself lured off course along the ruthless continuum:

Tyrannical. At the most extreme end of the highly ruthless spectrum, you have tyrannical leadership behaviour. This is where a leader displays high levels of pro-organisational behaviour, pursuing goals, tasks, and strategies that are all valuable to the organisation whilst behaving poorly to their subordinates: humiliating, belittling, and manipulating them to 'get the job done'.[10] Leaders who have slipped into this pattern of behaviour are culturally very toxic, with upper management valuing the results they generate for the business and perceiving little more than a strong task focus, whilst subordinates see their behaviour as abusive or even bullying.[11]

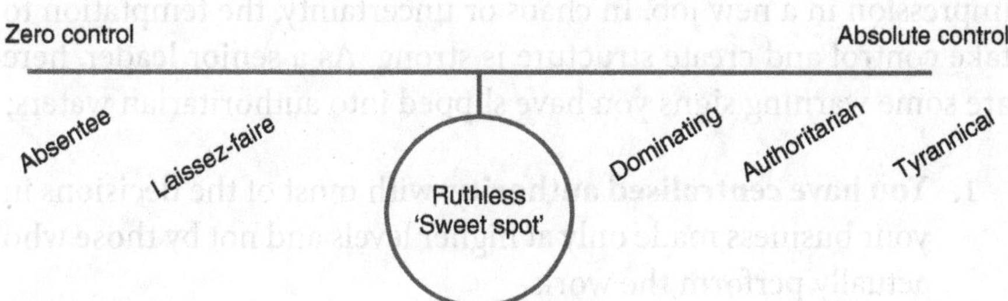

Figure 3.1 The ruthless leadership continuum.

Staying future-fit top tip. Pursuing business objectives and being a key contributor to results is great; however, as a leader, be wary of this 'key contributor' trap. Delivering outcomes that are valuable to the business is not a ticket to tread heavily and inconsiderately on those around you. When the pressure is on to deliver results, try to avoid tunnel vision on the task; think about those around you, and make sure the culture and environment you are creating and role modelling for people is also contributing positively to the business.

Authoritarian. Leaders who have slipped into authoritarian-like behaviour want their team to achieve the best performance, have a need for structure, and often a fear of alienation.[12] Leaders operating in a highly authoritarian way will make all the important decisions in their team, setting out clear rules, clear responsibilities, and simply require other people to follow their rules and ways of doing things to achieve the best performance. Focused on performance, they dictate how things need to be, moving and removing people like pawns in a game. This sole focus on results makes it difficult for leaders to maintain relationships and build trust.

Staying future-fit top tips. There are times where it is easy to wander off course into authoritarian territory; for example, when faced with a business crisis (perhaps while rolling out a challenging organisational change), or, when simply wishing to make a good first impression in a new job. In chaos or uncertainty, the temptation to take control and create structure is strong. As a senior leader, here are some warning signs you have slipped into authoritarian waters:

1. **You have centralised authority**, with most of the decisions in your business made only at higher levels and not by those who actually perform the work.
2. **You find yourself unilaterally making a lot of decisions** without consulting or listening to the advice, concerns, or opinions of others.

3. **You tend to use rewards and punishments to ensure compliance,** incentivising people with bonuses and promotions, whilst coercing others to fall into line.

If any of this feels familiar, try to step back. Think about the value other people, relationships, diverse thinking, and trust brings to performance. Reflect on what fears have triggered your threat response and prompted you to draw in the reins of control. Gently find ways to release your grip and empower those around you.

Dominating. Leaders displaying dominant behaviours achieve their goals by asserting their role as the boss and leveraging their power to insist others 'get on board' with the plan. At times of crisis or change (when a fast, well-coordinated response is called for), sometimes leaders need to step into this more dominating style to manage stakeholders with opposing views and move things forward. However, this technique should be used sparingly at critical moments. There are also more subtle dominant behaviours leaders should be vigilant to every day, such as hogging the discussion and suppressing talent. Specifically, leaders who exhibit dominant behaviours are more likely to feel threatened by rising stars in their team, attempting (consciously or unconsciously) to suppress that person by ostracising them, monitoring them, and preventing them from forming close friendships with others in the team.[13]

Staying future-fit top tip. When you are the leader, it is very difficult when you think you have the right answer not to immediately put it out there and end up dominating the conversation. However, by over-dominating the conversation, it is likely you are stifling creative ideas and missing important information that is relevant to decision-making. To achieve performance, stay focused on orchestrating conversations and ensure there is a lot of space in discussions for everyone to talk and contribute. Similarly, notice your behaviour towards top talent in your team: do you support and challenge them? Encourage them to stay connected to others in the team? Empower them to keep growing in their role? Or, consciously or unconsciously, have you been distancing them from others and monitoring them more closely?

Laissez-faire. Whereas leaders operating in the dominant and authoritarian space seek to achieve performance via controlling decisions, those who have slipped the other way into laissez-faire behaviours tend to avoid decision-making.[14] Leaders operating in a laissez-faire way have stepped back from the process, following the belief that leaders should hire or build capable teams and then step back to give those individuals lots of freedom in how they do their work and what decisions are made. This passive approach is far more prevalent amongst leaders because it has a lure to it: it feels like a good thing to do. However, there is a fine line between empowerment and laissez-faire. Step back from control too much and leaders will find this lack of decision involvement means they have forfeited control of the final outcome, caused decision making to become overly delayed and strung out, and risked conflict as team members jockey over roles and responsibilities.

Staying future-fit top tip. As Steve Jobs said, 'it doesn't make sense to hire smart people and tell them what to do; we hire smart people so they can tell us what to do'. A compelling quote but embrace this philosophy with caution. Empowering people is not the same as adopting a completely 'hands-off' approach, stepping back, and relinquishing all control over decisions and process. Empowerment requires leaders to set clear expectations, provide feedback, involve people in decision-making, be open to new ideas, and recognise work well done. It is about giving people space and stepping forward into the role you need to play as a leader, not stepping out of it.

Absentee. Leaders who find themselves in the 'absentee' category, have completely checked out of their leadership role. To coin a phrase: the wheel is still turning but the hamster is long gone. Having worked hard and been promoted, leaders here have slipped into enjoying the privileges, titles, and rewards of leadership whilst avoiding any meaningful involvement with their team, failing to provide any direction or feedback. Although the impact of this behaviour is often overlooked, quietly team effectiveness gets eroded with people becoming demotivated, less satisfied with their job, and stressed out by the ambiguity.

Staying future-fit top tip. If you find yourself straying all the way out into absent territory, it is worth talking to a coach or mentor to tune into what is causing the drift and discuss the impact it is having on you, others, and the business generally. To get back on track, you will need to drill right down into your motivations and purpose, asking yourself the big questions, such as: What gets you out of bed in the morning? Why do you lead? What imprint do you want to leave on the company and those around you?

Research and Psychology: The Evolutionary Pull of Authoritarian Leaders

Evolutionary psychology shows that under situations of threat or uncertainty, when unpopular decisions need to be made, we prefer more authoritarian leaders. People support and vote in leaders who appear more assertive, decisive, and self-assured in achieving their goals, the leaders perceived as being more capable of taking radical actions.[15]

(*Continued*)

High-threat environments are also more likely to provoke authoritarian behaviours in leaders themselves.[16] But, as a leader, beware of this lure towards authoritarianism when under threat. Research shows authoritarianism is associated with rigidity of thinking, intolerance, lower levels of empathy, and feelings of vulnerability.[17] Indeed, this feeling of vulnerability may explain the evolutionary preference for this leadership style when under threat, as it prompts leaders to monitor their environments more actively and react more strongly to negative events.[18]

In situations of threat or crisis, be cautious of this pull towards authoritarianism. Ensure the call to make radical decisions does not snuff out other skills you will need to effectively lead through the intense situation (skills such as empathy, adaptability, and relationship management).

Leading with Care: Staying Compassionate No Matter What

The word 'compassion' comes from Latin and literally means 'co-suffering'. However, compassion requires more than putting yourself in someone else's shoes and getting in the trench with them. True compassion can be defined as:[19,20]

> *Empathic concern for someone's suffering coupled with taking wise action to help.*

Compassion is not simply 'being nice'; it requires a leader to balance emotion, logic, and action. It's about being able to listen, understand, and feel what others feel, and having the courage and control to respond in the most helpful way. As Rasmus Hougaard, author and CEO, puts it: 'compassionate leadership is about doing the hard things in a human way'.[21]

Take the example of a doctor working in a busy emergency ward. Despite seeing numerous patients every day, the doctor needs to remain aware and empathetic to what each patient is going through. They must stay attentive to the pain and suffering each person may be experiencing, appreciating how frightening it is to face a surgical procedure or battle a life-threatening illness. And yet, the doctor cannot be swept up by emotions and empathy. They need to think logically and respond appropriately to provide the best possible advice, care, and treatment.

Research and Psychology: the Four Ingredients of Compassion

Although often conflated with 'showing kindness to someone', research shows that true compassion requires four key skills:[22]

1. **Cognitive empathy:** the ability for perspective taking

   Knowing and understanding, at an intellectual level, how another person feels and what they might be thinking is what helps guide us to an appropriate response in a distressing situation (rather than an impulsive one). It enables us to respond to a problem with brainpower.

2. **Emotional empathy:** the ability to share in someone's emotional experience

   Feeling what another person is feeling and sharing their state of mind is what moves us to comfort, reassure, and

(*Continued*)

help someone. The emotional system in our brain has a mirroring mechanism, which means, to varying degrees, individuals feel what others feel (whether that is joy, anxiety, anger, or sadness). Emotions are contagious, and they are what move us to want to act and help.

3. **Distress tolerance:** the ability to avoid being overwhelmed by negative emotions

   Accepting a level of pain, suffering, or discomfort is crucial if you are to face an intense or emotional situation and still do what needs to be done. Distress tolerance is the skill that stops us from letting our emotions take over and make a situation worse. It is what makes us remain capable of helping.

4. **Non-judgement:** the ability to not be condemning or critical of others

   Observing without evaluating is what helps us deal with a situation constructively. Our brains can be very quick to pass judgement and assign blame, but these two habits get in the way of compassionate action. Being non-judgemental is about accepting the reality of a situation rather than dissecting its causes.

Acting compassionately in tough moments requires you, as a leader, to connect and share in the suffering others are experiencing without becoming so entwined that you are no longer able to offer the best support. When times are tough, it can be tempting to hold tightly on to logic and shut off from the human impact. Or you may find yourself caring so much for people that it burns you out. You end up swamped in the emotions of it all. But, as we have briefly explored here, compassion does not mean wildly flinging open Pandora's box and taking on everyone's emotions. It is about balancing emotion with rational thinking and helpful action. Practising true compassion will protect you from burnout and help you perform effectively as a leader.

Let us look at a few ways you can practice compassion:

Meet people where they are and listen carefully	Make a habit of putting yourself in other people's shoes before you meet with them . . . ask yourself: • What might their perspective be? • What might they be thinking or feeling at this moment? Then, listen carefully: • What are they trying to tell you? • What is the key message they want to communicate? • What are they saying about their situation as they understand it? • *How* are they saying it? – What is their tone of voice and body language telling you? – What keywords and phrases are they using? (possibly repeatedly)

(*Continued*)

Accept reality for what it is	Keep yourself in the present moment by acknowledging and accepting the situation as it is right now . . . notice: • What thoughts of judgement or blame are popping up? • How much thinking effort is being spent unpicking the cause of the situation? • Are your thoughts resisting reality, stuck in the trenches of what 'should be'? Attempting to suppress all judgemental thoughts will backfire. Instead just notice them. Let them bob to the surface of your mind and leave them be. . . . focus on: • How can I best handle the situation as it is? • What is the best way for me to help this person?

The Caring Leadership Continuum: How to Stay on Track

A leader who is in the sweet spot of 'caring' acts with compassion to help people develop. They make sure others feel heard, respected, supported, and encouraged, whilst appreciating that giving true support often requires them, as a leader, to embrace a level of discomfort. For example, helping someone develop may mean making a difficult decision or giving someone feedback that they need, but may not want, to hear.

If you find yourself off track from leading in a caring way, most likely it is a thinking preference, fear of social rejection, failure to embrace discomfort, or simple bias that is taking you off course. These are traps everyone falls prey to on occasion. Whilst having a caring mindset sounds obvious, demonstrating true compassion is not always clear-cut or automatic when operating in the flow of work. As a leader, it is easy to sidestep the moments that matter, following a path that on the surface seems natural, logical, or paved with good intentions.

Let us look at the caring leadership continuum (see Figure 3.2) and specific ways you may be pulled off course.

People-pleasing. Leaders who are stuck in a people-pleasing behaviour pattern will find themselves constantly trying to keep everyone happy; as Dr. Beatrice Chestnut explains, such leaders tend to be 'friendly, upbeat, and generous (to a fault). Their focus of attention is on other people, on important relationships, and what other people think and feel about them. They pay a lot of attention to whether or not others like them and they strive to be indispensable and approved of in the eyes of others'.[23] Whilst this leadership style has many positive qualities (such as a deep sense of empathy and an ability to build great networks), people-pleasing is an extremely unhealthy behaviour pattern to get into. Performance-wise, leaders here find themselves avoiding conflict, failing to give clear direction,

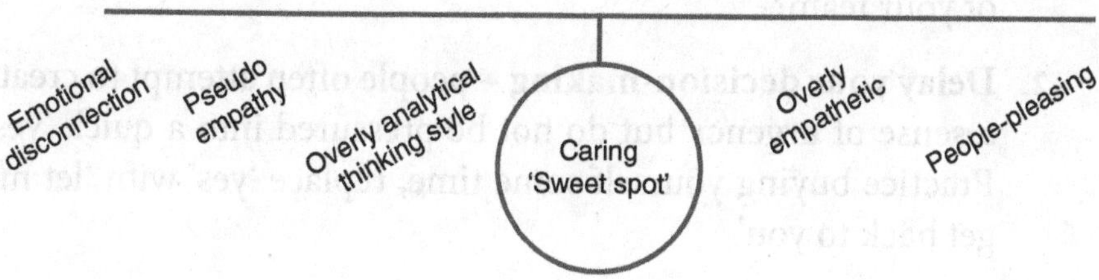

Figure 3.2 The caring leadership continuum.

not asserting themselves (ending up going along with subpar ideas), and struggling to make decisions or delegate tasks for fear of disappointing someone.[24] Furthermore, constantly putting the needs and feelings of others first can lead to resentment building up, especially when others do not reciprocate; however, rarely will a leader operating in 'people-pleasing' mode vent their frustrations directly to the person displeasing them.

Staying future-fit top tips. People-pleasing is an incredibly difficult pattern to get out of as it is linked to your personality type, childhood experiences, and neural mechanisms in your brain. Specifically, if you tend to get stuck in the habit of people-pleasing, it is likely you will have high levels of agreeableness (and often perfectionism) in your personality, as well as childhood experiences of a parent who was emotionally inconsistent or unpredictable towards you (i.e., sometimes loving, sometimes distant).[25] On top of that, neuroscientists have shown that, at a neural level, people-pleasers experience greater levels of mental stress and discomfort when disagreeing with others.[26] People-pleasing is therefore deeply ingrained but thankfully not a life sentence! You can shift your way of operating with insight and practice. Here are three top tips to get you started:

1. **Recognise the impact** – focusing on keeping people happy will be perpetuating certain situations that you find frustrating. Start observing yourself at work, notice how your 'need to please' shows up: how is it impacting you or the performance of your team?

2. **Delay your decision-making** – people often attempt to create a sense of urgency but do not be pressured into a quick 'yes'. Practice buying yourself some time, replace 'yes' with 'let me get back to you'.

3. **Stay focused on what matters (not what people will think)** – as a senior leader, not everyone is going to like, approve, or agree with you or your decisions. Stay focused on what you feel is the right course of action to take and what will move business performance forward, rather than getting fixated on what others will think or say of you.

Overly empathetic. Empathy is built into us as humans and deeply rooted in our biology. Our brains are wired to be sensitive to the emotions of others.[27] However, research shows we are more likely to be empathetic towards people we feel close to socially (i.e., friends, family, or someone we see as similar to us).[28] This bias can result in a leader watering down or avoiding difficult feedback, acting slowly on a performance issue, or being overly lenient and indulgent towards behaviour that would otherwise be unacceptable, and/or avoiding a tough decision because of the impact they know it will have.[29,30]

Staying future-fit top tips. It is tricky to spot when you arrive in overly empathetic territory. At the time, it just seems like a caring awareness for another person's situation, or a decision made based on being privy to more information. However, over-empathy towards those we feel closest to tends to result in decisions that feel unjust to others, as well as hindering the individual's own development. To avoid this common leadership trap, be acutely aware that your empathy has an 'in-group' bias and proactively counter it. Specifically, when considering a situation or decision in relation to someone new or who seems different to you, have an open mind, step back, and ask yourself:

- What do I need to get curious about here or understand better?
- What factors would I be weighing in if this person was more 'like me' or a close friend?

On the other hand, if it's someone you naturally feel a strong affinity towards, consider:

- What is the impact of my empathy towards this individual on others?
- What is the impact of my empathy on this individual's own development? Is it helping or hampering them?

To keep over-empathy in check, it is also well worth finding a 'not-like-me' sounding board; identifying a senior leader who thinks and behaves very differently to you, who can offer another perspective on key situations or decisions.

Overly analytical thinking style. We all have certain preferences and thinking styles when it comes to making decisions and approaching challenges. For example, some leaders naturally tend towards an analytical style, preferring to focus on facts, evidence, and applying logic. Whereas other leaders may have a more intuitive default style, preferring to focus on emotions, personal experiences, and concrete examples.[31] Research has shown that these preferences map on to two neural networks in our brain: the analytical network (AN) and an empathetic network (EN).[32] Neither style is better or worse, and to lead effectively, you must become adept at balancing both networks. If your go-to preference is the AN, you risk not listening, considering, or understanding other people's views and experiences enough, thereby missing key ideas or alternative possibilities. Similarly, when making (or communicating) a decision, you may find yourself overlooking the personal impact of that decision, which can make you appear 'uncaring' and leave you open to be blindsided by someone's reaction or feedback.

Staying future-fit top tip. Unfortunately, researchers have shown that our thinking style is likely to be unbalanced because the AN and EN do not work well together. In fact, if one network in our brain is activated, the other is deactivated, as they actively suppress each other.[33] And it is likely you will have a more dominant 'go-to'. Consequently, if your 'go-to' thinking style is more analytical, check yourself when it comes to staying in the sweet spot of 'caring'. For a moment, reflect on: How am I processing things at this moment? Am I really taking the time to listen and understand other people's views? Am I tuned in to the feelings and experiences of those around me? Have I given enough weight to factors like compassion and social connection?

Pseudo-empathy. Often we can think we are being empathetic and showing concern for someone else, but in fact, we are reacting to our own anxiety and needs. For example, as a leader, if one of your direct reports is struggling and distressed, you could find yourself doing whatever you can to fix the situation for them. However, what is likely happening here is that their distress is causing you to feel anxious, and you want them to stop acting in a way that distresses you. Your empathy is therefore self-focused rather than focused on them. Similarly, when a direct report is struggling to perform a task, as a leader, it can be tempting to rescue that person from the difficult situation. Whilst sometimes this may be necessary, this reaction can also be driven by a leader's need to feel indispensable. In both instances, what looks like a caring response is pseudo-empathy; it is the leader reacting to their own anxiety and needs, not based on what is good for the other person.

Staying future-fit top tip. Pseudo-empathy might not seem like the biggest mistake to make as a leader; however, by trying to fix people or fix their situation, it is likely you are stopping that person from learning and growing (i.e., having their own experience and discovering their own strengths). Many leaders want the people who work for them to be happy and feel like they have the best job, but you cannot make other people happy or fix the 'right' experience for them. Your role as a leader is to help others understand how they can make themselves happy, fix their own situations, and tackle their own challenges. Empathy requires you to listen, pay attention, and respond by helping someone work through their own challenges. Get yourself out of the way. In psychology, this is called learning to be 'self-differentiated'; differentiating your own experience from the experience of others and allowing others to have their experience. Whilst this may not always feel easy to do, in the long run, it is the pseudo-empathy behaviours of fixing and rescuing that can be more unhelpful, even if at the time they feel like being kind and doing someone a favour.

Emotional disconnection. Research suggests it is common for emotional intelligence (EQ) to erode as leaders rise in the ranks. One industry study from TalentSmart analysed the EQ profiles of the million-plus people in their database and found senior executives and CEOs, on average, have the lowest EQ scores.[34] As Simon Sinek explained, one cause of this may be 'the problem of abstraction', with many executive leaders having less and less meaningful interactions with their staff, ending up seeing people as resources or numbers on a spreadsheet rather than individuals.[35] Furthermore, as accountability for the bottom line increases, assertive, action-oriented leaders can begin to see caring about the emotions of others as a distraction and a luxury they cannot afford. This is an understandable coping mechanism but one that quickly slips into emotional detachment: 'I can't talk to everyone, so I won't talk to anyone', 'I don't have time to care about people personally, I have to delegate this to other talented people who get my philosophy', 'I can't worry about individuals when I'm accountable for the whole company'.

Staying future-fit top tip. The best-performing leaders are those with the highest levels of EQ.[36] Empathy, compassion, and meaningful interactions with people at all levels are essential if leaders are to make effective decisions and stay in touch with the business they are running. It is an illusion that emotional connection can be delegated; in truth, the emotions of executive leaders have an amplified impact on those around them. One meaningful interaction can make or break someone's day or shift their entire outlook on their job and the company. It is a daunting truth but avoiding connection with people and suppressing emotion and empathy is not the answer – it means you are flying blind. If you have slipped into this avoidance coping mechanism, tune back in: start noticing your emotions (how they influence your behaviour and impact on others), start getting curious (next time someone expresses a strong emotion, ask them about it, listen, and play back what you hear), and get into the habit of talking to people (with the aim to understand rather than solve).

Notes

1. Cummings, G.G., Tate, K., Lee, S., et al. (2018). Leadership styles and outcome patterns for the nursing workforce and work environment: a systematic review. *International Journal of Nursing Studies* 85: 19–60.
2. Wang, A.C., and Cheng, B.S. (2010). When does benevolent leadership lead to creativity? The moderating role of creative role identity and job autonomy. *Journal of Organizational Behavior* 31: 106–121.
3. Walters, A. (2019). *The Future of Leadership: Developing a New Perspective*. EY white paper.
4. Andy Coxall (2018). *Open Source Leadership*. TedX video.
5. Carucci, R. (2018). Leaders, stop avoiding hard decisions. *Harvard Business Review*.

6. Batten, J.D. (2001). *Tough-Minded Leadership*. Oregon, US: Wipf and Stock Publishers.
7. Kierein, N.M., and Gold, M.A. (2000). Pygmalion in work organizations: a meta-analysis. *Journal of Organizational Behavior* 21: 913–928.
8. Eden, D. (1990). *Pygmalion in Management: Productivity as a Self Fulfilling Prophecy*. Lexington: D.C. Heath.
9. Carucci, R.A., and Hansen, E.C. (2014). *Rising to Power: The Journey of Exceptional Executives*. Texas, US: Greenleaf Book Group.
10. Aasland, M.S., Skogstad, A., Notelaers, G., et al. (2010). The prevalence of destructive leadership behaviour. *British Journal of Management* 21: 438–452.
11. Einarsen, S., Aasland, M.S., and Skogstad, A. (2007). Destructive leadership behaviour: a definition and conceptual model. *The Leadership Quarterly* 18: 207–216.
12. Harms, P.D., Wood, D., Landay, K., et al. (2018). Autocratic leaders and authoritarian followers revisited: a review and agenda for the future. *The Leadership Quarterly* 29: 105–122.
13. Case, C.R., and Maner, J.K. (2014). Divide and conquer: When and why leaders undermine the cohesive fabric of their group. *Journal of Personality and Social Psychology* 107: 1033.
14. Eagly, A.H., Johannesen-Schmidt, M.C., and Van Engen, M.L. (2003). Transformational, transactional, and laissez-faire leadership styles: a meta-analysis comparing women and men. *Psychological Bulletin* 129: 569.
15. Kakkar, H., and Sivanathan, N. (2017). When the appeal of a dominant leader is greater than a prestige leader. *Proceedings of the National Academy of Sciences* 114: 6734–6739.
16. Nielsen, M.B., Skogstad, A., Matthiesen, S. B., and Einarsen, S. (2016). The importance of a multidimensional and temporal design

in research on leadership and workplace safety. *The Leadership Quarterly* 27: 142–155.

17. Harms, P.D., Wood, D., Landay, K., et al. (2018). Autocratic leaders and authoritarian followers revisited: A review and agenda for the future. *The Leadership Quarterly* 29: 105–122.
18. Ludeke, S. (2016). Authoritarianism: Positives and negatives. In Zeigler-Hill, V.E. and Marcus, D.K. (Eds.), *The Dark Side of Personality: Science and Practice in Social, Personality, and Clinical Psychology* (pp. 231–250). American Psychological Association.
19. Gilbert, P. (2009). *The Compassionate Mind*. Robinson.
20. Gilbert, P., Catarino, F., Duarte, C., et al. (2017). The development of compassionate engagement and action scales for self and others. *Journal of Compassionate Health Care* 4: 1–24.
21. Hougaard, R. and Carter, J. (2021). *Compassionate Leadership – Doing Hard Things the Human Way*. Massachusetts, US: Harvard Business Press.
22. de Zulueta, P.C. (2016). Developing compassionate leadership in health care: an integrative review. *Journal of Healthcare Leadership* 8: 1.
23. Chestnut, B. (2017). *The 9 Types of Leadership: Mastering the Art of People in the 21st Century Workplace*. New York, US: Simon and Schuster.
24. Kaplan, R.E., and Kaiser, R.B. (2003). Developing versatile leadership. *MIT Sloan Management Review* 44: 19–26.
25. English, C. and Rapson, J. (2006). *Anxious to Please: 7 Revolutionary Practices for the Chronically Nice*. Illinois, US: Sourcebooks, Inc.
26. Dominguez, J.F., Taing, S.A., and Molenberghs, P. (2016). Why do some find it hard to disagree? An fMRI study. *Frontiers in Human Neuroscience 718*: 1–9.
27. Decety, J., and Cowell, J.M. (2014). Friends or foes: is empathy necessary for moral behavior? *Perspectives on Psychological Science* 9: 525–537.

28. Montalan, B., Lelard, T., Godefroy, O., and Mouras, H. (2012). Behavioral investigation of the influence of social categorization on empathy for pain: a minimal group paradigm study. *Frontiers in Psychology* 3: 389.

29. Kaplan, R.E., and Kaiser, R.B. (2003). Developing versatile leadership. *MIT Sloan Management Review* 44: 19–26.

30. Cameron, K.S., Quinn, R.E., DeGraff, J., and Thakor, A.V. (2006). *Competing Values Leadership: Creating Value in Organizations*. Cheltenham, UK: Edward Elgar Publishing.

31. Epstein, S., Pacini, R., Denes-Raj, V., and Heier, H. (1996). Individual differences in intuitive–experiential and analytical–rational thinking styles. *Journal of Personality and Social Psychology* 71: 390.

32. Smith, M., Van Oosten, E., and Boyatzis, R. (2020). The best managers balance analytical and emotional intelligence. *Harvard Business Review Article*.

33. Boyatzis, R.E., Rochford, K., and Taylor, S.N. (2015). The role of the positive emotional attractor in vision and shared vision: toward effective leadership, relationships, and engagement. *Frontiers in Psychology* 6: 670.

34. Bradberry, T. (2017). Here's why your boss lacks emotional intelligence. *World Economic Forum Article*.

35. Sinek, S. (2014). *Leaders Eat Last: Why Some Teams Pull Together and Others Don't*. New York, US: Penguin.

36. Stein, S.J., Papadogiannis, P., Yip, J.A., and Sitarenios, G. (2009). Emotional intelligence of leaders: A profile of top executives. *Leadership & Organization Development Journal* 30: 87–101.

CHAPTER 4
AMBITIOUSLY APPRECIATIVE

Be grateful for what you already have while you pursue your goals. If you aren't grateful for what you already have, what makes you think you would be happy with more?

—Roy T. Bennett, author

What Is an 'Ambitiously Appreciative' Mindset?

Ambitiously appreciative leaders hold the following mindset:

- To achieve ambitious goals, they must be relentless and determined.
- It is important to set objectives that are aggressive.
- Performance and progress should be celebrated (not just attainment).
- They must appreciate the things outside work that matter, and make sure others have time to do the same.
- They must always value, make space for, and be aware of their own and other's well-being.

Elvin Semrad, a teacher in psychotherapy, once said: 'You can achieve whatever you want, as long as you are willing to pay the price'. Do you want to be CEO or head of sales in Europe? Pay the price. As a child, do you want to win an Olympic medal or become prime minister? Pay the price. If you put the effort of every living moment into reaching that goal, your chances may not be negligible.

At least that is the mentality. And it is true: no great achievement will come for free. But how do you give yourself relentlessly to a goal or job, put in all the hard yards necessary to succeed, and yet avoid being consumed by the challenge?

Future-fit leaders have a mindset that is both ambitious and appreciative. They know that to achieve ambitious goals you have got to be relentless and determined, whilst at the same time believe it is important to keep your goals in perspective and be sustainable. On the one hand, they are highly driven and never satisfied, yet they also celebrate great performance (even if certain objectives have not all been achieved) and continue to appreciate things that matter outside work. Simply put, their projects and goals are both everything to them and yet not everything.

This is potentially one of the trickiest mindsets for C-suite leaders to get right and keep in balance. Even Indra Nooyi, former PepsiCo CEO, said that while she was proud she had boosted revenue 80% during her tenure, looking back, there are times she wished she had prioritised her family, stating 'I've been blessed with an amazing career, but if I'm being honest, there have been moments I wish I'd spent more time with my children and family'.

To be clear, ambitiously appreciative is not a mindset of 'do it all' perfectionism. Leaders can be both relentlessly driven and highly appreciative, but that is not the same as stating leaders (male and female) must strive to excel in all aspects of their life all the time. Of course, certain compromises have to be made at certain times. As Oprah Winfrey is quoted to have said, 'You can have it all. You just can't have it all at one time'.

In 1975, Shirley Conran published a book called *Superwoman* a guide aimed at helping the working woman by offering advice on how to run a home, save time, save money, and have fun. By about 1984, the term 'superwoman syndrome' had been coined, referring to women who were constantly striving and stretching themselves, neglecting their health, to excel in multiple roles (for example, business leader, wife, mother, daughter, sister, aunt, volunteer, homemaker, best friend, and/or student).

This chapter is not about becoming some sort of superman or superwoman. It is more a prompt to stay vigilant to the whole picture and make your choices consciously. It is about intentionally choosing when to make what compromises and sacrifices in which aspects of your life. It is here to help prevent you sleepwalking into situations out of habit or blinkered thinking and then looking back and regretting certain decisions later.

Leader to Leader Story

Having worked his way up from shop floor to CEO, Steve Carson has a successful track record in various FTSE retail organisations. His journey to the top has taken hard work, commitment, and dedication. As Steve explains, 'relentless drive is one of the qualities that makes you stand out from the next person, who's not prepared to sacrifice in the way you sacrifice'.

But, as Steve reflects, 'there's a fine line between driving your performance and realising that there's more to life. All high performers are pushing themselves to that line, or sometimes beyond it, and you can step over the line before you realise you're over it'.

During certain phases of his leadership career, Steve has certainly found himself on the wrong side of 'that line': giving everything up for his job, continuously travelling, working across time zones, getting up at 5 a.m., sending emails until 11 p.m., going to bed at midnight, and getting up again for meetings or more travel the next day. Day after day, week after week, Steve recalls how 'over time your energy levels dwindle. You reach a point where there's just nothing left in the tank'. Often chasing a false horizon, telling yourself that if you can just keep pushing a bit longer, 'if you can get to the weekend' or 'keep pushing until the next month or next quarter', then it will all be okay. Things will get better and be different. It is just a little more, a little bit further.

Unfortunately, the horizon tends to be a mirage. There is always another thing around the corner.

For Steve, one of the biggest pause moments was when his father passed away suddenly. As he explains, 'it made me really stop and ask myself what is life all about, and have I got the balance right? Should I have spent more time with my father? I was working all hours under the sun. Was I there for him?' While it is impossible to do anything about that now, it did prompt him to consider 'am I giving enough time to my mum? To my wife and children?'

Whilst Steve remains driven and finds it incredibly hard not to sprint, constantly giving his all to succeed, he has discovered different ways to preserve some balance. He listens when people close to him, or his own body, start telling him he has gone beyond 'the line' and it is taking too much from him. He plans in 'sacred time' as far as possible in advance (for birthdays, anniversaries, school plays, sports matches) because, as he explains, 'there's always a thousand reasons why I can't be there. Always another meeting to attend'. Similarly, in the past five years, he has got much better at planning in time for himself. For exercise, mindfulness, reading, sleep, improved nutrition, time with friends. . . he finds ways to be the best version of himself. And, finally he consciously appreciates more in life (for example, his family growing up, the support of his wife, his health, and the beauty of nature whilst out walking his dog);

(*Continued*)

differentiating feeling lucky from feeling grateful and appreciative, as he explains, 'I used to say how lucky I am. But it's not really luck, not entirely. I work hard for much of it – it's more appreciation'.

By final words of caution, Steve remarks how 'the job is demanding of you. I've seen too many people lose marriages, not be close to friends or family, children, because they give everything. You've got to look after yourself, so that when you're with them you have the energy to connect with them. So, you don't just come home, sit on the sofa and fall asleep in 5 minutes because you're exhausted'.

You cannot keep striving and driving for more without appreciating and protecting what you already have.

Before we explore why this mindset is becoming so difficult for leaders to get right in the megatrends environment, let us first clarify what these two terms mean:

Defining Terms

- **Ambition:** is the persistent and generalised striving for success, attainment, and accomplishment.[1]
- **Appreciation:** a general state of thankfulness and ability to put goals in perspective.[2]

Why Being Ambitiously Appreciative Matters Amidst Megatrends

The megatrends environment is loading the dice against leaders, making it very easy to be consumed by relentless striving and much less easy to switch off, decompress, and feel content.

Today, if you are not constantly and fully exerting yourself by working, learning, taking on new challenges, striving to meet an impossible number of goals, then you are conditioned to view yourself as being 'lazy' or not doing enough. There is pressure to always be productive. A guilt that often lurks in the shadows of relaxation.

At the centre of this is what is known as 'hustle culture': a pervasive belief that what matters most in life is achieving professional goals by relentlessly working hard and sacrificing everything. It is a philosophy that has long been romanticised across performance domains, with books, films, and adverts retelling the story of individuals devoting every waking moment and sacrificing everything, until their hard work finally pays off.

This much hyped perception of what success looks like, and what it takes to be successful, has become distorted. Specifically, capitalist thinking, advancing technology, and social media have all converged to create a busyness epidemic. Let us explore what is happening in more detail.

Traditional 'Profit-Only' Thinking Distorts the Boundaries of What Is Expected and Rewarded

Within the business world, there has long been a drive to make sure people are working 'hard enough'. A capitalist desire to boost productivity, with those willing to work long hours and take on huge workloads celebrated and rewarded as dedicated high performers. However, as social psychologist Devon Price points out: our brains are not designed to be constantly productive.[3]

In fact, various studies have shown the average person is only productive 3–4 hours a day (on tasks that require a lot of mental effort, focus, and/or creativity). Yet still, most of us play the game. We look at what others around us are doing and use it as a gauge for what is reasonable. We talk about how busy we are. We police one another's behaviour (noticing who is a few minutes late to work or frequently 'offline'). We say yes to more and more work and responsibilities. We wear the badge of 'being super busy', working late, and working weekends like a badge of honour, especially at senior leadership levels. All the time, setting an impossible and unhealthy standard for ourselves and those around us.

Advancing Technology: Making It Possible to Be 'Always-On'

Technology has also made it possible to never switch off. Whether you are commuting to work, at the gym, on holiday, it is possible to always be plugged in. On average, people check their phones 58 times a day and, for those whose personal phone is their work phone, the quick inbox check is an easy habit to get into.

While checking the odd email or joining the odd call may feel harmless enough at the time, it means your mind is constantly tethered to work. Reading an email may take just a moment, but the effects ripple out, often triggering a change in your emotional state and setting off a chain of work-related thoughts. Furthermore, even when senior leaders consciously choose to subscribe to this 'always-on' way of being (stating it is a personal choice and not expected of others), their behaviour has a knock-on impact, setting a precedent, and driving a relentless pace of work. There is no disclaimer here; you are either part of the problem or part of the solution when it comes to driving an 'always-on' culture.

Social Media: Ramping Up the Expectations We Have of Ourselves

Social media is a hot bed of 'hustle culture' propaganda. On the one hand, the '#hustle' trend appears to be adding positive things to our society, with business leaders and influencers spreading inspiring and motivating messages; calling people to dig deep, work hard, and give everything to make their dreams and goals a reality. The problem is social media feeds us a distorted reality of other people's lives.

For one thing, influencers are not selling dreams; they are selling products. But this is easy for people to forget as brands get seamlessly woven into the compelling 'work harder' narrative. Secondly, on social channels, hustle culture is less about what you are ambitiously striving for and more a platform to signal how hard you are working.

Consequently, via social media, we are constantly bombarded with images and updates on what other people are doing; what they are learning, working hard on, striving for, and achieving. This view into other people's worlds is distorted and filtered in every sense, but the power of social comparison is strong. Our brains instinctively look to others to guide our behaviour and gauge what we 'should' be doing. The distorted reality promoted in social media therefore distorts the expectations we place on ourselves and exacerbates the feeling that we are never doing enough.

Burnout: The Price Being Paid

Work ethic, identity, and self-worth frequently become so closely intertwined, that it is common for people to only feel 'worthy' when they are being productive and doing things. This is particularly true, for those operating in the most senior levels of business. Being super busy, constantly productive in back-to-back meetings, always available and completely dedicated to the role and business, is just seen as part of the deal. After all, that is behaviour that got you where you are, right?

But, while hard work and a level of stress is part and parcel of the CEO position, burnout is not; C-suite leaders need to be aware of the assumptions they have about what life as an executive is 'inevitably like'. Furthermore, executive teams need to be able to openly discuss what is and is not expected at that level – and what impact role modelling certain working practices will have on the rest of the organisation.

The issue of C-suite executives pushing too hard, over-working, and burning out is not a new one. Back in 1897, Murray Finch-Hatton, a pioneering motorist, wrote to his fellow board members: 'Gentlemen – I believe you are aware that about three months ago, as the result of overwork, my health suddenly broke down, and my physician has ordered me at once to go to the Riviera'. Sadly, even after being declared unfit for work and stepping down as director, Finch-Hatton died the following year at just 47 years.[4]

Have things improved? Statistics suggest not.

In the healthcare sector (prior to the pandemic), a survey of 350 executive leaders showed:[5]

- 65% never or rarely take all of their vacation days due to their workload

- 51% say that on average, they are not getting an adequate amount of sleep every night
- Over half (51%) of respondents shared that burnout could cause them to leave their current position
- 75% of respondents know colleagues who have left the health-care industry entirely due to burnout.

Furthermore, research shows 54% of C-suite leaders across sectors are falling into the 'always-on' trap, finding themselves often or almost always fuelling the perception that it is important to be seen as hyper-busy, working weekends, always on, and exhausted.[6] And, the cost of this relentless lifestyle is high, with burnout being a significant predictor of several psychological and physical consequences, including insomnia, depression, type 2 diabetes, coronary heart disease, hospitalisation due to cardiovascular disorder, musculoskeletal pain, severe injuries, and mortality below the age of 45 years.[7]

Pressure to perform and push boundaries is not going to disappear. But a balance between relentless striving and appreciation must be found. Burnout is an occupational phenomenon that results from not being able to switch off, not being able to appreciate your input and achievements as 'good enough', and an inability to put work into perspective.

Within modern society, somewhere along the line, the recipes for burnout and success have got stuck together and confused. Thriving personally and professionally is not about relentless hustle; that is the recipe to burn bright and burn out. Lasting success is what comes from finding a balance of ambition and appreciation. It is these ingredients people need to tune into and master.

Let us now explore how to find the sweet spot in both.

Leading Ambitiously: The Relentless Drive to Achieve

Philosophers remain undecided whether ambition is a virtue or a vice. Most likely, it can be both.

Often ambition is perceived negatively within the specific context of politics and pursuit of power. And, this context is indeed where the word 'ambition' has its roots, coming from the Latin 'ambire' meaning 'to go around' (and canvas votes). However, within this mindset, we align more to the modern definition of ambition as a general 'desire and determination to achieve success'.[8]

From this lens, the virtues of ambition are clear. Without ambition, space programmes would not exist, the Human Genome Project would not have been completed, and the Sistine Chapel would never have been painted. There is no doubt ambition is a key ingredient of incredible achievements, but at what point does positive ambition become negative excess?

As researchers have identified, the thing with ambition is 'it does not cease once a certain level of attainment is achieved, nor is ambition compartmentalised toward success in only a single sphere. It is a habitual level of striving for or desiring accomplishment in situations associated with success'.[9] As Thomas Otway (1680) observed: 'Ambition is a lust that's never quenched' (p. 66).[10]

Similarly, in the first century CE, Seneca (1806) noted, 'Ambition is like a gulf, everything is swallowed up in it and buried; beside the dangerous consequences of it' (pp. 143–144).[11]

Research and Psychology: Summit Fever

Within climbing, 'summit fever' is a well-known phenomenon referring to the compulsion to reach the summit of a mountain at all costs. Indirectly, summit fever has killed countless climbers who wanted to reach their goal so badly they stopped accurately assessing their situation and considering other courses of action. Research suggests summit fever may result from the goal (in this study: reaching the summit of Mount Everest) becoming a core part of a person's social identity.[12] Furthermore, when individuals have invested so much in achieving a goal, 'sunk cost fallacy' also comes in to play, i.e. there is a massive fear that turning back would waste all the time, effort and resources already invested.

Although mountaineering is an extreme situation, the lessons for leaders in business still apply. Firstly, appreciate your different identities (e.g., friend, mother, sister, boss, football coach. . . whatever those may be) and remember achieving a goal or accomplishment never defines you entirely. Secondly, be wary of the 'sunk cost fallacy'; remember the big picture and track your investments in a project, be ready to cut your losses if you judge a tipping point has been passed.

Research suggests that the best way to keep this habit of perpetual striving in check is to focus on developing harmonious passion (rather than obsessive passion):[13–15]

- **Harmonious passion** is where an individual devotes time and energy to an activity or goal whilst remaining in control of their engagement. The activity therefore occupies a significant space in their identity and life without being overpowering and all-consuming. As the name suggests, the passion is kept in harmony with other important aspects of life.

- **Obsessive passion** is where an individual has lost control over the activity or goal and feels a constant pressure to engage in it. Like a cuckoo in the nest, the activity takes up a disproportionate place in the individual's identity and daily life. This in turn causes a rigid persistence in the activity, even when such persistence is ill-advised, counterproductive, and creating conflicts in other life areas.

Consequently, whilst we often see an Olympic athlete or a Michelin-starred chef as passionate, or quickly justify our own devotions of time, energy, and resources as investing in a passion, passion itself is a dual-carriage way. Road one: cultivating harmonious passion. This road takes you to higher levels of performance, vitality, well-being, career satisfaction, positive emotions, and more frequent experiences of flow state (where you are completely 'in the zone', feeling a sense of energised focus and enjoyable immersion in the activity).[16] Road two, obsessive passion, leads to more negative emotions, a decrease in well-being, with a final stop at burnout.

Two very similar looking roads, two very different destinations.

It is therefore important as a leader to distinguish between the two forms of passion. Cultivate harmonious passion with care and check in with yourself regularly to make sure you have not, somewhere along the way, taken the slip road to obsessive passion.

Developing Harmonious Passion

When we find a goal or activity that is meaningful to us, something we are willing to devote a large amount of time and energy to, our mind quickly absorbs it into our identity. For example, you are no longer just someone who plays basketball or leads a business, you start to say: 'I'm a basketball player' or 'I'm a managing director'.

In this way, our activities become woven into who we are and how we define ourselves, rather than just something we do.

Both types of passion (harmonious and obsessive), predict similar levels of commitment to an activity and are part of someone's identity.[17] The key difference is how healthily the activity has been integrated into your overall sense of self.

Here are a few ways you can check if your passion is healthily integrated:

	Harmonious passion	Obsessive passion
You feel. . .	**Free and in control** – there are no strings attached to your involvement, you engage in the activity when you want to	**Tied in** – your sense of self-worth or social acceptance is tied up in the activity
You are striving to . . .	**Improve and learn** – your focus is on developing mastery of an activity and self-improvement (i.e., deepening your skills, knowledge, and understanding)	**Outperform others** – your focus is on being the best and demonstrating your superiority *and/or* **Avoid negative judgements** – your focus is on ensuring others do not make negative judgements about you; you may want to avoid disappointing people or appearing inferior to others

(*Continued*)

	Harmonious passion	Obsessive passion
You persist. . .	**Flexibly** – when persistence seems counterproductive or potentially harmful, your involvement in the activity reduces appropriately or even stops	**Rigidly** – you persist even if it is clear the activity has become 'all-consuming', regardless of whether continued striving is ill-advised, highly risky, or likely to lead to negative consequences
You enjoy. . .	**A variety of activities and life experiences**	**Little else** – valuing this activity over and above all other areas of your life
You often. . .	**Take time to restore and unwind when you need it**	**Disregard the need for mental and physical recovery**

In a nutshell, harmonious passion is about pursuing a goal or doing an activity because you love it and enjoy it. Any activity or goal that you are passionate about will inevitably become part of your identity, but it should not be so self-defining that it becomes the central and sole defining feature of who you are. It is therefore important to take a broad view of your identity and to leave room for new activities and variety in your life.

The romanticised image of having complete and utter dedication to one's passion is compelling, but inaccurate. Lasting success and optimal performance in fact requires your passion(s) to exist in harmony with other areas of your life. In this way, passion can be a healthy driving force, not an all-consuming one.

To check if you are developing harmonious passion, ask yourself the following:

- Would I feel 'good enough' without this goal or activity in my life? Or, am I trapped in a battle of constantly trying to prove my worth via this goal or activity?
- Do I enjoy and value investing my time and energy in this activity? Or, do I keep going because others value it?
- Do I feel energised and driven to keep going? Or, obligated to?
- Would I pursue this no matter what the outcome? Or, am I mainly in it for the external rewards (i.e., status, recognition, approval)?

If your answers are all yes to the first questions, you are in the sweet spot of ambition. Keep striving to pursue your goals but keep checking to make sure your ambition has not become all-consuming and unhealthily obsessive.

The Ambitious Leadership Continuum: How to Stay on Track

It is easy for high-functioning people to keep powering through. Many high performers in organisations appear super-human in terms of their stamina and output, churning out results and high-quality work month-after-month, year-after-year. Especially at the executive level, there is a sense of expectation that you will always be on top of your game. That you have an endless reserve of time, energy, and dedication to plough into your work. It is almost baked into those at the executive level, as they have often got where they are because of this very ability to keep going and keep performing.

However, while high-functioning people can keep powering through, they do eventually crash.

As we will explore here, sometimes energy and drive simply wear out, with leaders feeling fatigued and 'checked out' from work, having lost all motivation to keep striving. Alternatively, leaders can be so swept up by ambition that their relentless 'must keep going' mindset is only stopped by a harsh and dramatic wakeup call (perhaps a life event, heart attack, or serious injury). Only then do circumstances force them to take time to pause and reflect.

While the fatigue or crash may seem sudden and unexpected at the time, there are warning signs along the way.

Let us explore what patterns of behaviour and thinking you should look out for on the ambitious continuum (see Figure 4.1).

Hyper-competitiveness. As author and University fellow Annie McKee states, it is when 'ambition is coupled with hyper-competitiveness and a single-minded focus on winning, that we get into trouble' (p. 4).[18] McKee goes on to explain how hyper-competitiveness can blind us to the impact of our actions on ourselves and others, causing us to start chasing goals for the sake of hitting targets, distancing us from the true meaning and purpose of our work. With resources stretched, rapidly changing markets,

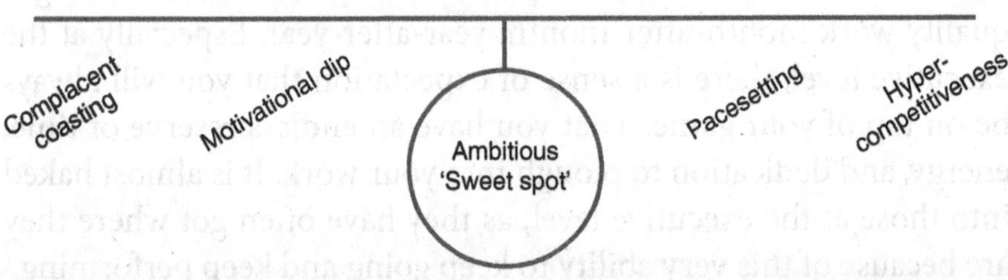

Figure 4.1 The ambitious leadership continuum.

and increasing pressure from disruptive start-ups, it is not hard to see how this competitive win-at-all-costs thinking sneaks in. However, it is ambition without hyper-competitiveness that serves leaders much better in the long run.

Staying future-fit top tip. Leaders need to avoid a 'zero-sum mentality', namely: perceiving that achieving a goal (one person's gain) must come at someone else's cost. Whilst this may sound an obvious and easy watch out for leaders, findings from research show how 52% of C-suite leaders often or almost always find themselves getting swept up in a false belief that they or their team is in a win-or-lose situation.[6] In reality, gains and losses are not always so obvious. Losing a pitch or business opportunity may feel like a win-or-lose situation, but there are often learnings to take from the experience and connections that have been made. In today's purpose-led business environment, staying focused on the company's mission and purpose is far more important than finding ways to outperform and 'win'. The best performing business leaders in the twenty-first century, will instead be looking for ways to connect, collaborate, and integrate their work with what others are doing, not win-at-all-costs against the competition.

Pacesetting. It is easy to spot a leader who has slipped into pacesetting; characteristically, they:[19]

- lead by example and displays of personal heroics
- have high standards and ensure those standards are met (even if they must jump in and do the work themselves to get it done)
- have an intense pace (for example, early starts, late nights, working weekends, emails sent at all hours), producing incredible output at incredible speed. While they may profess

that they do not expect everyone to keep up, their behaviour and output drives a pace and everyone needs to keep up

- view everything as a priority
- are quick to provide answers and solve challenges, often directing people to next steps rather than helping them discuss and unknot the problem themselves

This is a typical go-to leadership style for high achievers, with organisations often inadvertently nurturing an 'achievement-at-all-costs mentality' by promoting pacesetting talent, causing the style to run rampant and unchecked. However, whilst pacesetting can deliver results in the short-term and engage one or two high achievers (who can keep pace out ahead of the pack), research shows pacesetting is demoralising to most people and exhausts everyone in the long run.[20]

Staying future-fit top tips. It is vital for individuals who have strayed into pacesetting to get back on track, for themselves, those they lead, and for the good of the business generally. As counter intuitive as it sounds, performance and motivation will go up if you get into the habit of 'pressing pause' (rather than operating with the go button rammed down). Specifically, it is helpful to 'press pause' on two things:

1. **'press pause' on your focus:** check in on whether your focus has become distorted. Are you and your team still focused on the big picture, operating with a clear understanding of what the business (or the clients) are trying to achieve? Or, has the focus become to keep hitting targets? (finding and implementing whatever shortcuts are necessary to secure quick win results)

2. **'press pause' on your advice:** instead of jumping in with solutions, learn to leave space for others to think and contribute. Make your default response to people 'how can I help?' not 'this is what you should do'. If you have comments or ideas in a meeting, note them down for later. By adopting a slower coaching approach, you will nurture the talent in other people, rather than smother it out of them as you strive for immediate results.

In relation to pacesetting, it's important to remember the job of a senior leader is not to be irreplaceable and create a team or organisation whose success depends heavily on you. The best leaders look to create legacy by bringing on a team of talent, capable of performing without them and long after they have gone.

Motivational dip. Everyone, no matter how ambitious or successful, hits the motivational wall from time to time. Sometimes the scale of the challenge, or relentlessness of a job, can simply feel overwhelming and no longer worth it. Especially for ambitious individuals, prone to taking on big challenges, it is almost inevitable that at some point reality will kick in. The undertaking requires far more than you initially realised; the results take longer than you anticipated; the rewards do not seem as potent or attainable.

If your motivation has dissipated and you no longer feel able to keep going or capable of success, you have hit what author Seth Godin calls 'the Dip'.[21] Specifically, he describes 'the Dip' as 'the long stretch between beginner's luck and real accomplishment. The dip is the set of artificial screens set up to keep people like you out. . . Extraordinary benefits accrue to the tiny minority of people who are able to push just a tiny bit longer than most'. Like Indiana Jones, in the scene from The Last Crusade, where, according to the map he is following Indy must cross a seemingly invisible bridge to get to the

Holy Grail. Despite seeing no way forward, he keeps going, puts one foot in front of the other, holds fast to his goal, and the path appears in front of him. As Indy demonstrates, extraordinary accomplishment is not so much about talent or never-ending motivation, but the tenacity to keep going when others would quit.

Staying future-fit top tips. The biggest challenge any ambitious leader will face is not productivity or time management but motivation. Luckily, once you have recognised your motivation has dropped, there are a few tricks you can use to help you power through the wall:

What to do...	How to do it...
1. Tune into your 'why'	Check back in with why you are chasing this goal or doing this job, ask yourself honestly: Why did I want this? Why is it important to me? What made me excited about this in the first place? Are all those things still true? Or, has circumstance or time changed the value I place on what I am doing and why?
2. Increase your sense of urgency	If you feel the goal is still important to you, set yourself a deadline to get it done. Identify a 'Goldilocks time frame', a deadline that is not so short it is impossible (causing you to overexert yourself and become more demotivated when you fail) and not so long that you procrastinate and waste time on unimportant things. Set a deadline based on how long it has taken you to do a similar task in the past, minus a bit.

What to do...	How to do it...
3. Share your goals (and timeline)	Next, use the oldest trick in the book to make yourself accountable: tell someone else your goals and time frame. This will boost your motivation simply because you care what other people think of you. Speaking it makes it real. It is a sign of commitment.
Follow your plan not your mood	Our moods can be deceptive and unhelpful. We all have activities that we know we enjoy and benefit from, but still frequently 'don't feel like' beforehand. If we have been avoiding something we value for a while, guilt, self-doubt, and a sense of failure can also build up and stop us from resuming action. However, these are fake screens our primal mind conjures up to conserve our energy and resources. Just like how Indiana Jones followed his map to the Holy Grail (rather than let fear turn him back), you too should aim to follow your plan not your mood.
Celebrate small wins	When chasing a big goal, feeling a sense of progress and accomplishment as you go is critical. It may feel like a small chip in a big iceberg, but by noticing and celebrating the small wins, you reaffirm your ability to succeed. If you are waiting to celebrate at the end – you will likely never get there. The more frequently you, and those around you, feel that sense of progress, the more likely you are to keep going and achieve your ultimate goal.

Complacent coasting. This is where a leader is doing the minimum necessary to perform in their role. Anyone, at any level of a business, can find themselves coasting for various reasons, and executives are no exception. Having worked extremely hard for decades, pulling in the lion's share of the work, some senior leaders and high performers may find their drive to keep pushing eventually fizzles out. They feel like a spent force and that their exceptional contribution and dedication over the years entitles them to take more of a back seat. Leaders who have slipped into complacent coasting, gradually stop making the best use of their strengths, stop growing their skillset, and stop stretching themselves to take on new challenges.

Staying future-fit top tips. Many of us fall into some level of coasting in our career, but as tempting and justifiable as this path may feel, unfortunately, as executive coach Cary Shillcutt articulates: 'if you find yourself coasting, one of two things is happening: either you're going downhill or you're losing speed – neither is a good thing as a leader'.[22] Particularly in today's fast-changing markets, where lifelong learning and continuous reinvention are crucial, leaders who coast put themselves and their business at risk of becoming superfluous.

To avoid slipping into a state of complacent coasting (and taking your team or potentially your business with you) notice whether you have begun: avoiding challenging tasks, attending meetings passively, no longer paying attention to details, and solving problems as they arise rather than proactively. Then, check in with what is missing, for example: Have you no longer got a challenge or goal you feel energised to 'get your teeth into'? Do you know what is required to move yourself, the team, or the business forward but lack the energy to do it? If this sounds familiar, start getting curious. Find ways to open yourself back up to new ideas and challenges. Look around you to notice where you could add value. Shake up your network to find new people with fresh perspectives and insights. Get feedback from others, gathering ideas about what could be done better or differently. Work with a coach to unknot the fears that may be holding you back and identify a meaningful goal that re-energises you.

Research and Psychology: Rebooting Your Motivation by Keeping Your Brain Fired Up

Motivation is caused by a dopamine release in the brain. When we imagine achieving our goals, feel something important is about to happen, or expect to get a positive outcome, dopamine kicks in. Dopamine is the 'chemical messenger' (i.e., neurotransmitter) of our brain's reward anticipation system: if our expectation of reward increases, so does the amount of dopamine in our brain. Likewise, if our expectation of reward decreases, the level of dopamine drops.

Research shows that 'go-getters', who are willing to work hard for rewards and bear the costs of effort, have a higher release of dopamine in the brain area known to play an important role in reward and motivation (namely, the ventromedial prefrontal cortex).[23] Whereas those individuals who are less willing to work hard for rewards and make high-effort choices have high dopamine levels in another brain area (the anterior insula), which plays a role in emotion, risk perception, and cost–benefit decision-making.

Consequently, if you are feeling unmotivated, you can reboot your motivation neurologically by encouraging the dopamine

(*Continued*)

in the reward areas of your brain to fire up. Specifically, by recording small accomplishments, celebrating the work of teammates, and focusing on how you will feel when the goal is achieved are all great ways to get your 'go-getting' dopamine flowing.

Top tip: the fact of the matter is ambitious goals never happen overnight; you chip away at them bit by bit. Waiting to celebrate at the end, once you have attained your goal, will cause your motivation to evaporate. Instead, keep stoking the dopamine fire of belief and expectation by reinforcing a sense of progress, envisioning accomplishment, and focusing on what you have done (rather than what you still need to do).

Leading with Appreciation: Keeping Goals and Work in Perspective

It is easy to think that appreciation is just about having work–life balance but scratch the surface and this mindset refers to something much broader.

In the Cambridge dictionary, appreciation is defined as 'the act of recognising or understanding that something is valuable or important'.[24] In the Oxford dictionary, appreciation is defined as 'recognising and enjoying the good qualities of someone or something', 'having a full understanding' and 'feeling grateful'.[25]

Appreciation is therefore a melting pot term referring to full awareness, recognition, and enjoyment.

Leaders with an appreciative mindset recognise and make space for the important people, activities, and moments in their life outside their work and career goals (making sure others have time to do the same). They are thankful and enjoy what they have, and place huge value and importance on their own and other's well-being. In this way, their ambitious goals are both everything to them and yet not everything. The bigger picture of their existence is ever-present, helping them keep their goals in perspective. The appreciative mindset is therefore defined as:

A general state of thankfulness and ability to put goals in perspective.

The key point is that while we often view ambitious drive and contentment as uncomfortable bedfellows, they can sit side by side. You can be both. Contentment should not be confused with complacency, as author and speaker Tony Gaskins articulates: *'To be content doesn't mean you don't desire more, it means you're thankful for what you have and patience for what's to come'.*

In the next sections we will explore the two different components of appreciation: 1) being thankful for what you already have 2) keeping a sense of perspective.

Learning to Appreciate What You Have

Leading in the sweet spot of appreciation requires you to cultivate active contentment. This is a sense of inner peace (with who you are, what you have, and what you are doing in this moment), whilst simultaneously keeping sight of your vision for the future.

Here we briefly explore three ways you can nurture active contentment, with techniques positive psychology research has proven to be particularly effective.

5 minutes to reframe...	
Notice three good things	Often when we recount or think back on our day, we focus on the hassles, the things that annoyed us or did not go so well. This is because our brain has a negativity bias, prompting us to pay more attention to the 'bad stuff' that happens. We recall insults better than praise, react more strongly to negative events, and think about negative things more frequently. In evolutionary terms, this bias made sense: those who were more attuned to danger and paid more attention to the bad things around them were more likely to survive. However, to cultivate active contentment, you need to counter this bias. Every day, take a moment to think about or even a quick list of three things you feel grateful for since yesterday. Think about all areas of your life (family, friends, health, work, etc.) and all the interactions and events that took place. Big or small, it does not matter, just see what 'good stuff' springs to mind and notice what you are grateful for.

15 minutes for deeper reflection...	
Write a gratitude letter	You are probably thinking 'I don't have time to write a gratitude letter' or 'that's too cuddly for me'... if you are, keep reading. Studies have shown writing improves memory, helps your mind focus on what is important, and can offer health benefits (such as improved mood, well-being, and lower stress levels).[26–28] The power of writing therefore should not be underestimated.

While it may seem like a lot of extra work, evidence suggests writing is worth the effort. You can write the letter without any intent to deliver it to the person to whom you are writing it. So, get over any self-consciousness you may be feeling and give the following exercise a go:

1. Think back over the past several years of your life and remember an instance when someone did something for you for which you are extremely grateful or think of someone who you are glad to have in your life.
2. Pick someone who has been especially kind but who has never heard you fully express your gratitude or appreciation (this may be a parent, teacher, coach, teammate, spouse, relative, friend, neighbour, doctor, therapist, manager, mentor . . .).
3. Take 15 minutes to write a letter out.
   - Format it as you would a letter 'Dear so-and-so' (but do not worry about grammar, spelling, or the perfect phrasing)
   - Describe in specific terms why you are grateful to this individual and how they have impacted your life
   - Focus on the specific parts of their behaviour you appreciate and the details about how their actions positively affected you
   - Describe what you are doing now and how often you remember their efforts

As stated, you can keep the letter private or share it with the person in question. What matters is that you have taken the time to consider and express your gratitude and appreciation.

(*Continued*)

15 minutes for deeper reflection. . .

Identify your signature strengths	Whilst we often think about appreciation in an 'appreciating other people' sense, it is also important to appreciate yourself. Specifically, positive psychology shows that recognising and using your '*signature strengths*' leads to enhanced well-being, life satisfaction, and performance.[29] Everyone has different strengths, and your signature strengths are the ones you own, celebrate, and use frequently. When using them, you experience excitement, invigoration, and a sense success is inevitable. Some strengths may come to mind easily, but it is also likely you do not notice or undervalue some of your greatest strengths because they feel ordinary to you. To identify all your signature strengths, appreciate more fully the ways you are already using them, and explore new ways to harness your strengths in future, try the following: 1. Look up the 24 key strengths in the 'Character strengths and virtues: a handbook', which catalogues positive traits and their role in people's lives.[30] 2. Now, list out the strengths you possess that help you with: a. your relationships, b. your work, and c. your hobbies 3. For each domain, describe a specific time your strengths helped you and outline two new ways you could use your strengths more in a current situation.

Getting a Sense of Perspective

Often, we find ourselves so wrapped up in one aspect of our life, it is difficult to step back and get perspective on the whole picture. A situation, key decision, relationship, challenge, or goal takes centre stage in our mind, and we end up blinkered to everything else going on around us.

Leading with an appreciative mindset requires you to notice when you have become too blinkered and intentionally step back, make space, and appreciate the big picture.

Research suggests getting out into nature and finding ways to experience 'awe' are particularly effective ways to shift our attention away from ourselves and makes us feel like we are part of something greater. Firstly, the sounds, smells, even colours of nature have all been found to help reduce anxiety and shift us into a more relaxed state, giving our mind a chance to replenish, decompress, and think differently.[31,32] Specifically, a 50-minute walk in nature has been shown to help pull us out of our bubble by reducing levels of rumination (i.e., the amount of focused attention on negative aspects of oneself or life);[33] even just looking out a window onto a natural scene can prompt beneficial changes in our mind and body, nudging us into a more positive, prosocial, and appreciative mood.[34,35]

Secondly, finding ways to experience 'awe' can be hugely beneficial. Awe can be characterised by the phenomenon of 'perceived vastness', in other words, observing something physically large like the Grand Canyon or a clear night sky.[36] Studies have shown that awe can create a diminished sense of self (an effect known as 'the small self'), giving people the sense that they have more available time, whilst also increasing feelings of connectedness, and decreasing materialism. Consequently, a good way for leaders to boost their appreciative mindset may be to seek out 'awe-inspiring' experiences; perhaps choosing to visit a grove of giant trees, top star gazing location, music concert, historic landmark, or world-renowned piece of art.

There are many ways nature and 'awe' can help you as a leader to step back and get perspective; whether it is a long walk, carefully chosen office view, or a trip to see a talented musician or incredible athlete perform, you can boost your level of appreciation in a variety of ways.

Research and Psychology: Boosting Your Serotonin Levels

Serotonin is the neurotransmitter responsible for feelings of well-being and happiness. While serotonin does much more than regulate mood (influencing a wide range of systems in our body),[37] high levels of serotonin have been linked to improved mood, higher life satisfaction, and the drive to seek contentment.[38–40]

Consequently, just as it is important to find ways to boost your dopamine levels for the ambitious mindset, it is important to top-up your serotonin levels when it comes to enhancing appreciation and cultivating contentment.

Specifically, research suggests getting out into sunlight, eating foods containing the essential amino acid 'tryptophan' (such as spinach, pumpkin seeds, milk/soy milk, bananas, kiwi fruit, and dark chocolate), and doing aerobic exercise are all ways you can naturally boost your serotonin levels.

The Appreciative Leadership Continuum: How to Stay on Track

Compared with other mindsets, it is a bit harder to drift off course when it comes to the sweet spot of appreciation. However, there are still a few traps to watch out for.

Let's briefly explore the appreciative continuum (see Figure 4.2).

Excessive gratitude. It is possible a leader can slip into excessive gratitude in a number of ways. For example, rather than cultivating active contentment (i.e., appreciating what you have whilst keeping sight of your vision for the future), you just become content. Accepting of the status quo and no longer motivated to pursue goals and improvements. Similarly, although debated, it is possible a leader can be too thankful towards those they lead. When leaders show appreciation for everything, offering 'drive-by' praise even for the most basic day-to-day duties, the power of appreciation loses its potency. People may not value meaningful feedback when it is given for truly 'above and beyond' work or could start to think there is no room for improvement in what they do.

Staying future-fit top tips. In terms of staying actively content, remember that being appreciative of what you have does not mean you cannot desire more. Future-fit leadership is about being thankful

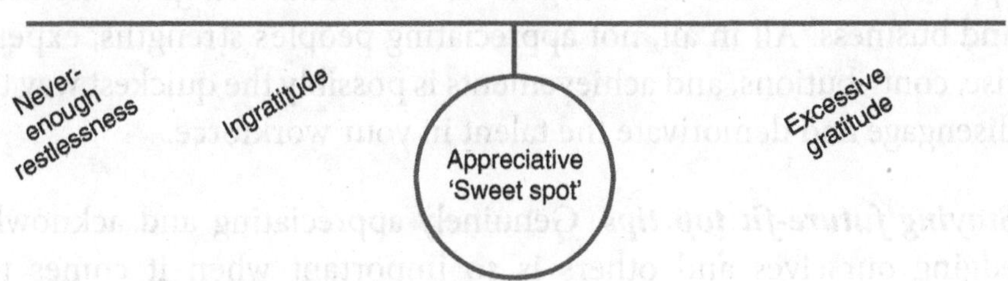

Figure 4.2 The appreciative leadership continuum.

for what you have and motivated to change things for the better. Keep your vision for the future, your lifelong goals, and ideal future-self strong in your mind. It is about simultaneously valuing what you have and the improvements you want to make happen. In relation to being overly appreciative of others, avoid this trap by keeping your praise and thankfulness genuine and specific. Use motivational feedback to reinforce the right behaviours and recognise people's specific achievements, contributions, and efforts. In this way, you will offer clear, motivating signposting for people when they are travelling in a positive direction (as opposed to confusing signposting, dotted about everywhere for random efforts and routine accomplishments).

Ingratitude. Sometimes when we are feeling low or anxious, it can be harder to notice or appreciate the positive attributes in ourselves or helpful things others do for us. In psychology, this is known as 'state-dependent-recall';[41] whereby a low mood, stress, and anxiety distort what we pay attention to and makes us more likely to recall negative events and information. During a tough moment or crisis, there is consequently a high chance a leader will, at some point, find themselves in a state of ingratitude, blinkered to the positive actions going on around them. Alternatively, ingratitude can seep in more insidiously to a leader's behaviour, particularly when a leader has fallen into the habit of mentoring people to be 'just like them'. Leaders stuck in the 'be like me' trap may get frustrated when people struggle to pick up aspects of the role as fast as they did and fail to appreciate the different strengths an individual brings to the role and business. All in all, not appreciating people's strengths, expertise, contributions, and achievements is possibly the quickest way to disengage and demotivate the talent in your workforce.

Staying future-fit top tips. Genuinely appreciating and acknowledging ourselves and others is so important when it comes to creating a healthy and productive work environment.[42] Showing gratitude to people has been shown to improve self-esteem, goal attainment, decision making, engagement, well-being, productivity, and resilience.[43–47] Throughout the organisation, people must feel their efforts and unique contributions are being recognised and valued, with executive leaders' role modelling appreciation during both big events and small daily interactions.

If you think you have slipped into a state of ingratitude, pause and take a moment to seek out the strengths and positives. For example, if you are operating in a high-pressure, highly stressful situation, take time to proactively counter the 'negative lens' bias. Make a conscious effort to pay attention to the small acts of kindness and meaningful contributions people are making around you. Alternatively, if you notice yourself being frustrated by a team member, try to seek out and notice the signature strengths they bring and uniquely contribute. Leadership is not about creating an organisation full of 'mini-me' clones; it is about bringing different skills, ways of thinking, and experiences together to unlock performance. Supporting people to be at *their* best, rather than emulate you at your best.

Never-enough thinking. There are two ways never-enough thinking shows up in a senior leader, they can be 'impossible-to-please' (instilling never-enough thinking in others) and/or 'never-off-duty' (putting themselves into a never-enough mode of operating). 'Impossible-to-please' is particularly common in prestigious, world-class organisations (who have talent queuing up, dreaming to get in). In these organisations, to maintain high performance, senior leaders can feel it is their duty to expect professional excellence from others as standard. There is almost a fear that if you show others appreciation, they will stop trying to improve and the benchmark for performance will slowly sink. Alternatively, 'never-off-duty' is where senior leaders themselves get swept up in the false belief that they can never afford to switch off and must be 'always-on', always available, always contributing, and always working hard to stay ahead. It is a trap anyone can fall into, but it is particularly tempting when it is on you to keep the business afloat and successful. But watch out. Both 'impossible-to-please' and 'never-off-duty' lead to toxic cultures, either driving people into the ground through unrealistic levels of perfectionism and excellence or ruining people's health and family life by setting the precedent for being 'always-on'.

Staying future-fit top tips. As a leader you may fall into the trap of being impossible-to-please for many different reasons. Perhaps you are pursuing excellence and want to cultivate an environment full of 'only the very best' talent, perhaps you yourself put everything into work and get little acknowledgement or thanks, or perhaps you feel insecure in aspects of your own role, which results in a tendency to be hypercritical of others. Either way, creating an environment devoid of praise and appreciation is never the best approach. To stay motivated, people need to feel a sense of competence and belonging;[48] we all need to experience pride, feel like we have done a good job, and that our skills and efforts are valued. Consequently, as a leader, never be afraid to recognise people's contributions and work. Appreciation is not an indulgence but a vital ingredient of high performance. Talent will thrive off the feeling of improving, accomplishment, and recognition. Similarly, if you notice yourself being hypercritical of those you lead, take an honest look inward. Is it everyone else that keeps failing you and not living up to your expectations? Or, if you are super honest, is there something you worry is lacking in yourself and your own performance that you are projecting on to them and reacting to?

In relation to 'never-off-duty', the constant striving to 'do more', 'be more', and be 'always-on' is habitual within our modern society. Left unchecked, the 'never doing enough' self-flagellation infiltrates our thinking until it becomes our default mode of operating. Sadly, this 'never-off-duty' trap is littered with false-beliefs and self-fullfilling prophecies. For example, it is easy to convince yourself that you can do a bit of work in the evening or on Sunday and 'get ahead' for the week, saving yourself time later on. . . Firstly, you will not get ahead or on top of things. There is no quiet week, no empty inbox, no time that will magically appear in your calendar later. Work is like a ravenous time-beast: the more you feed it, the more it expects. So, getting into the habit of working early mornings, evenings, late nights, and weekends is a false economy. Secondly, it is poor management of your energy and resources. Spending time working all hours may feel like the ultimate state in terms of productivity and efficiency – but, in fact, it is not. Your energy is limited; your mind and body needs time to rest, unwind, and rejuvenate. Working long hours today does not come free, it costs you tomorrow's performance.

By never switching off, you do yourself, and others, no favours in the long run. If you think you may have got stuck in the never-enough work whirlpool, have a read of Professor Mark Cropley's 'The Off Switch' or try a few of these simple strategies:[49]

- **Check emails judiciously.** While ideally, you will use your holidays and time outside work to digitally detox and switch off from work completely, as a senior leader, there will inevitably be moments where totally switching off is tricky. However, avoid having work constantly running in the background of your life. Instead, set aside dedicated time where you can fully concentrate on what needs doing, then switch off.

- **Find your favourite place.** Identify a place where you feel comfortable, able to unwind, relax, and be yourself. For some people this may be a quiet allotment, or spot in a park or garden; for others, it may be a local pub or music venue. Wherever it is, find that place and go there often. Cherish it and make sure it stays ever unpolluted by feelings of stress and thoughts of work.

- **Make a realistic to-do list.** Many of us start each day, week, even year, with a to-do list that is completely unrealistic. We inevitably end up rushed off our feet, completing a vast number of tasks and still feeling like we have failed and have not done enough. Give yourself a reality check. Start each day with a to-do list and calendar of meetings that is realistic (not the schedule of a superhero). Prioritise one or two big things that need to get done and a few side tasks.
- **Make a stopping-doing list.** It is easy to keep adding things to the 'to-do' list, making space for people, doing favours, capitalising on unexpected opportunities. . . but unfortunately, you cannot just keep adding things on. If you are already stretched thin, avoid the temptation to just keep saying yes to people and finding ways to power through. Prioritise what is important and declassify tasks and projects where necessary. You cannot do it all, you must decide what it is that you are not going to do to make it work.
- **See yourself through the eyes of another.** Trapped in our own bubble, it is easy to just look out and constantly compare ourselves to the lives, habits, and achievements of others. Particularly now, with the rosy filters of social media, this self-other comparison often makes us feel like we are not doing enough and could be doing or achieving more. However, it is important to remember we only ever see a sliver of people's lives, never the whole picture. It is also useful to reverse the image: imagine how you come across to other people? How might others be viewing your life, expertise, and achievements? Do you think it seems to other people like you are 'never doing enough'? Unlikely. Try to see yourself and your life the way other people must view it, before letting your mind badger you into thinking you are never doing enough.

Research and Psychology: The Importance of Active Rest

fMRI studies show our brains have a 'default mode' and highlight how even in a 'resting state' our minds remain active to differing degrees (ruminating, roaming, wandering, daydreaming).[50] Consequently, whilst we may define rest as the absence of a task, our brains always find a task or something to think about. If you have ever tried meditation, you will notice this – true 'rest' or stillness of the mind can be hard to come by. In fact, it takes sustained conscious effort to rest in this way.

Active rest or active mindfulness is about giving your mind a break by giving it a task to focus on. This activity might be one that is low effort but satisfying (for example, cleaning or weeding), it might focus your mind on your body (like running, surfing, or yoga) or it may be more creative (such as painting, playing piano, or baking a cake). It does not matter what the activity is – or even if you are good at it – what matters is that you help your brain rest and switch off by actively giving it something different to focus on.

Notes

1. Judge, T.A., and Kammeyer-Mueller, J.D. (2012). On the value of aiming high: the causes and consequences of ambition. *Journal of Applied Psychology* 97: 758.
2. Sansone, R.A., and Sansone, L.A. (2010). Gratitude and wellbeing: the benefits of appreciation. *Psychiatry (Edgmont)* 7: 18.
3. Price, D. (2021). *Laziness Does Not Exist.* New York, US: Atria Books.

4. Hill, A., (2019). A brief history of executive burnout. *Financial Times Article.*

5. Witt/Kieffer (2019). Impact of Burnout on Healthcare Executives. *Survey Report.*

6. Walters, A., and Maitland, A. (2019). The Future is Now: The New Context of Leadership. Lane4 white paper, available on request.

7. Salvagioni, D.A.J., Melanda, F.N., Mesas, A.E., et al. (2017). Physical, psychological and occupational consequences of job burnout: a systematic review of prospective studies. *PloS One* 12: e0185781.

8. Soanes, C., and Stevenson, A. (Eds.). (2004). *Concise Oxford English dictionary (Vol. 11).* Oxford, UK: Oxford University Press.

9. Judge, T.A., and Kammeyer-Mueller, J.D. (2012). On the value of aiming high: The causes and consequences of ambition. *Journal of Applied Psychology* 97: 758.

10. Otway, T. (1680). *The History and Fall of Caius Marius.* London, England: Angel & Crown.

11. Seneca (1806). *Seneca's Morals, By Way of Abstract: To Which Is Added a Discourse, Under the Title of an After-Thought (R. L'Estrange, Trans.).* New York, US: Dover.

12. Kayes, D.C. (2004). The 1996 Mount Everest climbing disaster: the breakdown of learning in teams. *Human Relations* 57 : 1263–1284.

13. Vallerand, R.J., Blanchard, C., Mageau, G.A., et al. (2003). Les passions de l'ame: on obsessive and harmonious passion. *Journal of Personality and Social Psychology* 85: 756.

14. Verner-Filion, J., Vallerand, R.J., Amiot, C.E., and Mocanu, I. (2017). The two roads from passion to sport performance and psychological well-being: The mediating role of need satisfaction, deliberate practice, and achievement goals. *Psychology of Sport and Exercise* 30: 19–29.

15. Vallerand, R.J., Houlfort, N., and Forest, J. (2014). Passion for work: determinants and outcomes. In M. Gagné (Ed.), *Oxford Handbook of Work Engagement, Motivation, and Self-Determination Theory* (pp. 85–105). Oxford University Press.

16. Forest, J., Mageau, G.A., Sarrazin, C., and Morin, E.M. (2011). 'Work is my passion': The different affective, behavioural, and cognitive consequences of harmonious and obsessive passion toward work. Canadian Journal of Administrative Sciences/Revue Canadienne des Sciences de l'Administration 28: 27–40.

17. de Jonge, J., Balk, Y.A., and Taris, T.W. (2020). Mental recovery and running-related injuries in recreational runners: the moderating role of passion for running. *International Journal of Environmental Research and Public Health* 17: 1044.

18. McKee, A. (2017). *Happiness Traps*. Harvard Business Review.

19. Spreier, S.W., Fontaine, M.H., and Malloy, R.L. (2006). Leadership run amok. *Harvard Business Review* 84: 72–82.

20. Goleman, D. (2017). *Leadership that Gets Results (Harvard Business Review Classics)*. Massachusetts, US: Harvard Business Press.

21. Godin, S. (2011). *The Dip: The Extraordinary Benefits of Knowing When to Quit (and When to Stick)*. Hachette, UK.

22. Shillcutt, G. (2019). Are You Coasting as a Leader? LinkedIn blog.

23. Treadway, M.T., Buckholtz, J.W., Cowan, R.L., et al. (2012). Dopaminergic mechanisms of individual differences in human effort-based decision-making. *Journal of Neuroscience* 32: 6170–6176.

24. *Cambridge Advanced Learner's Dictionary and Thesaurus* (2020). Cambridge University Press.

25. Hornby, A.S., and Cowie, A.P. (1995). *Oxford Advanced Learner's Dictionary* (Vol. 1430). Oxford, UK: Oxford University Press.

26. Silva, A.M., and Limongi, R. (2019). Writing to learn increases long-term memory consolidation: a mental-chronometry and computational modeling study of 'epistemic writing'. *Journal of Writing Research* 11: 211–243.
27. Mangen, A., Anda, L.G., Oxborough, G.H., and Brønnick, K. (2015). Handwriting versus keyboard writing: effect on word recall. *Journal of Writing Research* 7: 227–247.
28. Pennebaker, J.W., and Seagal, J.D. (1999). Forming a story: the health benefits of narrative. *Journal of Clinical Psychology* 55: 1243–1254.
29. Littman-Ovadia, H., Lavy, S., and Boiman-Meshita, M. (2017). When theory and research collide: Examining correlates of signature strengths use at work. *Journal of Happiness Studies* 18: 527–548.
30. Peterson, C., and Seligman, M.E.P. (2004). *Character Strengths and Virtues: A Handbook and Classification.* Washington, DC: APA Press.
31. Franco, L.S., Shanahan, D.F., and Fuller, R.A. (2017). A review of the benefits of nature experiences: more than meets the eye. *International Journal of Environmental Research and Public Health* 14: 864.
32. Atchley, R.A., Strayer, D.L., and Atchley, P. (2012). Creativity in the wild: Improving creative reasoning through immersion in natural settings. *PloS One* 7: e51474.
33. Bratman, G.N., Daily, G.C., Levy, B.J., and Gross, J.J. (2015). The benefits of nature experience: Improved affect and cognition. *Landscape and Urban Planning* 138: 41–50.
34. Zhang, J.W., Piff, P.K., Iyer, R., et al. (2014). An occasion for unselfing: Beautiful nature leads to prosociality. *Journal of Environmental Psychology* 37: 61–72.
35. Ulrich, R.S. (2002, April). Health benefits of gardens in hospitals. In *Paper for Conference, Plants for People International Exhibition Floriade* (Vol. 17, No. 5, p. 2010).

36. Allen, S. (2018). The science of awe. Greater Good Science: John Templeton Foundation.

37. Berger, M., Gray, J.A., and Roth, B.L. (2009). The expanded biology of serotonin. *Annual Review of Medicine* 60: 355–366.

38. Young, S.N. (2007). How to increase serotonin in the human brain without drugs. *Journal of Psychiatry & Neuroscience: JPN* 32(6): 394.

39. De Neve, J.E. (2011). Functional polymorphism (5-HTTLPR) in the serotonin transporter gene is associated with subjective well-being: evidence from a US nationally representative sample. *Journal of Human Genetics* 56: 456–459.

40. Tops, M., Russo, S., Boksem, M.A., and Tucker, D.M. (2009). Serotonin: modulator of a drive to withdraw. *Brain and Cognition* 71: 427–436.

41. Bower, G.H. (1981). Mood and memory. *American Psychologist* 36: 129.

42. Umlas, J.W. (2013). *Grateful Leadership: Using the Power of Acknowledgement to Engage All Your People and Achieve Superior Results.* New York, US: McGraw-Hill.

43. Chen, L.H., and Wu, C.H. (2014). Gratitude enhances change in athletes' self-esteem: The moderating role of trust in coach. *Journal of Applied Sport Psychology* 26: 349–362.

44. Jia, L., Tong, E.M., and Lee, L.N. (2014). Psychological 'gel' to bind individuals' goal pursuit: Gratitude facilitates goal contagion. *Emotion* 14: 748.

45. Zhang, Y., Chen, Z.J., and Ni, S. (2020). The security of being grateful: Gratitude promotes risk aversion in decision-making. *The Journal of Positive Psychology* 15: 285–291.

46. Emmons, R.A., and Mishra, A. (2011). Why gratitude enhances well-being: What we know, what we need to know. *Designing Positive Psychology: Taking Stock and Moving Forward*, 248–262.

47. Di Fabio, A., Palazzeschi, L., and Bucci, O. (2017). Gratitude in organizations: a contribution for healthy organizational contexts. *Frontiers in Psychology* 8: 2025.

48. Deci, E.L., and Ryan, R.M. (1985). *Intrinsic Motivation and Self-Determination in Human Behavior*. New York, US: Plenum.

49. Cropley, M. (2015). *The Off Switch: Leave Work on Time, Relax Your Mind But Still Get More Done*. New York, US: Random House.

50. Callard, F., Staines, K., and Wilkes, J. (2016). *The Restless Compendium: Interdisciplinary Investigations of Rest and Its Opposites*. London, UK: Palgrave Pivot.

CHAPTER 5
POLITICALLY VIRTUOUS

Leaders honour their core values, but they are flexible in how they execute them.

—Colin Luther Powell, politician and diplomat

What Is a 'Politically Virtuous' Mindset?

Politically virtuous leaders hold the following mindset:

- To enhance performance, it is important to be savvy in the circumstances (taking into consideration the implications, repercussions, and needs of certain situations).
- They must not use knowledge as power, but it is important to judge when telling everyone everything will be counter-productive.
- They must show integrity, live their values, and always aim to do 'the right thing' from the first opportunity.
- They must be willing to make practical compromises for the sake of progress.

Within this mindset, future-fit leaders exhibit both commitment to their values and the ability to navigate the political terrain, making the practical compromises required to be effective.

On the surface, this mindset should be relatively easy for those in the C-suite. Most executive leaders have a strong moral compass, aiming to show honesty, integrity, and care for people and wider society. They also have a high amount of political savvy, given that no one rises to the C-suite level without a strong aptitude for gaining power and influence.

So, this should be a short chapter then? Well, not quite.

When thinking in abstract terms of course we all want to 'do the right thing', but unfortunately senior leaders are frequently put in situations where it is not obvious what the 'right' thing to do is. Furthermore, far from being straightforward, our moral compass is context-specific and our values often conflict with one another. 'Living your values' and 'doing the right thing' are therefore far harder than you imagine when leading a business.

There is also the uncomfortable truth that virtue alone is not enough for effective leadership, as British Labour MP Jeremy Corbyn discovered. Corbyn made a political career out of championing unfashionable causes and showing unshakeable commitment to his values and beliefs. But, eventually his rigidly principled approach and unwillingness to compromise tied him in knots as party leader.[1] His history of constant defiance, based on acting with conscience, made it difficult for him to later demand loyalty and his refusal to compromise and 'play politics' blocked progress. The age-old debate inevitably surfaced, with Corbyn's supporters arguing power is meaningless without principle, while centrists argued principle is pointless without power.

Although the context of politics is different to that of business, the point remains that having unshakeable beliefs will only get you so far as a leader. A degree of compromise and political manoeuvring is inevitably required for meaningful progress to be achieved. However, power and playing politics can also be perilous ground for executives, as author, political scientist, and past congress candidate Sandy Maisel explains:[2]

> *I had a taste of the aphrodisiacal appeal of power. Others' lives revolved around mine. Others cared what I said, what I did. They looked after my schedule, drove me from place to place, provided for my every need. Someone was always at my beck and call to do whatever I said needed to be done. . .I found that appealing at first but quickly I became used to it. In the final analysis I found that to be frightening.*

To drive performance, leaders must therefore master the art of being both politically astute and virtuous. One mindset cannot exist successfully without the other. The taste of power at the C-suite level can be intoxicating; leaders who make political judgements without keeping decisions aligned to their values are at risk of slipping into power-hungry tactics that largely serve their self-interest. Similarly, if a leader follows their values dogmatically without weighing up the implications, repercussions, and needs of the specific situation, they risk hampering performance via unintended consequences and the trappings of their own idealism.

Leader to Leader

Since he was a kid, wanting to do the right thing has been a core principle for Will Gardiner. During college, this drive initially caused him to dismiss a career in business altogether; he wanted to do the right thing and have a positive impact on society – so he inherently felt a greater pull towards government and think tanks. However, the pace and energy of the business world lured him in. Over the course of his career, Will has held CFO roles at publicly listed UK organisations and is currently CEO of an energy company, which is the UK's largest provider of renewable electricity. The drive to do the right thing never went away, Will simply discovered multiple ways to have a positive impact. He explains, 'as a CEO, similar to any political leader – you do have a large capacity to effect change – and you have more freedom. And there are right things to do and wrong things to do'.

But doing the right thing is not always straightforward.

One dilemma Will and his team faced recently relates to their strategy to become carbon negative as a company. As Will describes, 'part of that plan, for several years now, has meant that we would want to stop running our coal units as of September 2022. However, the government has asked us to keep our coal unit open for another year, because the UK may need the energy generated to offset possible shortages resulting from the war in Ukraine'.

Delaying plans is not an easy choice. Will has stood up and made a lot of public commitments over the past 18 months, clearly stating their plan and timelines for getting off coal. Furthermore, 200 people have already been made redundant on the basis that the coal unit will not be running past September. On the other hand, reasons to delay are compelling: 1) ensuring the country has sufficient energy supply and 2) the opportunity to secure government support for long-term projects that will enable the organisation to become carbon negative. There is also undoubtedly 'money in it', profits to be gained from extending the coal run another year.

At the time of the interview, Will stated how it is an 'ongoing story', one that he did not have an answer to yet. However, he also described the situation to be all about short-term and long-term balance and knowing which red lines to draw: 'if I have to compromise on coal, I'll do it, because over the long-term it gives us a greater likelihood of achieving our ambitions than if we didn't do it. . . but, a very definitive agreement with the government would need to be reached on that'. In addition, he stated how, if they do end up extending the coal run, there would be 'a very live discussion in the boardroom

(*Continued*)

about where the money goes that we generate from that. Does that money go to our shareholders? Does it go into the community? Does it go towards environmental activities?' Each element of the decision, follow-on actions, and consequences were being carefully weighed. With care and intention, Will and his team aimed to reach a decision they could stand by.

While this specific situation remained 'in progress', reflecting on other dilemmas he has encountered throughout his career, Will had the following advice around embracing a politically virtuous mindset:

1. ***Be wary of promising too much*** – it is easy to get swept away promising too much, especially to shareholders. When you get trapped behind a promise or commitment to deliver something, you and your team can then become obsessed with it. And, when you are fixated on that one thing, it is a dangerous place to be as a leader. You will most likely miss the warning signs of issues occurring on the periphery that can turn into big problems for the company if not addressed.
2. ***Listen to your detractors*** – take time to hear, listen, and understand what your detractors and/or opponents might be saying. Engage with them, do not dismiss them. That way you do not start drinking your own Kool-Aid too much and believing your own story. You keep yourself grounded.
3. ***Make sure you have enough time*** – delegate effectively so other people do the things that are important and do them well, without it appearing that it is not important

to you because you delegated them. Then, with the time you are carving out, understand where your attention is going, because where you spend your time is what will happen. As a CEO, it is important not to get trapped into the day-to-day responsibilities. Your job is not to do a lot of stuff, it is to make several big decisions every year that determine which direction this business is going to go.

4. ***If things are not going well, acknowledge it*** – if things are not going well and it is an important enough thing for shareholders to believe you have failed at your job – so be it. There is a level of honesty with yourself and with them that you need to be comfortable with.

5. ***Optimise your influence for outcomes*** – when you are CEO, every step you take is watched. You must constantly be careful what you say and when you say it. Sometimes a quick response from you can short-circuit a committee decision, similarly a delayed response can leave space for others to surface critical issues. It is okay to play games with the process, so long as you carefully consider which outcomes you are trying to optimise for.

Throughout history leaders have been required to be politically virtuous. Chiefs, kings, queens, presidents, and CEOs are all expected to artfully manage intergroup relations, act with integrity, and serve the interests of society and those they lead. This paradox has long nestled in the core of effective leadership; however, in today's megatrends environment, it is trickier than ever to get it right.

Before we dig into what is amplifying the need for leaders to be politically virtuous, let us quickly define these two terms:

Defining Terms

- Being **Politically Savvy** is about effectively understanding and influencing others at work, leveraging relationships to achieve organisational, team, and individual goals.[3] It is about exercising power and being shrewd in the circumstances.
- **Virtuous leadership** is about demonstrating a deep commitment to high moral standards, leading with integrity and according to life-affirming values (such as fairness, honesty, equality, humanitarianism, and loyalty).[4]

Why a Politically Virtuous Mindset Matters Amidst the Megatrends

In *The Godfather*, when Michael Corleone comes up with a plan to kill a rival mob boss and a corrupt police chief in one manoeuvre, he makes a clear distinction: 'It's not personal Sonny. It's strictly business'. Repeatedly, this distinction is made in movies whenever characters are about to do something morally abhorrent. In the business world, whilst not quite as extreme as Godfather-style murder plots, the unwritten distinction between business and ethics has nevertheless lurked below the surface.

Historically, the business world has been predicated on the assumption that so long as you operate within the bounds of legality, anything goes in the pursuit of growing profit and market share. For centuries, big corporates and their successful leaders have taken whatever they can, via whatever means necessary, hiding behind the well-versed mantra: 'that's just business'.

Thankfully, times have changed. In 2019, nearly two hundred chief executives pledged to redefine the role of business in society, with 63% of global corporate leaders strongly believing a fundamental change in capitalism is underway.[5,6] The philosophy that an organisation exists purely to make money for shareholders is outdated. Global challenges such as scarcity of natural resources, climate change, and inequality are forcing organisations to recognise that they can either continue to be part of global problems or step up and become part of the solution. And, only the businesses that step up and positively contribute to society will continue to survive and prosper. Companies will need to justify their existence by 'doing good' both in *what* they aim to do (i.e., their purpose and mission) and *how* they go about doing it (i.e., their operations, processes, and culture).

'Doing the right thing' is therefore a fundamental part of leading a successful business in the modern age. However, while demand for moral leadership in business is high, with integrity and high moral standards frequently rated as the most important qualities for a leader to have,[7,8] research from the How Institute suggests CEO behaviours are falling short. Specifically, their survey findings suggest only 24% of CEOs demonstrate virtue, high integrity, and commitment to doing the right thing, and only 8% of CEOs consistently demonstrate moral leadership behaviours, which include a leader:[9]

- living their values and acting on their principles (even when doing so is uncomfortable, difficult, or inconvenient)
- constantly wrestling with questions of right and wrong, fairness and justice
- refusing to sacrifice principles for short-term gain.

These findings paint a bleak picture. But those in the C-suite are caught in the perfect storm. Pressure is mounting to 'do the right thing, first time around' on numerous unchartered societal, environmental, political, and economic issues. Meanwhile, the hyperconnectivity afforded by social media also means executives are now under increased scrutiny and much more likely to be called out and castigated for ethical lapses, scandals, or improper conduct. In fact, these days, CEOs are more often dismissed due to ethical lapses than for poor financial performance or board conflicts.[10] Both action and inaction on core issue can undo a career.

Alongside a focus on ethics, today's business environment is also characterised by a rapid rate of change. AI, data, and robotics are transforming what is possible in terms of the experiences and services organisations can provide, with an increasing number of disruptive start-ups capitalising on new opportunities as they emerge. For those in the C-suite, driving change and innovation is a business imperative; after all, if you do not constantly reinvent your business, somebody else will. Leaders are therefore needing to wade into new and unchartered territory at pace.

As well as the ethical awareness, successfully leading any form of change in an organisation requires political savvy.[11] Senior leaders must be skilled at managing friction and resistance to change, utilising information, and carefully influencing relationships to make stuff happen. Positive change is always the output of successful political manoeuvring. As business ethics professor Al Gini once stated:

> *The term power comes from the Latin 'posse' – to do, to be able, to change, to influence, or effect. To have power is to possess the capacity to control or direct change. All forms of leadership must make use of power. The central issue of power in leadership is not 'will it be used?' but rather 'will it be used wisely and well?'*

In this sense, being virtuous and being political must be intertwined if you wish to sustain high performance amidst the megatrends. Legality trails way behind the possible, especially when it comes to AI, data, and robotics, so leaders cannot rely on the law as a handrail for determining 'what is right'. Ethical decisions will be being made at every level in the business and C-suite leaders must set the standard, navigating the business towards positive change with integrity and via influence.

Leading Politically: Being Savvy in the Circumstances

'You're going to love it here, there's lots of office politics' is something no one has ever said.

In an organisational context, the notion of 'politics' has poor connotations. Political manoeuvring and behaviours are seen as negative attributes, with the idea of a person being highly political quickly conjuring up images of someone who is covert, dishonest, and manipulative. TV series like *House of Cards* depict this perception of politics perfectly; a toxic environment, where super-smart, ambitious highflyers stop at nothing to get power, demonstrating a predilection for ruthless pragmatism, manipulation, and betrayal.

But that is not what political competence actually means and spurning political savvy from leadership discussions is both naive and unhelpful. Organisations are social systems and embracing politics is an important part of leadership. Politically skilled leaders exhibit higher leadership effectiveness, lead better performing teams, and have followers with higher job satisfaction.[12] In fact, political skill is the strongest predictor of job performance, over and above intelligence and personality.[13] Undoubtedly, a political mindset is a must-have for any leader aiming to make a difference and leave a legacy.

What is important is to untangle power from being political savvy. Firstly, power. Power is an important place to start because any form of politics is fundamentally about power: acquiring it, enhancing it, and using it for personal and public interest.[14] Power can be defined as:

the possession and control of valuable resources or other people.

As we will discuss later in this chapter, it is in the struggle for power that many senior leaders find themselves lured off track. As political scientist Harold Laswell explained, politics is about 'who gets what, when, and how'.[15] More precisely, office politics is the behind-the-scenes influence that determines who gets a say in decisions, what changes happen, and which teams and projects get resourced. It is the inherently inequitable system that operates in all companies, giving influence to those who understand the 'unwritten game' and have effectively networked their way into the 'inner circle'. This is also what makes most of us dislike office politics so much, as it tramples all over our innate desire for fairness and transparency.

However, whilst numerous initiatives and movements are working hard to create more equity and increase the diversity of the 'inner circle' that resides at the top of many companies. Like it or not, there will always be an unwritten game for leaders to navigate. Being politically savvy is therefore a must-have for anyone looking to initiate significant, positive, and lasting change, and can be defined as:

the ability to effectively understand and influence others at work.

Politically savvy C-suite leaders can make a difference in the world because they are skilled in leveraging relationships to achieve organisational, team, and individual goals. They always embrace the importance of networking and influencing.

Let us now explore how to lead in the politically savvy sweet spot.

The Five Key Ingredients of Politically Savvy Leadership

Ingredient 1. Benevolent Motivation

The first thing you need to interrogate is your *willingness* to expend energy on the political game. Ask yourself:

- Are you motivated to engage in strategic politicking, both publicly and behind the scenes?
- If yes, what is the real goal underpinning that drive?
- If no, what is holding you back? And what is the cost of you not investing energy in it?

Whilst it may be tempting to think politics should get easier once you have reached the C-suite and hold a position of power and influence, it is as you move closer to the epicentre of power where political savviness becomes most critical. Motivation to expend energy on political behaviours therefore must remain high.

However, those at senior leadership levels also need to keep interrogating their political motivations and goals. Power is addictive. Having status, autonomy, and resources makes us feel good; it triggers our brains reward system urging us to strive for more and keep precious hold of the power we have gained. As Abraham Lincoln is quoted to have said: *'nearly all men can stand adversity, but if you want to test a man's character, give him power'*. The Ring 'that rules them all' in the Lord of the Rings is a good depiction of how power can be irresistibly corrosive to even the purest of characters. However, in reality, power is even more corrosive, because it is rarely given (or found in a cave) but hard-won over years of steady effort. Making it all the more precious to hold on to.

Political will must consequently be kept under the microscope of honest self-reflection. The goals underpinning political behaviour can either be self-serving (i.e., a need for achievement, power, and status) or benevolent (i.e., a drive to create meaningful positive change, give voice to core issues, improve practice and services, and generally make a business a better place to work).[16] The former self-serving elements are inevitably always present to some degree, but it is the latter all senior leaders must remain deeply and authentically focused on.

To lead as a political savvy leader, you therefore need both the will to engage in politics and the discipline to stay focused on the benevolent bigger picture. In other words, driven to make a positive, meaningful, and lasting difference and have an impact that extends beyond yourself, even beyond your company.

Ingredients 2–5. The skills of politically savvy leaders

Tactically speaking, politically savvy leaders excel on four interrelated, yet distinct, skills.[17] In the following table, we explore these four skills in more detail and outline questions you can use to assess your politically savvy strengths and development areas.

Skill	Are you . . .	Top tip
2. Social astuteness – *the ability to shrewdly observe others, detecting their motivations and agendas*	. . .able to insightfully observe yourself and others? • accurately interpreting their thoughts and emotions • constantly, paying attention to subtle social cues • often pausing to consider and understand the motivations that lie beneath people's outward behaviour • consistently making a good impression on others • . . .able to do all this in diverse social settings, not just the ones you are most used to?	**Adopt a hawk's eye view** It is easy to get lost in a blur of thoughts and to-do lists. But, in the rush for action, we often miss vital information. When interacting with people, slow down, zoom out, and zoom in. Like a hawk, consider the wider context of someone's situation, notice the subtleties in their tone, language, and mannerisms. Similarly, observe yourself how you are feeling, and how you might be coming across to them.
3. Interpersonal influence – *the capacity to persuasively communicate with and mobilise others*	. . . able to: • put people at ease? • quickly establish rapport with people? • exercise a compelling or charming interpersonal style?	**Develop charisma** Dr Robert Cialdini outlines the seven principles of persuasion.[18] However, influence also requires the less tangible 'charisma'. We often think of charisma as something people just have, but it can be crafted. As behavioural expert and author Olivia Fox Cabane explains,[19] mastering the art of charisma is about becoming a good conversationalist (creatively starting conversations, asking questions,

(*Continued*)

Skill	Are you . . .	Top tip
		and sharing stories), using expressive body language, mirroring people's energy and body language. Above all, pay attention to others who exude charisma; observe what they do, learn their secrets, try out their techniques and fine-tune them to fit you.
4. Networking – *the ability to build, maintain, and use relationships and connections*	. . .investing time: • connecting with the right people so you have greater insight – and greater say? • building quality relationships with others at different levels across the business? (informing your understanding of what's going on) • leveraging relationships to secure resources and get things done? (rather than relying on formal channels and processes) • prepping for conferences and events, so you know which other attendees are most relevant for you to connect with?	**Make small 1% builds everyday** Particularly for those with an introvert preference, the idea of networking can seem daunting and energy draining. However, even (perhaps especially) for those in the C-suite, both your internal and external network are still mission critical. The best approach is to make small 1% builds to your network every day. Your internal network will give you a view on aspects of the business you cannot see from the top (what is working well, not working, what the atmosphere is like). So, make time to get to know key people within your company on a deeper human level. Similarly, keep building your external network to keep fresh ideas for your company feeding in. Ask questions, be open, speak from the heart, and

Skill	Are you . . .	Top tip
		importantly, when connecting with people, stay focused on what value you can provide them (rather than 'how can they benefit me?').
5. Apparent sincerity – *skill in conveying honesty and authenticity while influencing others*	. . . able to: • communicate your sincerity in your words, voice, and behaviour? • make others perceive you to be honest, open, and forthright? • convey a genuine interest in others?	**Accept trust is a 'slow burn' process** *Apparent* sincerity sounds very false, but do not be mistaken. This is not about faking or putting on a show of honesty; it is about being sincere and genuine with others. However, the 'apparent' is important because what is crucial is what other people perceive you to be (not whether you think you are being honest). Sincerity is in the eye of the beholder. Whilst there are obvious quick wins (such as putting your phone away when having a conversation, actively listening, and maintaining good eye-contact), unfortunately, there is no short-cut when it comes to sincerity. Trust takes time to develop and express. Convey sincerity and authenticity by doing what you say you are going to do, treating everyone equally and fairly, sticking to your values and the truth, and allowing others to see you express a range of emotions.

The Political Leadership Continuum: How to Stay on Track

Staying in the sweet spot of politically savvy leadership can be particularly tricky. People tend to fall into one of two camps. Either they detached themselves mentally from engaging in politics, believing progression and power should all lie above ground – with the rules of play out in the open, giving everyone equal access to resources, influence, and decision making. Or they jump in to 'the reality' of how things get done and then get swept up in the game, losing sight of the bigger purpose around why they were seeking more power in the first place.

Unfortunately, veering off in either direction will have a negative impact. Being apolitical may feel like the moral high ground, but it will render you ineffective in your role as a senior leader. Similarly, getting too swept up in the game of acquiring status, autonomy, and influence will likely lead to an Icarus-esque experience. As your power accumulates, people defer to you more and more, you have increasing free reign on decisions, you may begin to lose touch with reality, and take questionable risks. Ultimately you fly too close to the sun and your career and power will likely implode in on itself, leaving you in the ashes of your past high-flying success.

Here, we will briefly explore how to catch yourself from wandering off into the more perilous paths of the powerless or power-hungry (see Figure 5.1).

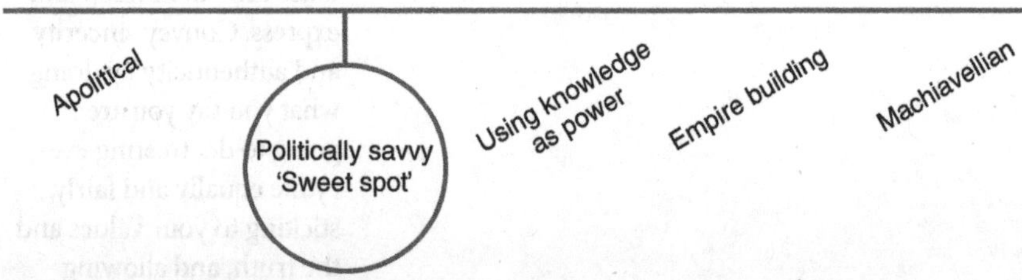

Figure 5.1 The political leadership continuum.

Apolitical. As Aristotle pointed out, 'man is by nature a political animal', so like it or not, politics will have a big influence on what happens to you, your projects, and your department(s) whether you participate in 'the politics' or not. Furthermore, aside from the performance implications of not embracing a politically savvy mindset (mentioned earlier in the chapter), evidence suggests that not engaging in politics can increase your level of psychological strain, reduce your job satisfaction, and your level of commitment.[20] Consequently, it is an 'if you can't beat them, join them' situation. By developing your political will and politically savvy skills you will find you are much more actively involved in organisational life and able to constructively make a difference. In turn, you will also find that your well-being and job satisfaction increases.[21]

Staying future-fit top tips. Often leaders who find themselves in the apolitical camp, perceive all office politics negatively. However, it is important to distinguish between bad politics and good politics.[22] Bad politics is the sneaky sort. The backstabbing, sucking up, and rumour-mongering people sometime use to advance themselves ahead of others. No one wants that in a business. But, there is also good politics. Good politics involves advancing one's own interests whilst remaining focused on the higher purpose. It is manoeuvring via morally acceptable means, mastering the art of the politically savvy skillset to get your own and your team's contributions recognised, have your ideas taken seriously, and influencing the key decisions being made by the executive team.

Using knowledge as power. According to authors John French and Bertram Raven, there are six distinct sources of power:[23,24] legitimate (endowed by a role or position), coercive (an ability to enforce consequences), reward ('do this and I'll give you that'), referent (attracting and maintaining loyalty through force of personality), expert (a high level of in-depth specialist expertise), and informational (the possession of knowledge others do not have). One of the most effective sources of power is information. Having access to facts and information others do not have can be hugely advantageous; it also indicates a special relationship with other power holders (emitting an indirect signal of status and influence). However, the use of knowledge as power is dangerous territory for leaders to venture into. Collecting, withholding, or even concealing knowledge is playing with fire in terms of people's trust. Once discovered to have held back potentially valuable information from people, it can be very difficult to regain people's confidence (even when done with good intentions). Furthermore, having a reputation as a 'knowledge hoarder' and 'information trader' will make others more guarded. One by one, relationships become very weak and transactional, not based on genuine connection and loyalty, but a wary mistrust and the perceived temporary value each person holds.

Staying future-fit top tips. In the long-run, and in an ideal world, it is best to avoid using knowledge as power. However, as a senior leader, you will inevitably find yourself being privilege to a lot more information than others in the business. In some situations, it will be crystal clear what information needs to be kept confidential, but there will also be many grey areas to deal with, where you will need to judge when telling everyone everything would be helpful or counterproductive. In these grey areas, total honesty and transparency is often impossible and it is part of the role to accept some of the discomfort that may cause you personally. It is also helpful to stick to the more 'socially acceptable' forms of knowledge hiding.[25] Specifically, rather than using 'evasive hiding' (giving other people partial or incomplete information, which may provoke more questions and uncertainty), it is more socially acceptable to either play dumb (i.e., pretend you do not know anything or are unaware of what someone else is talking about) or implement 'rationalised hiding' (i.e., explain that you would like to tell them but cannot for specific reasons and are bound by external factors). Employing these techniques should help you navigate the murky world of honesty and transparency at the senior leadership level, helping you protect relationships and avoid the lure of using knowledge as power.

Empire building. Empire building is when a leader has become focused on increasing their own power and prominence within a company, spending time securing head count, amassing large departments, acquiring budget, and establishing their central position in 'the general running of things'. To them, their function is the motor that drives the boat. Leaders here most likely started out with the best of intentions, seeing it as their role and responsibility to help their department grow and make a difference. However, whilst this leadership dedication initially led to more resources and the department expanding, over time, the taste of accumulated power is intoxicating. Leaders here become ever intensely focused on demonstrating the integral importance of their own functions and are no longer operating for the greater good, despite protestations and possibly self-deception (for it is likely they truly believe that the more power they have, the better it is for the company). Eventually, leaders who have strayed into empire building are easy to spot because they are way off course, operating with departments that are either big and siloed or all-consuming.

Staying future-fit top tips. Empire building is the enemy within. It is the enemy within an organisation that blocks it from being balanced, collaborative, and effective; and it is the enemy within ourselves. The urge to gain new territory, secure resources, and keep hold of what has already been acquired is incredibly primal; it is an ancient survival instinct playing out in the modern battlefield of business.[26] However, leading from such a survival mode is always a slippery slope, so it is important to pause and reflect: Why is your brain constantly in fight and defend mode at work? As author and organisational psychologist Dr. Nicole Lipkin explains, when you start to notice yourself (or someone else) needing to control everything, empire building for the sake of empire building, chances are you (or they) are feeling threatened.[27] Self-worth has become entangled with the external domain (i.e., the size and importance of the department they lead), and consciously or unconsciously, there's a constant fear someone will take it all away. Whilst for a time empire building may feel like you are onto a winning formula, it is a very perilous path with a sharp fall from integral to obstructive. If you think you may have strayed into empire-building territory, reflect on the following (perhaps with the help of an executive coach):

- What threats are you experiencing or perceiving in your work environment?
- What needs to be true for you to feel good about yourself or successful in your role?
- How do you imagine others perceive you? And what impact is this having?
- If you were watching yourself in a movie, what would you be noticing about your character? And, what would you be recommending they do differently?

Machiavellian. In the sixteenth century, Niccolò Machiavelli wrote '*The Prince*', describing strategies leaders could use to gain political power and prestige.[28] Specifically, Machiavelli prescribed how while leaders should try to appear virtuous, *acting* virtuously can be detrimental, endorsing how leaders should instead do whatever is necessary to acquire and maintain power. His philosophy was based on the premise that while people admire honour, generosity, and courage, by nature people are self-interested, deceitful, and profit-driven; a worldview akin to the 'dog-eat-dog', 'that's just business', philosophy mentioned earlier. In psychology today, Machiavellianism refers to one of the Dark Triad personality traits, describing leaders who are focused on their own interests, are unprincipled, cynical, and willing to manipulate, deceive, and exploit others to achieve their goals.[29]

While a Machiavellian personality may sound very extreme and far removed from life in the C-suite, studies often find individuals with this personality trait at higher positions within organisations.[30] Individuals high in Machiavellianism tend to do well in business. They desire status and control more and often apply softer manipulation tactics to get ahead, such as charm, exchanging favours, offering compliments, managing their physical appearance, joking with people, forming alliances, and compromising.[31] The line between the charismatic and the Machiavellian leader is consequently a fine one, with charismatic leaders likely to possess Machiavellian tendencies when influencing others.[32] On a more sinister note, leaders who are high in Machiavellianism are also more skilled at lying, tend to withhold important information from others (to minimise other people's power and influence), and find subtle ways to bully or undermine others. They pull the strings in the background. However, like a stealth hurricane, their tactics in pursuit of power leave a trail of destruction on other people's jobs, health, and home life. All actions justified in the belief that if the tables were turned, other people would do the same to them.

Staying future-fit top tip. Machiavellianism is a personality trait and, while certain aspects of personality can shift across our lifespan, our traits are relatively stable across time and situations.[33] Consequently, here we will not look at how to reduce trait levels of Machiavellianism but briefly outline one way to avoid slipping into Machiavellian tendencies. The secret: reflecting on what it is you are trying to control. Holding a position of power is associated with two forms of control: control over others and personal control. And it is the drive to control others that is most corrupting.[34] Particularly if you perceive your senior leadership position to be unstable, you may find this drive to exert power and control over others amplifies – leading you to undervalue and objectify people, treating them as objects on a chess board to be manoeuvred and played to your advantage. What is much healthier for you (and those you lead) is to focus on power as a way to satisfy personal control; the innate need we all have for autonomy and influence over our own lives. By focusing on the control power grants you over your own life, you are much more likely to pursue goals that make a difference, build positive relationships, and leave a meaningful legacy with societal-level consequences. Essentially, it is about reflecting on what you want to do with your life (i.e. with the power you have) rather than worrying about how to control others (i.e. keeping hold of power).

Leading Virtuously: Doing 'the Right Thing' at the First Opportunity

Virtue in the Oxford dictionary refers to:[35]

Behaviours or attitudes that show high moral standards

When leading virtuously, it is important to focus on behaviours. It is your actions that matter most. Do you do the right thing at the first opportunity?

'Doing the right thing' may sound simple enough, as we all like to think we have a strong moral compass. However, as you climb the leadership ladder, evidence suggests your moral compass gets weaker, with research indicating that senior executives are 64% less likely to challenge unethical behaviour compared with employees in the lowest-ranking positions.[36] Specifically, findings show that for high-ranking leaders, their identity becomes so strongly meshed with that of the organisation, it causes them to be much less likely to see unethical practices as being wrong in the first place.

Consequently, 'doing the right thing' and demonstrating a deep commitment to what you believe is not always easy, particularly for leaders at the top.

Here, we will explore how leading with a virtuous mindset requires two things:

1. an ability to spot ethical issues early on
2. the moral courage to act (both in the moment and over time, in the face of personal risk or challenges).

Let us look at each of these in more detail.

1. Identifying Ethical Issues Early On

More than three years before the CEO of an automotive manufacturer appeared before a congressional panel about the company's response to safety issues, employees had warned company bosses that cost-cutting measures were impacting the safety of the cars. In the memo, employees had even connected early mechanical issues to five deaths and used that to warn executives. However, the alert went unnoticed.[37]

Ultimately, millions of cars had to be recalled, with the unintended fault linked to a number of fatal road accidents. When called to testify at a congressional hearing, the CEO acknowledged how the company grew too fast to keep up with safety controls and that priorities had become confused as the business expanded rapidly. Condolences were extended to those affected and the organisations values of safety and quality reaffirmed. In a post-recall investors meeting, the CEO further emphasised their mission to create a car company that can grow sustainably, without the overreach that triggered past quality problems.

With hindsight or in a safe training environment, spotting ethical issues is easy. Looking back, it's clear senior leaders should have listened to the warnings coming from front-line employees. It is also a comforting illusion to think that you would never make such a critical mistake. However, back in the real world of C-suite leadership, where there is substantial time pressure, numerous appointments and events, a surplus of information, several topics on the board agenda, and business-critical decisions being made every day, spotting ethical issues is harder than it is comfortable to admit. It is frighteningly easy for those early warnings, micro-decisions, and small pieces of information to slip under the radar of busy executive teams – information that should be acted on is ignored, until it is too late.

Doing the right thing at the first opportunity requires leaders to be aware of, and proactively counter, the biases that create a fog around ethical issues. Whilst there are several biases everyone in the company should be alert to, as we enter a new society-focused era of business, C-suite leaders need to be particularly mindful of what we will refer to as 'fishbowl thinking'.

Fishbowl Thinking

'Fishbowl thinking' is where senior leaders unconsciously overlook wrongdoing if it benefits them or the company.[38] In the past, thinking about 'the fishbowl' (i.e., what is right for 'us, our teams, our company') was good enough. The old management cliché of thinking about 'the bigger picture' meant thinking about the whole company and higher strategic aims. Today, however, people expect business leaders to think and act with society in mind. The 'bigger picture' refers to how a company operates, what service it offers or product it creates, how employees are treated, how future generations are considered, whether sufficient value is created for shareholders, the impact a company has on the environment, whether the supply chain is ethical and sustainable, and generally how the company positively contributes to societal issues.

Whilst this may sound 'woke', leaders who fail to make this gear shift in thinking will pay the price. Doing what is right at the first opportunity requires leaders to consider 'what is right' from a 360-degree, wide-angle perspective and be alert to a range of ethical issues that could be emerging. For example, it is no good producing a product that makes the world worse, but having great policies around equity, diversity, and belonging. Likewise, it is not enough to offer a fantastic service that makes the world better but engaging in unfair competition or having poor employee well-being.

In sum, to spot ethical issues early on: senior leaders must look outside the fishbowl of their own organisation.

Ethical Fading

Aside from fishbowl thinking, there are several other ways good companies and well-intentioned leaders can fail to identify ethical issues early. Unfortunately, as humans, we tend to rationalise unethical choices by distancing ourselves from the consequences of our actions in a process known as 'ethical fading'.[39] Poor choices are typically the result of a gradual process, in which unethical decisions become shrouded in a veil of acceptability via self-deception.

The table below highlights key forms of ethical fading to watch out for:[40]

Type of fading	Example in business	Top tip
Euphemistic language – often we use business jargon or euphemisms, but the words we use can shield us from the true nature of what we are discussing or doing.[41] For example, presenting 'bribes' as 'soft commission', 'lies' as 'alternative facts', or describing 'right sizing' instead of 'firing people'. The language is softened, but the actions remain the same.	Over a decade ago, the Chairperson of a multinational information technology company led an investigation to uncover board leaks using a technique termed 'pretexting', (i.e., obtaining personal information under false pretences). This distancing from the reality of what they were doing (i.e. 'spying'), later unravelled into a widely publicised spying scandal, which led to charges against company the company's executives and board members, alongside a jail sentence for the investigator involved.	As a senior leader, listen closely to the language yourself and others are using: is an action or process being sugar-coated? Is there another word for what you are doing that, if used, would change your perspective, or raise concerns?
Ethical numbing – when we are repeatedly exposed to ethical dilemmas, we stop seeing the ethical issue. What may have initially seemed shocking becomes commonplace, it is just 'the way things are done'.	Two former executives (the company's president and vice president) slow slide into fraud started in the early 90's with the senior leaders allowing sales representatives to book revenue a bit early, if the quarter was ending and they just needed a few days to cement the sale. Rather than shipping the product to the customer, the 'as-good-as-confirmed' order	

Type of fading	Example in business	Top tip
Ethical numbing (*Continued*)	would be sent to a nearby warehouse and recorded as sold, violating accounting principles, which state a sale can only be recorded once goods are en route to the customer. However, so long as the sale went through quickly, it remained a difficult manoeuvre to detect on accounts. Over the next year, the leaders relaxed the policy further to allow sales representatives to book revenue two weeks before a sale was complete; until eventually the sales teams were doing whatever necessary to meet sales expectations, culminating in the two company executives being convicted and sentenced for financial fraud. Again, this may sound like an extreme example and obvious failing, but when the pressure to deliver results is high, unethical decisions can easily be downplayed and rationalised as acceptable practice.	Pay close attention to the processes and behaviours which have become accepted norms in your business. Listen out for when yourself or others are justifying behaviour with: 'it's just how we do things here' or 'we have to do it this way because . . .' When under pressure, it's easy to make or go along with dubious ethical decisions that are later impossible to untangle from.

(*Continued*)

Type of fading	Example in business	Top tip
Routinisation – if what we were doing in the past was okay, and our current practice is almost identical, then it too must be okay. This is another common way in which unethical practices can slide under the radar. A researchers Ann Tenbrunsel and David Messick put it: 'a series of small steps can lead to a journey of unethical and illegal activities'.[39] This type of ethical fading is known as 'routinisation', and it involves ethics never even being brought into question because ethics is assumed at every stage (i.e., 'we're doing the same as before, just with a slight modification').	The early stages of the Facebook Cambridge Analytica scandal could be seen as an example of this. Global Science Research, in collaboration with Cambridge Analytica, paid hundreds of thousands of users who agreed to take a personality test and have their data collected for academic use on an app called 'thisisyourdigitallife'. However, the app also collected the information of the test-takers' Facebook friends, creating a data pool tens of millions strong. Despite Facebook's platform policy only permitting collection of friends' data to improve user experience in the app, the harvested data was later used to create tailored adverts and targeted campaign messages to influence US presidential elections.[42] Thus, the steps from ethical research study to illegal misuse of data were complete.	As a senior leader, always be wary of small changes to existing routines. Don't automatically assume a new practice is ethical just because it's only marginally different from what was being done before. Ask yourself: Is this incremental change a risk? Does it raise ethical questions?

At the heart of every failure to spot an ethical issue always lies self-deception. Deception that it could never happen to you, deception it is not as bad as it seems, deception it is only a small change, deception it is not you but the system, deception it is just the way the world works or deception it is beyond your remit to worry about as an individual or business leader.

Everyone can fall prey to these self-deceptions and spotting ethical issues early on is the responsibility of everyone in the business. However, as a senior leader, you set the tone. Your actions have an amplified impact. You determine and role model whether ethical issues are downplayed and swept under the rug or identified early and acted upon.

2. Acting with Moral Courage

Being able to identify ethical issues is not enough, to do what is right also often requires moral courage. Virtuous action takes grit and perseverance.

In Finnish, this is referred to as 'sisu'. Whilst difficult to translate accurately, sisu refers to 'inner strength' and 'guts', as author Joanna Nylund explains, sisu is all about:[43]

> *stoic determination, hardiness, courage, bravery, will-power, tenacity and resilience. . .it's an action-oriented mindset. You don't brag about having sisu; you just let your actions do the talking.*

'Sisu' or 'moral courage' requires you as a leader to do the right thing despite the potential risks or personal hardship you may have to endure. As Rushworth Kidder, author of the book *Moral Courage* describes:[44]

> *moral courage is the bridge between talking ethics and doing ethics. . . without moral courage, even the best virtues grow weak from inactivity. With moral courage a more ethical world is slowly constructed.*

Specifically, morally courageous leaders do the following:[45]

- recognise and respond to unethical practices
- question practices or actions they do not believe are right
- are willing to take actions that may go against the status quo
- are willing to speak up when others remain silent.

Research and Psychology: Priming Yourself to Overcome Fear and Do What Is Right

Moral courage is the ability to overcome fear to do what is right. It is about taking action when it is not easy. In the moments where moral courage is called for, it will be very tempting for you as a leader to keep quiet and do nothing. You will be fully alert to the potential negative consequences of 'doing the right thing'. At best, action might risk humiliation or social rejection; at worst, you could lose your job and everything you have worked hard for over the years.

Social acceptance, status, income, and security are all powerful triggers, and the most primitive part of your brain will be urging you to freeze and not act, to protect yourself, your family, not risk it, and stay safe.[46] An instinctive survival mechanism kicks in. Meanwhile, your mind's moral alarm bells are ringing, but with less clarity. Morality does not lie in one brain

(*Continued*)

region but across many areas of the more recently evolved neocortex.[47] In these regions, your brain will be frantically trying to process the morality of the situation and deciding how you 'should' act, making rapid inferences about others' beliefs and intentions.

A battle therefore wages between the primitive region of your brain, urging you to inaction, and your sense of morality. Unsurprisingly, the most primitive part of your brain often wins. The moment to act slides by, the instinct to freeze and do nothing proves too strong.

Top tip. Do not rely on moral courage simply being there when you need it. It is a skill that must be trained and ready to use. Prime yourself to be ready to act when it counts.

Displaying moral courage can have profound effects, but moral courage is not an innate reflex; it needs to be cultivated beforehand from within. Try using the following tips to help you build your moral courage:

1. **Make a choice to take action** – try not to think too much about how you might handle an ethical issue, or what type of issue you could face, just make a deal with yourself right now that as a senior leader, if you notice something unethical or ethically dubious occurring in your business, you will call it out. Do not leave that decision to the moment. If you want to lead with a virtuous mindset, make the decision right now that you will be the type of leader who 'does the right thing at the first opportunity', regardless of whether you feel alone and despite the potential personal risk.

2. **Practice exhibiting courage in small ways** – courage comes with practice. Do not wait for the big moments or dramatic situations to test your moral fibre; rewire your brain and get used to taking action in spite of fear. There are small ways we can be courageous every day, whether it is speaking candidly about a topic that others are avoiding, providing honest feedback, or stopping to help someone even if it means being late for your next meeting. Whenever opportunity allows it, practice small acts of moral courage.
3. **Deal with what is, not what might be** – our minds are great at creating extra problems that do not exist yet. In situations where there is ambiguity, our thoughts can jump to imagining the worst-case scenario. This cognitive distortion is known as 'catastrophising' or 'magnifying' because very quickly a situation looks much more dire than it actually is. For example, when a loved one does not answer their phone, you may quickly worry they have been in an accident; similarly, by simply asking a challenging question or following-up on an issue you may worry, you will be fired from your role or ostracised from the senior team. Start noticing these moments when your mind surges forward to imagine the worst-case scenario and get in the habit of focusing your mind on 'what is' rather than 'what might be'. This will help keep your mind from edging into a stress-response and enable you to think clearly when ethically murky situations crop up.

As a final call to action: with moral courage, there is no grey area. Every time you stay silent, look on, and do nothing, whilst a morally dubious decision or behaviour goes by, you are setting the precedent. Every time you do not act you are making the choice to be complicit. Especially as a senior leader, your actions set the tone for what behaviours and decisions are viewed as acceptable. It is therefore imperative you become a role model of ethical awareness and morally courageous action.

The Virtuous Leadership Continuum: How to Stay on Track

A leader who is in the sweet spot of the 'virtuous' mindset will identify and take action around ethical issues at the first opportunity. They look at the decisions in the business from a wide-angle 360-degree lens, not only considering the business impact (for example, on employee well-being, performance, and company profit margins) but also, and at equal measure, the impact on wider society and the environment. They do not sweep bad decisions under the rug or buy-into the attitude that 'if it's legal, it's ethical'. They take ownership for 'doing the right thing', even when others remain silent or their actions go against the status quo in the business.

The 'virtuous' path is not an easy or comfortable one to take. It is a foggy road plagued with doubt about 'what the right thing to do' is and the potential risks of action or inaction. Consequently, it is very easy to lose your bearings and end up down a road where you find yourself stranded on your moral high ground or down an unethical path you never intended to end up down.

Let us explore a few ways you can slide off course on the path to leading virtuously (see Figure 5.2).

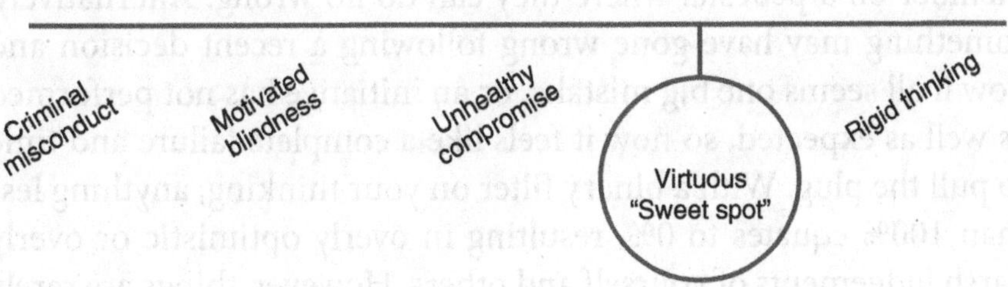

Figure 5.2 The virtuous leadership continuum.

Rigid thinking. When anxious or facing a high amount of ambiguity, it is easy for a leader to slip into the comfort of rigid thinking. In psychology, this is known as 'splitting' or 'black and white thinking' and involves our mind avoiding complexity and uncertainty by thinking in extremes.[48] From this standpoint, there are no grey areas, no moral ambiguity. Things are neatly packaged. People, events, and situations are either all good or all bad. Beliefs and facts are either completely right or completely wrong. Other people are either 'with' or 'against' you. For senior leaders, getting stuck thinking in absolutes can make life incredibly difficult, hindering your ability to collaborate or see alternative solutions in difficult situations. Over time, leaders can even begin to feel surrounded by enemies as those with different viewpoints, or who do things they disagree with, quickly flip across from being an ally to an adversary. Leaders operating with a rigid, all-or-nothing mentality can also be very difficult to work for. For example, with their mood switching between extremes (either happy or sad, calm or angry) and changing their mind over issues at the drop of the hat, unable to dwell in the grey area of a decision.

Staying future fit top tips. Thinking in absolutes is a very common trap. Right now, there is probably an aspect of your life that you have split into an 'either–or', 'all-good' or 'all-bad' situation without even realising it. For example, perhaps you see another leader in the business as utterly incompetent or have put a talented team member on a pedestal where they can do no wrong. Alternatively, something may have gone wrong following a recent decision and now it all seems one big mistake, or an initiative has not performed as well as expected, so now it feels like a complete failure and time to pull the plug. With a binary filter on your thinking, anything less than 100% equates to 0%, resulting in overly optimistic or overly harsh judgements of yourself and others. However, things are rarely that clear-cut. Sometimes 'doing the right thing' requires a leader to take a hard stand, but it also requires leaders to be able to step back and consider all sides. To find the acceptable middle ground and discover what is doable. Without the ability to embrace those grey areas of a situation, you will find yourself pinned on the precipice of a false extreme, unable to move forward or reverse back from an untenable position. Try to challenge yourself when you notice your thoughts jumping to extremes. A key indicator will be the language you are using, for example, words like 'always' and 'never' will start cropping up. Listen out for this distortion and dramatisation in your narrative and use it as a prompt to pause and reconsider the shades of grey you are overlooking.

Unhealthy compromise. Finding acceptable compromises is part and parcel of leading a business; without sacrificing lower priorities for higher ones, it is impossible to navigate real-world pressures and constraints. Deprioritising elements of the strategy, putting aside a personal preference to move a decision on, reallocating resources are all compromises that crop up. However, whilst many of the compromises leaders make are healthy, some can be unhealthy. An unhealthy compromise is when you find yourself sacrificing what you believe is important, surrendering your higher values and priorities for lower ones. For example, going along with a decision or idea you think is flawed simply because of who is pushing it, or manipulating the truth of a situation to win an award or look good in front of shareholders. Fortunately, when you make an unhealthy compromise, you will know about it – something will just feel wrong. Unhealthy compromises gnaw away at us, leaving a nagging sense of doubt and diminishing our passion for what we do, perhaps even replacing vitality with a deep sense of dread or bitter disillusionment.

Staying future-fit top tips. As author Elizabeth Doty explores in her book *The Compromise Trap*,[49] people end up making unhealthy compromises when the price of doing the right thing goes up. When they feel that have no choice but to conform. Unfortunately, we are all vulnerable to the pressure to conform, as our brains expect conflict when we do not conform and rewards when we do.[50] However, unhealthy compromise is a self-depleting cycle: you do not feel strong or secure enough to 'do the right thing', so you cross a line or betray something you value, which in turn takes a bite out of your self-respect and confidence. As Doty articulates:

> *People often frame dilemmas about compromise as a choice between self-interest and 'doing the right thing'. However, it's all self-interest: surviving and living your values.*

Unhealthy compromise is therefore the silent killer of successful careers. It is the gradual eroder of confidence, passion, health, status, power, and relationships. Consequently, regardless of the situation, it is important to remember three things: 1) you always have a choice, 2) surrendering your higher values has a less visible, but no less potent cost, and 3) 'doing the right thing' does not automatically mean conflict. More precisely, you do not have to take an antagonistic approach when you see something wrong; you can draw a line to protect what is important to you and work with people to find a better solution.

Motivated blindness. It is a well-documented psychological phenomenon that people see what they want to see, overlooking systematic failure or another person's unethical behaviour when it benefits them to stay ignorant. This is what is known as 'motivated blindness'. For example, managers are less likely to notice, and more likely to explain away any hint of unethical behaviour from an employee whom they hired and who performs well for them.[51] At a managerial level, this type of 'motivated blindness' can be problematic, but in a C-suite leader, it can be catastrophic. Motivated blindness contributed to crises such as the 2008 global financial meltdown and emissions scandal, where for years, executive-level leaders refused to notice and act on critical information that could have limited damage. As these examples show, motivated blindness can be extremely damaging to an organisation, industry, and society. It is not something those in senior leadership positions cannot afford to get wrong. Ignorance may feel safe, but conveniently overlooking an ethical issue is no excuse.

Staying future-fit top tips. No matter how smart or successful you are, we can all become prey to motivated blindness. In fact, it is when you and your team are excelling that it is most tempting to overlook the details and not ask too many questions. Researcher Maz Bazerman, author of *The Power of Noticing*, recommends three things senior leaders can do to avoid motivational blindness:[52]

1. **Never stop asking questions.** How is your success coming about? Is it sustainable? Are corners being cut to make this happen? What are the risks?
2. **Avoid turning a blind eye to 'minor things'.** Remember massive failures are often the result of small mistakes, compounded over time.
3. **Notice what is missing.** It is easy to focus on the information you have and what is happening, but it is important to notice: What information is missing? What is not happening? What are we not doing? What is not being discussed?

Criminal misconduct. You might be tempted to skip this paragraph thinking criminal misconduct is not something you would ever find yourself involved in. This is a thought shared by most C-suite leaders who have found themselves facing criminal and/or civil trials. Under the pressure to handle rapid expansion or tackle intensely challenging market conditions, the moral high ground can, however, slide far and fast from under you for a variety of reasons. In one research study, for example, 13 C-suite executives were interviewed to explore how they had become involved in financial fraud and revealed five different types of fraud immersion narratives:[53]

- **Social cues** – where certain practices were inherited and seen as 'just the done thing' in the organisation. Moral awareness became dampened with the desire to be super-successful prevailing in the culture. The ethical line became blurred as certain boundaries were crossed incrementally. As this C-suite executive explained:

  You get to here so it must be okay to go here. And if you're here, it surely is okay to go here. It's really fuzzy where you cross the line. At what point do you cross the line where that act becomes illegal? I don't know. I don't know.

- **Social conformity or compliance** – where executives had an 'inner voice' telling them that 'something is not right', but they choose to ignore it or perceive they did not have a choice in the situation. Some executives described how they were passively compliant:

  I put my head in the sand. My role continued to diminish as we hired other people in, my influence continued to drop down as the company grew. I was excluded. I said, you know, fine. I put my head in the sand, and just said okay, you know, I don't really have a position up here anymore, I'm safe, I'm just going to work here until I retire, and walk away and forget.

  Meanwhile, others described how they found themselves conforming fully due to peer pressure:

It was illegal, it was wrong. I knew it, you know. I could rationalise all the other things that we did as. . . part of the game, but it was very distinctly wrong and I knew it. I'm not a confrontational person and my basic nature is to not confront people. . .it's almost like a teenager and peer pressure. A teenager will do things because of peer pressure. They'll smoke a cigarette or do whatever. Because they want to fit in, they want to be liked, you know. And I think that was a lot of what motivated me.

- **The clan culture imperative** – where leaders fully embraced their new identity within the C-suite group: a tight-knit community where commitment and loyalty were heavily prized above all else and the group's common goal, underlying values, and assumptions were accepted without question. These leaders when interviewed used the pronoun 'we' more often than 'I' in their narratives, as this executive articulated:

  *Our incentive for the crime was not so much economic. It was more about loyalty to the group. Within the group, running with the same people you've been dealing with, I never thought about it, never had a morality discussion. Ever. Ever. Complete indifference. There was no discussion of morality whatsoever. We didn't give a s***. We really didn't care. Morality was for you, not for us.*

- **Rational choice system chaos** – in these narratives, leaders were simply overwhelmed by the sheer level of complexity of trying to figure out the extent of the issue; a challenge sometimes exacerbated by convoluted technical issues (for example, a segregated information system or ERP system conversion). One executive explained how it was difficult to figure out the magnitude of the rot. He focused his attention on gathering information and attempting to fix the problem; however, amidst the systemic chaos, ended up down a rabbit hole focusing on the wrong objective.

Staying future-fit top tip. C-suite leaders who end up with charges of criminal misconduct are not necessarily bad or evil people, with no moral compass. They are often well-intentioned leaders who really lost their way when placed in a bad situation.[54] As a leader, heed the lessons from these first-hand accounts. Be wary of taking on inherited practices. Listen to your inner voice if it is telling you something is not right. Notice when you are getting overly caught up in group mentality. Seek help when the issue feels too complex for one person to understand and solve.

Notes

1. Iszatt-White, M., Whittle, A., Gadelshina, G., and Mueller, F. (2019). The 'Corbyn phenomenon': Media representations of authentic leadership and the discourse of ethics versus effectiveness. *Journal of Business Ethics* 159: 535–549.
2. Cronin, T.E., and Genovese, M.A. (2012). *Leadership Matters: Unleashing the Power of Paradox*. London: Paradigm publishers.
3. Ahearn, K.K., Ferris, G.R., Hochwarter, W.A., et al. (2004). Leader political skill and team performance. *Journal of Management* 30: 309–327.
4. Kraemer Jr, H.M. (2011). *From Values to Action: The Four Principles of Values-Based Leadership*. New Jersey, US: John Wiley & Sons.
5. Business Roundtable (2021). *Statement on the Purpose of a Corporation.*
6. Diligent Institute (2020). Stakeholder Capitalism: Translating Corporate Purpose into Board Practice. *Survey Report.*

7. Giles, D. (2016). The Most Important Leadership Competencies, According to Leaders Around the World. *Harvard Business Review.*

8. BritainThinks (2019). What makes a great leader? Britain Thinks Leadership Study. *Report.*

9. The How Institute for Society (2020). The State of Moral Leadership in Business. *The How Institute Report.*

10. PWC (2018). CEO Success Study: Succeeding the long-serving legend in the corner office. *Survey Report.*

11. Cheema, I. (2008). Leaders' Political Skill, Organizational Politics Savvy, and Change in Organizations-A Constellation. In *IACM 23rd Annual Conference Paper*. Servant Leadership Research Roundtable, School of Global Leadership & Entrepreneurship. London, UK: Regent University.

12. Kranefeld, I., Blickle, G., and Meurs, J. (2020). Political Skill at Work and in Careers. In *Oxford Research Encyclopedia of Psychology*. Oxford, UK: Oxford University Press.

13. Munyon, T.P., Summers, J.K., Thompson, K.M., and Ferris, G.R. (2015). Political skill and work outcomes: A theoretical extension, meta-analytic investigation, and agenda for the future. *Personnel Psychology* 68: 143–184.

14. Cronin, T.E., Genovese., M.A. (2012). *Leadership Matters: Unleashing the Power of Paradox.* US: Paradigm.

15. Carpenter, W.S. (1936). Politics: Who gets what, when, how. By Harold D. Lasswell (New York, US: Whittlesey House. 1936. Pp. ix, 264.). *American Political Science Review* 30: 1174–1176.

16. Blickle, G., Schütte, N., and Wihler, A. (2018). Political will, work values, and objective career success: A novel approach–The Trait-Reputation-Identity Model. *Journal of Vocational Behavior* 107: 42–56.

17. Ferris, G.R., Treadway, D.C., Kolodinsky, R.W., et al. (2005). Development and validation of the political skill inventory. *Journal of Management* 31: 126–152.

18. Cialdini, R.B. (2006). *Influence: The Psychology of Persuasion, Revised Edition*. New York: William Morrow.

19. Cabane, O.F. (2013). *The Charisma Myth: How Anyone can Master the Art and Science of Personal Magnetism*. London, UK: Penguin.

20. Blickle, G., Schütte, N., and Wihler, A. (2018). Political will, work values, and objective career success: A novel approach–The Trait-Reputation-Identity Model. *Journal of Vocational Behavior* 107: 42–56.

21. Hochwarter, W.A. (2003). The interactive effects of pro-political behavior and politics perceptions on job satisfaction and affective commitment. *Journal of Applied Social Psychology* 33: 1360–1378.

22. Kaiser, R.B., Chamorro-Premuzic, T., and Lusk, D. (2017) Playing Office Politics Without Selling Your Soul. *Harvard Business Review*.

23. French, J.R.P., Jr., and Raven, B.H. (1959). The bases of social power. In D. Cartwright (Ed.), *Studies in Social Power* (pp. 150–167). Ann Arbor, MI: Institute for Social Research.

24. Raven, B.H., and Bertram, H. (2004). *Power, Six Bases of Encyclopedia of Leadership*. Thousand Oaks: Sage.

25. Connelly, C.E., Zweig, D., Webster, J., and Trougakos, J.P. (2012). Knowledge hiding in organizations. *Journal of Organizational Behavior* 33: 64–88.

26. Simmons, A. (2006). *Territorial Games: Understanding and Ending Turf Wars at Work*. New York: AMACOM.

27. Lipkin, N. (2013). *What Keeps Leaders Up at Night: Recognizing and Resolving Your Most Troubling Management Issues*. New York: AMACOM.

28. Machiavelli, N. (1995). The Prince [1513]. In S. Milner, (ed.) *The Prince and other Political Writings*.

29. Furnham, A., Richards, S.C., and Paulhus, D.L. (2013). The Dark Triad of personality: A 10-year review. *Social and Personality Psychology Compass* 7: 199–216.

30. Spurk, D., Keller, A.C., and Hirschi, A. (2016). Do bad guys get ahead or fall behind? Relationships of the dark triad of personality with objective and subjective career success. *Social Psychological and Personality Science* 7: 113–121.

31. Dahling, J.J., Whitaker, B.G., and Levy, P.E. (2008). The development and validation of a new Machiavellianism scale. *Journal of Management* 35: 219257.

32. Bedell, K., Hunter, S., Angie, A., and Vert, A. (2006). A historiometric examination of Machiavellianism and a new taxonomy of leadership. *Journal of Leadership and Organizational Studies* 12: 50–72.

33. Roberts, B.W., Walton, K.E., and Viechtbauer, W. (2006). Patterns of mean-level change in personality traits across the life course: A meta-analysis of longitudinal studies. *Psychological Bulletin* 132: 1.

34. Cislak, A., Cichocka, A., Wojcik, A.D., and Frankowska, N. (2018). Power corrupts, but control does not: What stands behind the effects of holding high positions. *Personality and Social Psychology Bulletin* 44: 944–957.

35. Hornby, A.S. and Cowie, A.P. (1995). *Oxford Advanced Learner's Dictionary (Vol. 1428)*. Oxford: Oxford university press.

36. Kennedy, J.A., and Anderson, C. (2017). Hierarchical rank and principled dissent: How holding higher rank suppresses objection to unethical practices. *Organizational Behavior and Human Decision Processes* 139: 30–49.

37. Calloway, J. (2005). *Indispensable: How to Become the Company that Your Customers Can't Live Without.* New Jersey, US: John Wiley & Sons.

38. Bazerman, M.H. (2020). A New Model for Ethical Leadership. *Harvard Business Review.*

39. Tenbrunsel, A.E., and Messick, D.M. (2004). Ethical fading: The role of self-deception in unethical behavior. *Social Justice Research* 17: 223–236.

40. Wilmot, D., and Walker, L. (2019). Shining the spotlight on ethics. *Lane4 Article, Available on Request.*

41. Rittenburg, T.L., Gladney, G.A., and Stephenson, T. (2016). The effects of euphemism usage in business contexts. *Journal of Business Ethics* 137: 315–320.

42. Cadwalladr, C., & Graham-Harrison, E. (2018). 50 million Facebook profiles harvested for Cambridge Analytica in major data breach. The *Guardian* (March 17).

43. Nylund, J. (2018). *Sisu: The Finnish Art of Courage.* London, UK: Octopus Publishing Group.

44. Kidder, R.M., and McLeod, B. (2005). *Moral Courage.* New York, US: William Morrow.

45. LaSala, C.A., and Bjarnason, D. (2010). Creating workplace environments that support moral courage. *The Online Journal of Issues in Nursing 15.*

46. Rock, D. (2009). *Your Brain at Work.* New York: HarperCollins.

47. Pascual, L., Gallardo-Pujol, D., and Rodrigues, P. (2013). How does morality work in the brain? A functional and structural perspective of moral behavior. *Frontiers in Integrative Neuroscience* 7: 65.

48. Oshio, A. (2009). Development and validation of the dichotomous thinking inventory. *Social Behavior and Personality: an International Journal* 37: 729–741.

49. Doty, E. (2009). *The Compromise Trap: How to Thrive at Work without Selling your Soul.* California, US: Berrett-Koehler Publishers.

50. Stallen, M., and Sanfey, A.G. (2015). The neuroscience of social conformity: Implications for fundamental and applied research. *Frontiers in Neuroscience* 9: 337.

51. Bazerman, M.H., & Tenbrunsel, A.E. (2011). *Blind spots: Why We Fail to Do What's Right and What to Do about It*. New Jersey, US: Princeton University Press.

52. Bazerman, M. (2014). *The Power of Noticing: What the Best Leaders see*. New York, US: Simon and Schuster.

53. Suh, I., Sweeney, J.T., Linke, K., and Wall, J.M. (2020). Boiling the frog slowly: The immersion of C-suite financial executives into fraud. *Journal of Business Ethics* 162: 645–673.

54. George, B., and McLean, A. (2012). Why leaders lose their way. In *Contemporary Issues in Leadership* (pp. 175–185). Oxfordshire, UK: Routledge.

CHAPTER 6
CONFIDENTLY HUMBLE

Because one believes in oneself, one doesn't try to convince others. Because one is content with oneself, one doesn't need others' approval. Because one accepts oneself, the whole world accepts him or her.

—Lao Tzu, philosopher and writer

What Is a 'Confidently Humble' Mindset?

Confidently humble leaders hold the following mindset:

- It is impossible for them to successfully achieve ambitious goals alone.
- They must inspire others to have confidence in them, so they back their beliefs, vision, decisions, and overall ability to deliver results.
- They show vulnerability and openly acknowledge their limitations.
- It's vital for them to learn from others and harness all the ideas, expertise, and strengths of those around them.

Future-fit leaders are therefore confident and inspirational as individuals and humble and vulnerable as team players.

The requirement for leaders to be both confident and humble is not new, and the balancing act is certainly not easy. History is littered with examples of leaders, often highly talented individuals, who got the balance badly wrong and paid the price in terms of performance.

Take Linda Wachner.[1] While starting out as a junior buyer at Foley's Department Stores, Wachner wasted no time in making her mark in the industry. Rising through the retail ranks, she rescued declining cosmetics company Max Factor, restoring the business to profit in just two years. She then turned her attention to clothing manufacturer Warnaco, taking over as CEO after successfully leveraging a buyout. Wachner transformed the company despite the brutal economic climate, building a collection of household brand names such as Calvin Klein Jeans and Speedo swimsuits. In 1992, *Fortune* magazine named her America's most successful businesswoman, and by

1998, Warnaco's share price was at an all-time high of $44.375, with total company sales around $2.1 billion.

However, Wachner's retail success was about to unravel. Having proved her competence time and time again, she strongly believed in her strategy and her ability to deliver results. She also believed she needed to have all the answers – but as a former subordinate of Wachner's commented to the *New York Times* 'there is some genius there, but she could not run a $2 billion corporation by herself'.[2] Sure enough, in 2001 Warnaco Group filed for bankruptcy protection with debts of $3.1 billion and Linda Wachner left her position as CEO.

America's most successful businesswoman had fallen into the trap. She had excelled in confidence, solely guided by her own expertise and gut instinct, and overlooked the necessity of humility.

Like all the paradoxical mindsets, confidently humble is a work in progress. There is no perfect leader who has completely mastered 'confidently humble'. That said, there are some leaders who often show 'both/and' thinking, exhibiting both confidence and humility blended together in their leadership.

The 44th President of the United States, Barack Obama, is one such 'confidently humble' example. Rising to be president takes a huge amount of self-confidence; in the words of Obama, confidence is a 'prerequisite of the job'. It is one thing he states himself and the 45th President, Donald Trump, had in common.[3] To run for President, you need to believe you can take on the top job, successfully inspire a campaign team to invest in you, and convince a nation to vote for you. And, to those who have worked closely with Obama, he has that 'special something' by the bucketload, exuding poise, self-assurance, and charisma.[4]

In just three hours, on attending three different California fundraisers, Barack Obama raised an extraordinary $7.8 million for the Democratic Party. During his speech at the third event, Obama confidently stated to a crowd of 1,300 people that 'I will win. Don't worry about that'.[5] By the end of the month, August 2008, Obama had raised more money in a one-month period than any previous presidential candidate had done.[6]

However, it is a fine line to tread: Obama's words and actions are sometimes perceived as brash. . . sometimes arrogant. . . sometimes well-grounded.[4] All-in-all though, he is certainly perceived as confident.

As well as inspiring confidence from others and displaying confidence in himself, during his tenure Obama simultaneously demonstrated a huge degree of confidence in others. Confidence in others is where the line starts to blur between confident and humble.

For example, in 2010, the Deepwater Horizon oil-spill occurred. A critical device had malfunctioned and engineers at the oil and gas company were rapidly trying different techniques to try and plug the leak. Obama certainly did not know how to solve the problem but his humility shone through his confidence in others around him. He put the dilemma to his energy secretary Steven Chu (a Nobel prize-winning physicist) and his team of government scientists. Chu returned to Obama with a drawing of 'a little hat' (in Obama's words), with some numbers scribbled next to it. Ultimately, this sealing cap was successfully bolted on, providing enough of a temporary fix for engineers to permanently seal off the flow. As Obama reflected later, his humility meant he was not intimidated by those around him and their incredible expertise. His success came through confidence in them: 'my role as leader was not to come up with the little hat, because I wouldn't have thought of it. I would have thought it didn't look complicated enough. . . my job was to ask Steven Chu, who had the Nobel prize in physics'.[7]

Consequently, whilst exuding confidence, a humble mindset is at the heart of the advice Obama gives others on leadership:

> *Anyone who wants to be a leader, ask yourself, 'How am I helping other people do great things?' I can't be an expert on everything, and I can't be everywhere, but I can assemble a team of people who are really good, really smart and really committed, who care about their mission and have integrity. Give them the tools and get rid of their barriers and help coach them so that they can do a great job. If they do, then by definition I will too – because that's my job.*[8]

Defining Terms

- **Confidence** can have many meanings and is often seen as both a feeling of being certain of your own abilities as well as the act of having trust in people, plans, or the future.[9]
- **Humility** is both an accurate self-assessment of one's abilities and achievements and the ability to keep those achievements in perspective.[10]

So, how easy is it to stay confidently humble at the top? How do you balance:

- Listening and learning from all those around you (no matter who they are or what they do), whilst still holding your own opinions and ideas?
- Focus on and trust in others, yet still back yourself to deliver your targets?

- Show openness and vulnerability when people are also looking for you to lead, be decisive, inspire them, and deliver what is expected?

The answer is: it is not very easy. It is a fine line to always be treading but adopting a confidently humble mindset is critical to success in a megatrend's environment.

Leader to Leader

Julie-Ann Haines's career has spanned a range of industries, shifting from roles in retail and consumer goods marketing to financial services. Even within her current organisation, which is the largest building society in Wales, she has progressed through a variety of roles moving from head of strategy, to director of IT, to chief customer officer, and now CEO. A big part of her leadership brand is her down-to-earth approachability, her willingness to be vulnerable, admit mistakes, and listen hard to her employees. But she has also learnt to embrace her own super strength, the value she brings as a generalist, with an eclectic portfolio of career experiences. Furthermore, despite being willing to be vulnerable, she knows when to hold firm, own the space, and gain people's trust and confidence in her and her ability.

This paradoxical blend of confidence and humility was demonstrated clearly in a talk she gave to branch managers, not long after being promoted to chief customer officer. As Julie-Ann explains, 'I was acutely aware that they didn't know me and had had a very different leader prior to me. A specialist leader very typical for finance, with a lot of gravitas and physical presence, as well as 30 years' experience in the financial services market. And here was me, turning up with the badge and the role, in my late 30's, a completely different individual in terms of background and experience'.

Right from the start, Julie-Ann openly acknowledged that daunting feeling to her branch managers, recounting how 'it was a big deal to me turning up in that room and I talked about that. I talked about the big shoes to fill'. However, her focus remained tight on helping them get to know her more, understanding her background, passions, core values, and showcasing her ability to take on the role.

Specifically, during the talk, Julie-Ann spoke about her values of 'being down-to-earth and accessible'. She also shared how she had worked at her dad's petrol garage, at the age of 12, and therefore recognised how the branch manager's job was one of the hardest that you could do, in terms of being customer-facing. At the same time, she carefully positioned herself as 'someone who is going to do good things for their part of the business'. She showcased her superpower as a generalist, outlining how her varied background and experience working in different sectors was a unique strength that she brought to the role. She also talked about her 'in-tray': the big-ticket items on her plate and some of the challenges and stakeholders she would be dealing with. The aim of the 'in-tray' being to help people understand that whilst she was approachable and down-to-earth, she was also there to 'do a big job', 'somebody who means business' and is taking on the most pressing issues and business-critical challenges.

(Continued)

To follow up on the talk, Julie-Ann also did a series of dinners, where branch managers could discuss in a one-to-one format with herself and the CEO, 'what was on their mind, what they were worried about and what they felt should be factored into leadership thinking'. As Julie-Ann explains, these dinners really helped build trust and deepen relationships. They gave people an opportunity to share and ask things more informally, to be heard, and, on occasion, hear where Julie-Ann and the CEO disagreed with them, where they intended to take a different direction to the one the manager wanted and why.

Listening to people, asking questions, taking time to understand the root cause of different opinions, absorbing honest feedback (from people at all levels), being able to admit mistakes, contributing value as a generalist, and holding firm when necessary are all trademarks of Julie-Ann's confidently humble leadership. Whilst she by no means professes to be perfect, she does urge leaders to understand their own 'secret sauce': to discover and harness both their own and other's super strengths. As she states: 'everybody has to work out what their secret sauce is and anchor back to that. If that's my secret sauce what does it mean I'm not so good at? And therefore, how do I have people around me that can help me fill those gaps?'

Why Confidence and Humility Matter Amidst the Megatrends

The megatrends are creating a context of high uncertainty. Technology is evolving at an incredible pace; data is adding to the amount of information available for decision making; start-ups are cropping up (seemingly overnight and out of nowhere) disrupting well-established markets, and there is high political volatility. Uncertainty is everywhere, and in such times, it is important for leaders to have a mindset of humility whilst simultaneously displaying confidence that inspires others.

More precisely, humility is key because to thrive in today's business environment, leaders must be aware that no one person can have all the right answers. Success in the modern world hinges on the ability to unleash the expertise of others and collaborate effectively. Research also shows that humble leaders perform better because they 'legitimise uncertainty' for their employees.[11] By admitting and acknowledging their own uncertainty, as well as articulating what they do and do not know, this helps to validate the uncertainty others are feeling. People are also more likely to be comfortable with uncertainty if they feel safe to ask questions – not that a precedent has been set and they should have all the answers. Furthermore, research shows leaders with a humble mindset are also more likely to create an adaptable workforce, where employees are empowered to suggest and implement small day-to-day changes that improve performance.[12]

At the same time, when uncertainty is high, confidence and trust become even more critical to get right. People want leaders they can put their faith in, who have a strong track record, will focus on what is important, and deliver the results required.[13] Amidst uncertainty, leaders need to make decisions and provide a sense of control. Furthermore, CEO research shows that leadership charisma is a predictor of performance under conditions of uncertainty, as highly charismatic leaders articulate a vision and sense of mission more strongly, show determination, communicate high performance expectations, and help others feel good in their presence.[14] They rally people together and heighten people's sense of belief, fuelling their confidence to overcome any setback necessary to attain the vision.

Leading Confidently: Trusting Yourself and Inspiring Others to Trust You

The word 'confidence' comes from the Latin *fidere*, meaning 'to trust'. However, when you dig deeper, this trust is a mix of belief, expectation, and action. As the Cambridge dictionary defines, confidence is:[15]

> *A feeling of being certain of your abilities and an act of having trust in people, plans, or the future.*

To lead with confidence, it is vital to separate the feeling from the action. But before we get into that, let us briefly explore what confidence is in a bit more detail.

Confidence is undeniably important. Surgeons, elite athletes, C-suite leaders. . . whatever the domain, confidence consistently appears as a key skill possessed by successful high performers.[16,17] It is also often referred to in absolute terms, something that someone either 'has' or 'does not have'. But confidence is neither broad, nor can it ever be 'possessed' outright.

Firstly, confidence is not general but domain specific. For example, it is possible to lack any confidence in your ability to sing or draw but have lots of confidence in your ability to deliver a presentation or develop a strategy. So, the idea of 'possessing' confidence in its entirety is a misnomer; we can only ever possess specific segments of confidence. Secondly, confidence is a fragile thing. It is not something we can build and then 'have'; it is something that must be earned and nurtured indefinitely. As two-time Olympic gold medallist and FIFA World Cup champion, Mia Hamm explained:[18]

The thing about confidence I don't think people understand, is it's a day-to-day issue. It takes constant nurturing. It's not something you go in and turn on the light switch and say, 'I'm confident', and it stays on until the light bulb burns out. Many athletes have admitted that confidence is a fragile psychological state.

When it comes to leading with confidence, sadly there is no 'free lunch' or quick fix. Cultivating confidence takes time and day-to-day effort. Even for top world-class performers, success alone does not automatically equate to high levels of confidence; it depends on how they interpret the cause of their success (i.e., a result of luck and good fortune, or earned through ability and effort).

Finally, while not always done, it is also useful to distinguish between confidence and self-esteem. As discussed, confidence is about having belief in yourself and your abilities and showing acts of trust. Self-esteem is about whether you appreciate and value yourself; with the word 'esteem' derived from the Latin *aestimare* meaning 'to appraise, value, rate, weigh, or estimate'. Consequently, it is possible to be highly self-confident and yet to have profoundly low self-esteem; as is the case for many celebrities and exceptional performers, who perhaps have high levels of confidence in their ability to perform (potentially in front of thousands of people) but then commit suicide or struggle with drug addiction due to profoundly low feelings of self-worth. To be clear, the discussion here focuses on how to build self-confidence, not self-esteem.

Now that we are aligned on what confidence is, let us explore how to 'put in the hard yards' and cultivate confidence on a daily basis.

Three Confidence Habits to Get Into

As Dr. Russ Harris explains in his book *The Confidence Gap*,[19] there are a few key habits to master if you want to lead with confidence, namely the ability to:

1. separate feelings from action
2. commit to practice
3. exercise task-focused attention.

Habit 1. Separating Feelings from Action

It is easy to view self-confidence as some sort of 'optimum state', where you have absolute belief, cool-calm-collected feelings, and total trust that things will 'come good'. In other words, as an ability to act free from fear, insecurity, and self-doubt. But this is not true.

Confidence is not the absence of fear. It is about not letting fear dictate your actions.

Nelson Mandela, for example, recounted how there was much fear on Robben Island, where he and other prisoners were continually subjected to gruelling conditions, beatings, starvation, and torture. But he knew that as a leader, to inspire others and give them strength, he needed to hide his fear, 'put up a front', and inject confidence and belief into those around him.[20] He understood that he could not control his feelings but could control his facial expressions, posture, the way he walked, and how he talked to people. Prisoners who were with him said watching Mandela walk across the courtyard, upright and proud, was enough to keep them going for days. Mandela, of course, felt fear, but he did not let fear determine his actions; he triumphed over it. By focusing on controlling his actions, rather than his thoughts and feelings, he learnt to trust himself to act no matter how he felt.

Although confidence can be defined as both a feeling and an action, as Russ Harris explains, you can't always wait for the feelings of confidence to come first:

> *If you wait for feelings of confidence to show up before you start doing the things that are truly important to you, the chances are you're going to be waiting forever. These feelings are not likely to magically appear out of thin air.*

Top tip	In your mind. . .
Learn to unhook	Our minds have evolved to be very good at preserving resources (i.e., telling us we are too busy and too tired) and assuming the worst (i.e., predicting failure, rejection, or other unpleasant outcomes). Start noticing the type of thoughts that hook you in and eat away at your confidence to act, for example: • I can't do this. • This is too hard; I'm out of my depth. • Other people seem to do this so much better than me. Then ask yourself: 'If I let this thought dictate my actions, will it help me create the life I want?' If the answer is no, create space around the thought. . .

(*Continued*)

Top tip	In your mind...
	Do not try to eliminate it, just acknowledge that the thoughts are just words that create feelings. Of course, they often have a powerful influence on our actions, but we always have a choice. We can choose how we behave and choose to pursue actions that matter to us, even when it is hard and our mind is nagging at us to do what is easy and comfortable. Try out some of the following techniques to help separate yourself from your thoughts and recognise they are nothing more or less than words: • Replay the unhelpful in a silly voice, using an accent, or in the voice of a famous actor. • Imagine the thought as words scrolling across your laptop screen. Do not try to change the words, just play around with the font, colours, spacing, and format. • With a sense of humour, thank your mind for its input and opinion on the matter. Perhaps with a gently added 'and, that's why you're not in charge here'.

Habit 2. Committing to Practice

We all love the promise of a quick fix and the idea of 'natural ability'. And, sure, some people are naturally talented in certain areas and get better results with seemingly much less effort. But, unfortunately, most of the time, if you want to get good at anything, if you want to build that feeling of trust in your ability, the bottom line is you are going to have to practice. Even those people who seem 'naturally gifted' invest huge amounts of time honing their skills in practice.

The fact is if you want to have feelings of confidence in your ability, you need to develop your ability. No matter how successful you are as a leader, there is always more you can improve and work on.

Top tip	In your mind. . .
Break it down	As discussed earlier, confidence is specific not general. It is no good as a leader aiming generally to 'be more confident'. You need to break it down: • What exactly do you want to be confident in? • How will being confident doing *x* help you to lead or perform better? • What will working on this give you? • What is the impact of not working on this? Once you have established if/why it is worth the effort, break the actual 'ability' down further: • What exact skills do you need to get good at? • What precise elements do you need to start practising to get good at those skills? • How much will you practise those elements? When? Where? Really home in so you can transform 'wishes' and 'hopes' for confidence into effective actions and skills you can trust.

Habit 3. Exercise Task-Focused Attention

Just for a second, think of a leader you know who appears to exude confidence . . .

One thing they are probably very good at is giving their full and undivided attention to the task at hand. For example, picture a leader who is highly charismatic and always talking easily with people. . . chances are they are always absorbed and engaged in the conversation with the person they are talking to. They are fully present and focused on that moment.

At any one point in time, there is always so much that can pull at our attention: our internal dialogue, the micro-events happening around us, the lure of our digital world and all the distractions and updates just there at our fingertips. Our minds are also great time-travellers, often contemplating on our future to-do lists, anticipating events that have yet to occur, and ruminating over the past.

By fully focusing on the task at hand, spotlighting that which is most important to spotlight, we give ourselves the best chance of performing well (whether it is *the* key moment to deliver that speech or a micro-moment to practice storytelling).

Top tip	In your mind. . .
Spotlight your attention	The phrase 'be present' is overused, but the reality is being able to focus all your attention on the task at hand will help you be more effective and develop trust in your ability. Mindfulness training is of course the best long-term way to learn to stay focused and absorbed in whatever task you are doing. However, do not assume it always requires extra time out of your day. Practice spotlighting your attention during your daily routine: • **When brushing your teeth:** focus in, notice the sounds, the feeling of the brush on each tooth, the taste of the toothpaste. . . • **When walking to lunch or work:** do not go on internal autopilot, notice what has changed, listen to the sounds around you. . . • **When stacking the dishwasher:** listen to the noise each item makes when it slots in, notice the colours and patterns food and drink has left on the surface, observe how your arm, fingers, and shoulder feel in the movement of stacking. . . While it may seem like a silly 'spotlighting' exercise, by practising tuning your mind into the present moment, you will find it easier and easier to focus your attention when it matters. It is a habit that, if strengthened daily, will improve your effectiveness as a leader.

The Confident Leadership Continuum: How to Stay on Track

Building your confidence is the first step in becoming a confidently humble leader. You need to spend time focusing in and practice taking actions with confidence (rather than waiting for the feeling of confidence to simply emerge).

However, as discussed, confidence is a fragile thing. It is easy to be pulled out of that sweet spot of confidence (where you have authentic pride in how you operate), and into the jungle where you suffer from a lack of confidence or perhaps overconfidence. We call this jungle – the confidence continuum (see Figure 6.1).

To become future-fit, leaders must resist the pulls of behaviours such as overconfidence, arrogance, or even narcissism. Similarly, it's important to avoid confidence dips and the patterns of thinking that accompany imposter syndrome.

Let us look at the different ways you can get lost off track in terms of confidence and explore how to stay future-fit.

Narcissism. At the broadest level, narcissism is the degree to which an individual has an inflated sense of self and is preoccupied with having that self-view continually reinforced.[21] Individuals high in levels of narcissism are more likely to exhibit feelings of superiority,

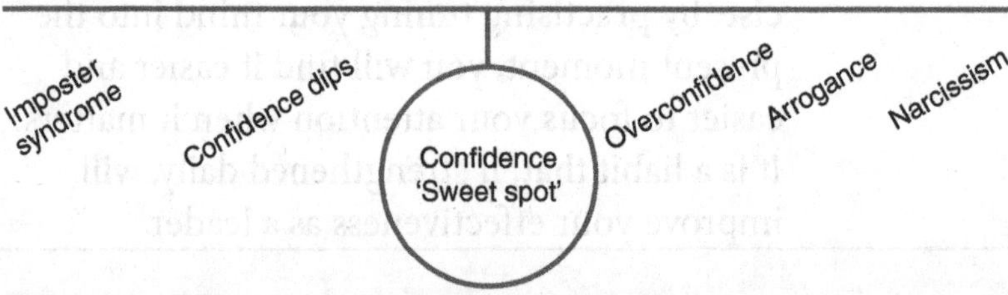

Figure 6.1 The confident leader continuum.

a sense of entitlement, show envy, arrogance, lack of empathy, display an aptitude for manipulating others, and tend to overestimate their capabilities.[22,23] It is a highly complex psychological construct, studied both as a personality dimension and clinical disorder.[24] However, whilst it is easy to dismiss narcissism as a clinical extreme, only thinking of it as a personality disorder, psychologically speaking, narcissism is a personality trait that every person possesses to some degree. Like any trait, it exists on a spectrum, with everyone showing flickers of narcissism from time to time (perhaps forgetting to consider others, feeling envious, expecting special treatment, or using manipulation tactics to get a certain outcome or response from others).

Staying future-fit top tips. Look out for where you exhibit flickers of narcissism and the situations that trigger it. Observe yourself and pre-empt how you can choose to act differently in future (e.g., not succumbing to a knee-jerk comment or response triggered by envy but appreciating others success without feeling threatened by it). Additionally, if you find yourself impulsively drawn to making a bold decision for the sake of it, take care. Research shows leaders high in narcissism are much more likely to take on bold, highly visible tasks, seeking the stream of admiration repeated bold actions will bring (if they pull it off).[25] Consequently, when tempted to take on an excessively risky proposal or idea 'for the hell of it', take a moment to reflect on your motives: do you think this is truly the best course of action? Or are you chasing the praise and kudos such action could bring?

Arrogance. A commonly used term, arrogance is when an individual behaves as if they are better, more important, or in some way superior to others. Arrogant behaviours typically involve disparaging others: disrespecting colleagues and their ideas, purporting to be more knowledgeable than others, avoiding blame and/or pinning blame on others, and discounting feedback. Sometimes success will propel a talented individual into arrogance, generating a deep-seated belief that they know best or are the best and that other people simply cannot do what they do. However, sometimes the real drive behind arrogant displays is a defensive one; with leaders attempting to hide their own insecurities by exaggerating their own competence and importance.[26]

Staying future-fit top tips. Arrogance is a strong word, which most people will have an aversion to. Unfortunately, when you are talented, very senior, and have a proven track record of high performance, arrogant thinking and behaviours can insidiously start to slip in. For example, a leader may believe someone is highly capable because they 'see a lot of themselves and their own traits' in that person – this is a form of arrogance and can massively prevent an organisation from harnessing the benefits of diversity. To avoid this more insidious form of arrogance, it's important to remember there are always multiple ways to do something and achieve a great result, always new ideas and innovations to add in, or different angles that have not yet been considered. In relation to more blatant displays of arrogance, senior leaders should also stay vigilant. No matter how important or how under pressure you may feel, it's never acceptable to put others down or disparage them (even in small ways, you think people will barely notice). Everything senior leaders do has an amplified effect on those around them. If you notice yourself slipping into certain arrogant behaviours (perhaps dismissing valuable feedback or attempting to pin blame), pause and reflect. What's triggering that response in you? Are there any insecurities or fears you have deeply buried? How might surfacing those help you lead more effectively?

Overconfidence. As a leader, you will trust in your own ability based on your past experiences and self-knowledge. What distinguishes confidence from overconfidence is whether that belief accurately reflects reality. As with confidence, overconfidence will most likely be specific, relating to a domain, goal, or task – for example, as a leader, you may be confident in your public speaking skills but overconfident in your negotiating ability.

Staying future-fit top tips. Maintaining a realistic view of your abilities requires two skills:

1. The ability to objectively review performance yourself.
2. The ability to collect and use feedback from others.

The latter is increasingly challenging for leaders as they become more senior. As an executive, having someone who observes your behaviour regularly and is willing to tell you what you may not want to hear is gold dust. Most people (understandably) want to avoid offending their boss, and many executives, whilst often saying they welcome constructive feedback, react in a way that suggests they do not.

Consequently, particularly as an executive, you must work hard emotionally here; creating a safe dynamic and allowing yourself to be vulnerable enough to seek feedback from your direct reports (rather than just other executive colleagues). This will require you to master sitting quietly, listening actively, and asking probing follow-up questions. It also requires clarification that 'constructive feedback' is both positive and developmental. Not an easy space for anyone to embrace but consider it the toll that must be paid on the path to staying confident.

Research and Psychology: How to Avoid the Pride Trap

Pride in one's own achievement is often perceived as a negative: something leaders should try to avoid as much as possible. As the late Anglican priest and theologian John R.W. Stott is quoted to have said, 'pride is your greatest enemy, humility is your greatest friend'. It could, however, be argued that it

(*Continued*)

depends on the type of pride. Researchers have distinguished between authentic pride and hubristic pride, with the former being much more beneficial to performance than the latter.[27,28]

Authentic pride arises from a self-evaluation of 'doing', whereas hubristic pride arises from a self-evaluation of 'being'. Both are self-conscious emotions, but the key difference is how a leader attributes their success. In the case of hubristic pride, a leader will attribute their success to internal, stable, and uncontrollable factors like natural talent. However, in the case of authentic pride, success is attributed to internal, unstable, controllable causes like effort.[29] Authentic pride has been linked to achievement, accomplishment, confidence, productivity, and self-worth.[30–32] Consequently, only hubristic pride should be considered 'an enemy'.

Top tip: Don't feel embarrassed to be proud of your achievements. However, make sure this pride is paired with acknowledgement of all the hard work and collective support that has made that success possible.

Confidence dips. When it comes to human performance, confidence is an incredibly important factor, but it is also a fragile psychological state. In sport, research has shown confidence positively predicts athletes' effort and persistence, their ability to think effectively, cope with adversity, concentrate, make decisions and, additionally, buffers the impact of anxiety on performance.[33] However, it can easily be lost momentarily or for longer durations of time if biases and negative thinking habits set in. These dips in confidence can be triggered by any number of factors: a poor performance, an unexpected failure, a stressful life event, or a negative home or workplace relationship.

Staying future-fit top tips. Awareness of self-talk is key when it comes to climbing out of a confidence dip. We all have a constant internal dialogue (a voice in our head) offering a running commentary on situations and decisions, whilst also labelling and rationalising our feelings for us. This inner voice can be helpful or unhelpful, critical, or motivational.

The critical voice often follows five thought patterns, which are embedded into our thinking early on in childhood from repeated interactions with our parents or caregivers, namely 'please others', 'try hard', 'be perfect', 'hurry up', and 'be strong'.[34] When experiencing a confidence dip, it is likely your critical inner voice is being given far too much airtime. Perhaps repeatedly telling you things which may be linked to a perceived failure in connection to one of the imprinted thought patterns, such as:

> I'm under too much pressure, I can't handle this stress.
> I'm not qualified enough for this job. Others will be disappointed in me
> I should be strong enough to cope with this on my own.
> I can't fail, this project must run completely perfectly.

The more these thoughts are repeated, the more ingrained into our thinking they become, and the more opportunity they have to negatively influence our behaviour. It is a dangerous downward spiral and one that must be dealt with quickly.

If you find yourself in this spiral, pause and notice:

- The first trick your mind is playing is to get you hooked onto the thought. So, step back and think '*I notice* that I'm thinking I'm out of my depth'; rather than simply thinking 'I'm out of my depth'. Create some space and distance between yourself and your thought (however, small it may seem).

- Secondly, rather than try to suppress the negative thoughts ('I shouldn't be thinking that'), just neutrally thank the critical voice for its input, and consciously try to give positive thoughts more airtime, paying attention to all the positive truths (such as good performances and supportive colleagues).

As discussed earlier in the chapter, it's important to remember thoughts are just thoughts. They have no real power – there is always a choice in how we behave and what actions we take.

Imposter syndrome. This is a pattern of thinking that occurs when people, who are often highly successful and intelligent professionals, feel they do not deserve their accomplishments, or they have somehow faked their way to success.[35] Despite a successful track record and plenty of evidence of their competence in role, leaders with imposter syndrome constantly perceive themselves as being out of their depth, believing their achievements to be the result of chance or extraordinary effort. They consequently have a deep-seated fear of being 'found out' or somehow 'exposed' as a fraud. Leaders with imposter syndrome tend to downplay or dismiss their successes, often place a lot of pressure on themselves not to fail, and can struggle to enjoy success, as it brings with it increased visibility and pressure (compounding their fear of 'exposure', that their luck will run out, and they will not be able to succeed the next time).[36] Left unchecked, imposter syndrome can also lead individuals to procrastinate (avoiding certain tasks in case it exposes their incompetence) or to workaholism (for example, with leaders starting every project feeling a constant need to prove themselves all over again and replicate the immense efforts that underpinned their past achievements).[37]

Staying future-fit top tips. While there are different types of imposter syndrome and it is a complex fear to overcome,[38] at the heart of imposter syndrome is an inability to internalise success. This can be turned around by consciously starting to notice how you talk about your performance; letting yourself acknowledge and value how you contributed to your own previous achievements, taking confidence that it wasn't 'all luck' and that you can build on the positive momentum of success. Here are two starter-for-10 tips to try out:

1. **With a coach: reflect on your biggest past achievements and for each one list out the factors that contributed to your success.** Be patient, if you battle with imposter syndrome it's likely your brain will freeze-up, unable to think of anything. As contributing factors start to come to mind, notice if you talk about things in an overly external and pessimistic way, such as putting your success down to luck, timing, and other people, or believing that particular success was a 'one-off because. . .'. It is a hard habit to break but try to get real. This is not about being modest. Balance out your list with internal factors: actions you took, things you did, skills you used that contributed to those achievements.
2. **Watch out for the 'effort-only trap'.** It's likely on at least one, if not all, of the lists you complied (for the above exercise), you've written 'put in a huge amount of preparation and hard work'. Many individuals who struggle with imposter syndrome secretly harbour a drive to be the very best, constantly putting pressure on themselves to perform to the highest possible standard and deliver the exceptional results others have come to take-for-granted they will produce.[39] When you internalise your success as only a by-product of your overpreparation and intense effort, thinking 'I did contribute heavily to my success: I worked really hard' you risk spiralling into the 'effort-only' trap. The follow-on assumption

being: 'in future I must work equally hard or even harder because the challenges I face will be more difficult'. This thinking pattern inevitably spirals you further into workaholism and burnout. Instead, remember success is cumulative – you don't need to start all over putting in the same, if not more, effort each time. Appreciate all the factors that help contribute to your success such as building-up expertise and a growing network of support. Don't let your mind trick you into thinking you must simply work hard and harder to meet grander and grander targets. Success breeds success, and you can harness that momentum.

Leading with Humility: Harnessing the Knowledge and Skills of Those Around You

Historically, humility referred to individuals being 'submissive and lowly', with the word originally deriving from the Latin *humus* meaning 'Earth, soil, and ground'. However, this mindset is not about leaders being subservient or submissive to others. By blending modern definitions, humility here is defined as:[40,41]

> *the tendency to consider yourself as having no special importance that makes you better than those around you; humility involves having an accurate self-view, an ability to keep accomplishments in perspective, and an awareness of one's fallibility and limitations.*

Many definitions emphasise '*having an accurate perspective of one's place relative to other people*', and here lies the challenge for those in senior leadership positions. On paper, as part of the organisational hierarchy, those in the C-suite are significantly higher in rank than everyone else. Therefore, it would be partly accurate to view oneself as 'better', more powerful, more integral to the running of the organisation, more knowledgeable (being privy to more information) and generally more important. However, a humble mindset is not about rank.

Leading with humility is about being able to accurately see oneself as imperfect, appreciating the strengths of others, and recognising the limits of one's knowledge. In psychology, this is specifically referred to as 'intellectual humility'.[41] To clarify the difference, humility is a general tendency of being able to accurately see oneself as imperfect and not as the centre of the universe. Whereas intellectual humility is about knowledge, having a willingness to recognise how your knowledge and understanding are imperfect and the ability to operate with a genuine openness and curiosity towards others (i.e., to their beliefs, opinions, ideas, knowledge, and understanding).

Curiosity is a word that is bandied about a lot in company values, but genuine curiosity and openness, genuine displays of intellectual humility, can be tricky in practice. For example, as researchers Tenelle Porter and Karina Schumann from the University of California, point out:[42]

> *A person might recognize that their understanding of an issue is limited and conclude that this means that no one has the capacity to understand it. Likewise, someone may think that because they do not know something, others must not know it either. What is needed for intellectual humility, then, is both an acknowledgement of one's partial understanding and an appreciation for the knowledge that others can possess.*

So, is humility about always holding your own views and knowledge lightly? About always being self-effacing and yielding to others at all times? Not quite.

Research shows how a paradoxical combination of strong professional will and humility are found in the best CEOs.[43] As Laszlo Block, a previous senior vice president at Google, stated in 2014:[44]

> *What we've seen is that the people who are the most successful here, who we want to hire, will have a fierce position. They'll argue like hell. They'll be zealots about their point of view. But then you say, 'here's a new fact', and they'll go, 'Oh, well, that changes things; you're right'.*

Leading with intellectual humility is not about always kowtowing to others. Evidence shows how those with high intellectual humility do not have less confidence or lower self-esteem relative to those who are not so intellectually humble.[42] Humble leaders are willing to assert their position and have a strong point of view, but they are also always aware that their skill set, knowledge, and character have limits and are imperfect. There is a non-threatening acceptance and recognition that others possess different strengths and knowledge, and, at any point in time, their own beliefs and understanding may be inaccurate or outdated.

Consequently, humble leaders can:

- embrace their own beliefs with confidence while simultaneously remaining open and flexible
- exchange and respect differing viewpoints without causing or taking offence
- admit their mistakes and weaknesses
- effectively harness the strengths, knowledge, and skill sets of those around them.

How to Develop Intellectual Humility

Below is a list of the key ingredients research highlights as essential for developing intellectual humility.

Key ingredients	Ask yourself...
Accepting your own ignorance	We are all overconfident in our ignorance from time to time. As social psychologist Professor David Dunning stated: 'not knowing the scope of your own ignorance is part of the human condition. . .But the problem with it is we see it in other people, and we don't see it in ourselves.' As Dunning elaborates,[45] we all operate our daily affairs under the shadow of our own inevitable ignorance. It is simply not possible to know everything about everything. There will always be holes in our knowledge and expertise. Your ignorance will, by definition, be invisible to you. Consequently, this is not about building self-awareness, it is about accepting the fallibility of your knowledge. **Ask yourself, are you. . .** • **able to ask when there is something you do not know?** • **open towards the fact that the knowledge you hold as certainty could be misguided and misinformed?** • **often 'over-claiming'?** (i.e., seeking to show others you have knowledge in many topic areas) • **frequently 'reaching around'?** (i.e., reaching back or around to any knowledge you have that might appear to be relevant, and then using it to answer questions or form a judgement)

(*Continued*)

Key ingredients	Ask yourself. . .
Showing vulnerability	Many of us fear that if we admit to being wrong, we will be perceived as less competent and trustworthy by others. But research suggests this is not the case; in fact, when we do see someone admit they are wrong, we are more likely to view them as communal and friendly.[46] Being vulnerable (for example, admitting you do not have all the answers or that 'things are challenging'), whilst terrifying for most senior leaders to do, is also important to building relationships and earning people's trust. As Brené Brown articulates, having to be the 'knower' or always being right is a form of armour many of us use to protect ourselves.[47] But, as Brown explains, vulnerability is not a sign of weakness, it is a sign of strength and courage. **Ask yourself, are you. . .** • **often focusing on wanting to 'be right' rather than wanting to 'get it right'?** • **able to own your mistakes, say sorry, and make amends where possible?** • **able to be frank with people and have the guts to tell them the truth?**

Key ingredients	Ask yourself. . .
Being open to the knowledge, ideas, and perspectives of others	Every day, we encounter difference: people with different perspectives, different experiences, different insights, different ideas, and different opinions to us. Embracing a humble mindset requires leaders to be open to the knowledge, ideas, and viewpoints of others, no matter how different or challenging they may be to our own. Unfortunately, 'being open' is easier said than done. Many of us can wish to appear open but deep down still believe we are right. We play the game of influence under the guise of curiosity. Our brains *affinity bias* also does not help us to harness difference,[48] as we tend to surround ourselves with people who have similar interests, appearance, experiences, beliefs, and backgrounds. In other words, we gravitate towards those who are most like ourselves, who think the same way and see the world as we do. **Ask yourself, are you. . .** • **willing to listen to others' ideas and opinions, even when they may be in direct opposition to your own?** • **able to actively seek advice and feedback from others, without feeling that your own ideas are being criticised?** • **prepared to change your mind in light of new information?** • **operating in an echo chamber? (i.e., surrounded by people who are 'like you' and see the world as you do)**

The Humble Leadership Continuum: How to Stay on Track

As with confidence, learning to lead with a humble mindset requires us to be aware of what pulls us out of that circle of humility. We can start to behave in a way that is insincere, with a false humility, or let our feelings pull us towards an inferiority complex (see Figure 6.2).

To become future-fit leaders must be skilled at maintaining a truly humble mindset, resisting both the temptation of false humility behaviour and the pitfalls of feeling somehow inferior to others.

False humility (a.k.a. 'the humble brag'). This refers to behaviours where someone depreciates their gifts, talents, and accomplishments for the sake of receiving praise or admiration from others – it is pride masquerading in humble words.[49] Underneath this type of behaviour is a self-serving need. By attempting to appear humble or belittling ourselves, we call for attention to be focused on us, seeking others to recognise our 'hidden brilliance'. Power comes in many forms (e.g., intelligence, money, privilege, beauty) and denying or diminishing that is in itself expressing power.

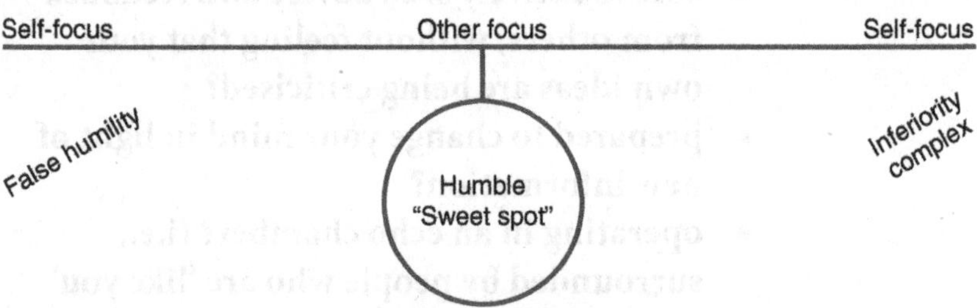

Figure 6.2 The humble leadership continuum.

Staying future-fit top tips. Avoiding false humility is hard to do. Intuitively, when someone compliments us, we are very socially aware of not wanting to appear falsely humble or overly arrogant. It is the clearest confidently humble clinching point almost everyone has experienced. To get this right, you need to be skilled in the art of gracefully accepting praise. If you deny, self-insult, or downplay your role, you risk downgrading or not acknowledging the other person's recognition and appreciation of you. The simplest thing to do is to display thankfulness for and appreciation of another's kind words. Also, try to avoid the tempting lure of compliment one-upmanship, in other words, immediately offering a compliment in return. Simply accept the praise and show gratitude.

Inferiority complex. This is a constant and intense feelings of not measuring up to standards or to others, with an individual experiencing persistent feelings of inferiority, insecurity, and inadequacy. These feelings of inferiority can be cause by personal experiences, social interactions, romantic relationships, social disadvantages, physical challenges, and cultural messages.[50] A leader with an inferiority complex might find they often doubt themselves and want to give up quickly on certain tasks. Feelings of inferiority can also cause an individual to:

- act as if inferior (thus reinforcing the low opinion they have of themselves)
- compensate (be intensely driven to excel and overachieve in a different domain)
- overcompensate (set superiority goals, aiming to excel in the specific challenging domain, or project an image to others of security and dominance)
- undercompensate (over-rely on support and becoming dependent on others who they perceive as stronger or more competent).

Staying future-fit top tips. Although an 'inferiority complex' is at the extreme end of the spectrum, we all experience feelings of inadequacy from time to time. For example, for whatever reason, in some situations you may feel less intelligent, less attractive, less socially adept, or less well-situated in life than others. The trick here is to notice the warning signs that this feeling is not so much 'passing' but something more deep-rooted and persistent. For example, do you find yourself:

- constantly comparing yourself with others?
- worrying that other people seem better or more qualified than you?
- struggling to believe that people are sincere when they compliment you or give you positive feedback?
- avoiding certain social interactions?

Going through life with a deep-seated belief that others are in some way better than you or that you are somehow inadequate can be incredibly challenging. For leaders, who think they may struggle with an inferiority complex, therapy and mental health support can be hugely valuable. For those who just feel inferior sometimes: surround yourself with positive people (who help you find the best version of you), be kind to yourself (perhaps adopting Michelle Obamas daily mantra of 'Am I good enough? Yes I am'),[51] and focus on the unique strengths, values, and positive assets you possess.

Notes

1. Eisenberg, D. (2001). Washed Up at Warnaco? *Time Magazine Article.*

2. Kaufman, L. (2001). Questions of Style in Warnaco's Fall. *The New York Times Article.*

3. Ian Talley (2017). Obama Says He and Trump are Opposites–But Share Self-Confidence. *The Wall Street Journal Article.*

4. Carrier Budoff Brown (2008). Obama: The Journey of a Confident Man. *Politico Article.*

5. Ben Smith (2008). Obama: 'I will win'. *Politico Blog.*

6. Jeff Zeleny and Michael Luo. (2008). Obama Raises a Record $66 Million in a Month. *The New York Times Article.*

7. Kindra Cooper (2019). Former President Barack Obama on Why a Leader is Only as Good as His Employees: Ryan Smith's interview with President Obama at Qualtrics X4 Experience Management Summit. *CCW Digital.*

8. Advice given by Barack Obama in 2016. *During the President's Town Hall Event Q&A Session with Local Young People, in London, Lindley Hall.*

9. Oney, E. and Oksuzoglu-Guven, G. (2015). Confidence: A critical review of the literature and an alternative perspective for general and specific self-confidence. *Psychological Reports* 116: 149–163.

10. Richards, N. (1992). *Humility*. Philadelphia, PA: Temple University Press.

11. Owens, B.P. and Hekman, D.R. (2012). Modeling how to grow: An inductive examination of humble leader behaviors, contingencies, and outcomes. *Academy of Management Journal* 55: 787–818.

12. Cable, D. (2018). How Humble Leadership Really Works. *Harvard Business Review.*

13. Ahern, S. and Loh, E. (2020). Leadership during the COVID-19 pandemic: Building and sustaining trust in times of uncertainty. *BMJ Leader Leader-2020.*

14. Waldman, D.A., Ramirez, G.G., House, R.J., and Puranam, P. (2001). Does leadership matter? CEO leadership attributes and profitability

under conditions of perceived environmental uncertainty. *Academy of Management Journal* 44: 134–143.

15. *Cambridge International Dictionary of English. (1995).* Cambridge: Cambridge University Press.

16. Woodman, T.I.M. and Hardy, L.E.W. (2003). The relative impact of cognitive anxiety and self-confidence upon sport performance: A meta-analysis. *Journal of Sports Sciences* 21: 443–457.

17. Hollenbeck, G.P. and Hall, D.T. (2004). Self-confidence and leader performance. *Organizational Dynamics* 33: 254–269.

18. Vealey, R.S. (2009). Confidence in sport. *Sport Psychology* 1: 43–52.

19. Harris, R. (2011). *The Confidence Gap: From Fear to Freedom.* London, UK: Hachette.

20. Richard Stengel (2008). Mandela: His 8 Lessons of Leadership. *Time Magazine.*

21. Campbell, W.K., Goodie, A.S., and Foster, J.D. (2004). Narcissism, confidence, and risk attitude. *Journal of Behavioral Decision Making* 17: 297–311.

22. Bogart, L.M., Benotsch, E.G., and Pavlovic, J.D.P. (2004). Feeling superior but threatened: The relation of narcissism to social comparison. *Basic and Applied Social Psychology* 26: 35–44.

23. Miller, J.D., Hoffman, B.J., Gaughan, E.T., et al. (2011). Grandiose and vulnerable narcissism: A nomological network analysis. *Journal of Personality* 79: 1013–1042.

24. Chatterjee, A. and Hambrick, D.C. (2007). It's all about me: Narcissistic chief executive officers and their effects on company strategy and performance. *Administrative Science Quarterly* 52: 351–386.

25. Wink, P. and Donahue, K. (1997). The relation between two types of narcissism and boredom. *Journal of Research in Personality* 31: 136–140.

26. Johnson, R.E., Silverman, S.B., Shyamsunder, A., et al. (2010). Acting superior but actually inferior? Correlates and consequences of workplace arrogance. *Human Performance* 23: 403–427.

27. Lewis, M. (1993). Self-conscious emotions: Embarrassment, pride, shame, and guilt. In M. Lewis and J.M. Haviland (Eds.), *Handbook of Emotions* (pp. 563–573). New York, US: Guilford Press.

28. Tangney, J.P., Wagner, P., Fletcher, C., and Gramzow, R. (1992). Shamed into anger? The relation of shame and guilt to anger and self-reported aggression. *Journal of Personality and Social Psychology* 62: 669.

29. Carver, C.S., Sinclair, S., and Johnson, S.L. (2010). Authentic and hubristic pride: Differential relations to aspects of goal regulation, affect, and self-control. *Journal of Research in Personality* 44: 698–703.

30. Tracy, J.L. and Robins, R.W. (2004). Putting the self into self-conscious emotions: A theoretical model. *Psychological Inquiry* 15: 103–125.

31. Tracy, J.L. and Robins, R.W. (2007a). Emerging insights into the nature and function of pride. *Current Directions in Psychological Science* 16: 147–150.

32. Tracy, J.L. and Robins, R.W. (2007b). The psychological structure of pride: A tale of two facets. *Journal of Personality and Social Psychology* 92: 506–525.

33. Vealey, R.S. (2009). Confidence in sport. In: Brewer, B.W. (ed.), *Sport Psychology* (pp. 43–52). Oxford, UK: Wiley-Blackwell.

34. Kahler, T. (1975). Drivers: The key to the process of scripts. *Transactional Analysis Bulletin* 5: 280–284.

35. Jackson, E.R. (2018). Leadership Impostor phenomenon: A Theoretical Causal Model. *Emerging Leadership Journeys* 11: 74–85.

36. Gill Corkindale (2008). Overcoming Imposter Syndrome. *Harvard Business Review Article.*

37. Rakestraw, L. (2017). How to stop feeling like a phony in your library: Recognizing the causes of the imposter syndrome, and how to put a stop to the cycle. *Law Library Journal* 109: 465.

38. Rahman, D. (2022). Overcoming imposter syndrome in dentistry. *BDJ In Practice* 35: 30–31.

39. Sakulku, J. (2011). The impostor phenomenon. *The Journal of Behavioral Science* 6: 75–97.

40. *Cambridge International Dictionary of English.* (1995). Cambridge: Cambridge University Press.

41. Krumrei-Mancuso, E.J. and Rouse, S.V. (2016). The development and validation of the comprehensive intellectual humility scale. *Journal of Personality Assessment* 98: 209–221.

42. Tenelle Porter and Karina Schumann. (2018) Intellectual humility and openness to the opposing view. *Self and Identity* 17: 139–162.

43. Collins, J. (2006). Level 5 leadership: The triumph of humility and fierce resolve. *Managing Innovation and Change* 234.

44. Haggard, M., Rowatt, W.C., Leman, J.C., et al. (2018). Finding middle ground between intellectual arrogance and intellectual servility: Development and assessment of the limitations-owning intellectual humility scale. *Personality and Individual Differences* 124: 184–193.

45. Dunning, D. (2011). The Dunning–Kruger effect: On being ignorant of one's own ignorance. In *Advances in Experimental Social Psychology* (Vol. 44, pp. 247–296). Academic Press.

46. Fetterman, A.K., Curtis, S., Carre, J., and Sassenberg, K. (2019). On the willingness to admit wrongness: Validation of a new measure and an exploration of its correlates. *Personality and Individual Differences* 138: 193–202.

47. Brown, B. (2018). *Dare to Lead: Brave Work. Tough Conversations. Whole Hearts.* New York, US: Random House.

48. Turnbull, H. (2016). *The Illusion of Inclusion: Global Inclusion, Unconscious Bias, and the Bottom Line.* Business Expert Press.

49. Eragula, R. (2015). Humility in leadership. *Advances in Economics and Business Management* 2: 786–789.

50. Liu, Y., Xu, C., Kuai, X., Deng, H., Wang, K., and Luo, Q. (2022). Analysis of the causes of inferiority feelings based on social media data with Word2Vec. *Scientific Reports* 12: 1–9.

51. Obama, M. (2019). *Becoming.* London, UK: Penguin Press.

CHAPTER 7
RESPONSIBLY DARING

Pure pragmatism can't imagine a bold future. Pure idealism can't get anything done. It is the delicate blend of both that drives innovation.

—Simon Sinek, author and inspirational speaker

What Is a 'Responsibly Daring' Mindset?

Responsibly daring leaders hold the following mindset:

- They have the opportunity and responsibility to do something meaningful, that makes a difference and has a lasting impact.
- They must be realistic when working with their purpose and beliefs.
- They believe everything is worth trying and anything is possible.
- They must stay positive and see the opportunities in difficult moments.

Future-fit leaders drive innovation and business transformation via a blend of pragmatic idealism. They dream big, take risks, and carefully steward their organisation into the future. They are relentlessly positive, believe anything is possible; at the same time, they stay realistic about what can and needs to be achieved to create long-term value and safeguard the business.

The 'responsible' side of the mindset is about leaders taking responsibility for two things:

1. **for making a difference** – creating long-term value not just for investors but for multiple stakeholders, including employees, customers, shareholders, people within their supply chain, the environment, society, and future generations to come.
2. **for safeguarding the business** – 'keeping the lights on'; protecting people's jobs and livelihoods by ensuring the business stays successful, profitable, and runs smoothly.

Leading responsibly, both in terms of having a lasting positive impact and 'keeping the lights on', critically requires leaders to stay realistic about what can and needs to be done. They are driven to do something meaningful and tackle the world's biggest challenges, but they also know they need to be pragmatic to turn those dreams into reality and deliver on promises.

The 'daring' side of the mindset does what it says on the tin. This is about leaders having an entrepreneurial 'anything's possible' spirit, having the courage to back audacious missions and ideas, maintaining optimism in the face of adversity, taking calculated risks, and embracing experimentation.

Anders Eldrup is one example of a leader who acted in a responsibly daring way, boldly pivoting a well-established, successful business in a new direction to safeguard the company long-term and positively contribute to society. To understand Eldrup's mindset, it is useful to travel back to when his career began in 1973, the same time his home country of Denmark was hit by the oil crisis. With 90% of Denmark's energy coming from oil and over 90% of that oil coming from the Middle East, Denmark was hit hard when the price of oil quadrupled.[1] This formative experience planted the seeds of a responsibly daring mindset, with the oil crisis showing Eldrup the danger of placing all of one's eggs in one basket and instilling in him a drive to help re-establish Denmark's economy. For nearly 30 years, Eldrup worked in Danish politics before taking up the CEO position at DONG in 2001, after which he quickly expanded into DONG Energy (taking it from a company that just imported and traded natural gas, to one that produced and traded electricity, heat, oil, and natural gas and distributed electricity and natural gas). By 2008, DONG Energy was a successful, profitable, and stable energy company. It took a conventional approach and was doing well in the market. It was then that Anders Eldrup pushed to pivot and transform the organisation.

Having spent three decades establishing itself as a company focused on the generation of conventional fuels, signs were showing how the world was beginning to shift. Specifically, leaders noticed how despite government support, strong local opposition had caused an attempt to build a coal-fired power plant in Northeast Germany to fail.[2] Noticing the changing market, Anders Eldrup, together with his senior vice president Jakob Askou Bøss, formulated a new '85/15' strategy, proposing the business flip from generating 85% conventional fuels and 15% renewable, to generating 15% conventional fuels and 85% renewable.

Now from the comfort of your current living room (or wherever you may be reading this from), with climate crisis in mind, this 85/15 strategy may sound like a no-brainer move to guarantee future success in the energy sector. But the pressure on Eldrup and Bøss to 'play it safe' and stick with what was tried and tested was huge. Internally, fossil fuels were core to the growth strategy, with the company having set a world-class standard in running coal-fired power plants. Scepticism even ran high within the Danish government, as politicians saw the move to trade oil and gas for renewable as too risky, with the prime minister even requesting Eldrup to personally explain his strategy.[3]

Despite the pressure and scepticism, Eldrup fully committed to the 85/15 goal, and a few things helped turn this dream into reality. Firstly, Eldrup set a realistic time frame. He knew the transformation would not happen overnight so aimed to pivot the company to green energy within one generation (roughly 30 years). Secondly, initial strategic discussions focused on existing strengths, identifying where they already had the right competencies and a critical mass of resources in place, exploring where they were in the best position to differentiate (with onshore and offshore wind emerging as the strongest option). Thirdly, they were not afraid to attempt what had not been done before (i.e. build an offshore wind project bigger than 160 megawatts). They dreamed big and bold, understood what made the task difficult, and recognised the importance of partnerships in overcoming those specific challenges.

In 2012, Henrik Poulsen took up the reins of CEO and continued the journey of focusing on green growth. In 2017, following the company's profound strategic transformation from black to green energy, the decision was made to change the organisation's brand identity and name to Ørsted. Whilst it may seem like a 'first-mover' fairy tale, the journey from DONG Energy to Ørsted was hard. Shareholders and board members repeatedly challenged the strategy shift and the costs nearly derailed the entire business, ballooning the company's debt. It took a responsibly daring leader, Anders Elrup, to initiate this transformation and hold his nerve, eventually passing the baton on to a string of dedicated successors. It is the courage to reinvent in the right direction that lies at the core of this business approach, as Martin Newbert, chief commercial officer and deputy group CEO at Ørsted, articulates:[2]

> *The ability to reinvent ourselves has proven to be key. In 2006, DONG Energy consisted of some oil and gas licenses. Then it reinvented itself through the merger of six domestic energy companies. A few years later, the company reinvented itself again by establishing a wind-power business unit that became a global leader within a few years. Scanning new horizons and spotting new business areas are essential to Ørsted's strategy and our ambition to become a global renewable-energy major.*

As this story highlights, while 'responsibly daring' may seem like two opposites that are impossible to unite coherently, they are two sides of the same coin. Taking responsibility for making a difference and safeguarding the future success of the business is what enables leaders to dream big and bold in their visions for the company. It is responsibility that fuels the daring acts that will keep the business successful in years to come. As author, mountaineer, and speaker, Stacy Allison, stated:

> *Only when we accept full responsibility for our lives, do we have the confidence and courage to risk.*

Leader to Leader

The belief that anything is possible was instilled in Alison Kay as a young child. Alison's father had taken bold risks in his own life to change his family's story, so whenever she struggled, her father was there, refuelling the mindset that 'of course you can do it'. Similarly, her piano teacher imparted the belief that 'anything is possible' and urged her not to give up when things got tough. Each time Alison found a piece of music too difficult to learn, saying in frustration, 'I can't, I can't do this. . . ', her teacher would calmly reply 'Alison. . . there is no such word in the English dictionary as can't'.

This baked-in attitude that 'anything is possible' and 'everything is solvable' blended with a strong future-focused drive defined Alison's leadership style. From her years as an executive within the power and utilities sector to her current role as managing partner of one of the largest professional services networks in the world, Alison is no stranger to mapping out and tackling an audacious challenge. Shortly after stepping into her role as managing partner, for example, Alison launched a nine-month 'outside-in' review to understand how the world of professional services was evolving and what changes would be necessary to keep the high-performing business at the forefront of the market. Based on conversations with clients, fellow partners, her team, and even her teenage daughter (and her daughter's friends!) Alison recognised a paradigm shift was underway. The new world of work was set to look vastly different from the working world she had entered years ago, and she felt the business would need to break free from tradition to stay current. The 'outside-in' review confirmed Alison's suspicions, revealing vast opportunities for the organisation to become industry-leading by being responsible and creating long-term value for its clients, its people, and the communities it serves.

Following the findings from the review, Alison proposed an audacious strategy, requiring a level of investment never before seen in the UK and Ireland regions, boldly aiming to achieve double-digit growth over a five-year period. First and foremost, however, the growth was to be intentional: putting people, clients, and the firm's purpose (to 'build a better working world') at the centre of all decision making. Part of that, meant placing some 'big bets' to enable clients as they moved towards net zero and saying no to some work, both daring new concepts for the business to embrace.

When put on the table, the strategy, of course, came under scrutiny and faced pushback. It was a bold proposal, and the business was already doing well; there was no burning platform to change – but Alison knew the organisation would fail

(*Continued*)

to realise its full potential unless it made significant strides in key areas such as digital transformation and its people experience. As Alison explains, 'much of the resistance came from people looking at the level of ambition and just feeling it was an insurmountable thing to try to tackle'. Whilst Alison understood the concerns, she held firm, and held her nerve. She knew it was the right strategy: 'we'd heard the feedback from our clients, the government agencies, our people. We had the robust data we needed – it was a non-negotiable change. The question at that point was figuring out how to make it happen'.

However, as Alison recalls, 'when you get to the stage of thinking about how to make a change happen, very quickly, traditional thinking comes into play'. It was clear, for example, that reducing the administrative burden would be an essential part of evolving the people experience but immediately traditional solutions would get proposed (such as hiring more people and setting up a dedicated admin team). Alison wanted something more radical than that. She proposed the team find a way to use AI and technology to take away 60% of admin effort. As she explains, 'I had no idea if that was possible or not – but if you don't set the challenge out there it won't happen. Nobody knows how or if it can be done, but if you set the challenge it's amazing what people can do and what they rise to'.

Whilst work to deliver the strategy is ongoing, so far Alison and her team have delivered a level of double-digit growth and consistency never before achieved in the global business, with record numbers of recruitment and acquisitions over the past 18 months. At the helm of the transformation, Alison remarks how 'at times it feels I'm walking a tight rope above Niagara Falls. But if I just keep looking forward at what we're aiming to achieve and bringing people with me then we'll be fine'. With her sheer dogged belief and tenacity, Alison and her team continue to power forward and achieve exceptional results in responsibly daring ways.

Before exploring how to lead in a responsibly daring way, let us first clarify exactly what these two terms mean:

Defining Terms

- **Responsible leaders** hold themselves accountable for making a difference and for the health of their organisation, both now and in the future.[4] They seek and serve multiple stakeholders (balancing the needs of people, planet, and profit) and sensibly provide solutions to problems by focusing on what is possible.[5]
- **Daring leaders** are optimistic about the future; they think big, think creatively, experiment, and take risks.[6]

Why Leading in a Responsibly Daring Way Matters Amidst the Megatrends

Two things in today's business environment make adopting a responsibly daring mindset particularly crucial: firstly, the pace at which leaders need to keep their organisation constantly adapting and evolving and, secondly, the shifting expectations towards long-term value creation.

Let us first dig into the pace of change.

The Requirement to Continuously Transform

A survey of 305 chief executives of Forbes Global 2000 companies revealed how leading with compassion, setting an example of experimentation and risk-taking, and driving a transformative mindset across the company are the top three characteristics CEOs need to effectively manage the challenges and opportunities, now and in the years to come.[7]

The rate of transformation required from organisations today is fundamentally different. Over the pandemic, leaders accelerated their digital transformation timelines, on average, by around six years; with companies in the construction and energy industry accelerating timetables forward around eight years.[8] However, this was not a blip or one-off surge; continuous transformation is the 'new normal'. In fact, one survey showed how, in Europe, 62% of CIOs expect the pace of change to increase significantly.[9]

As technology continues to advance and rapid industry disruption becomes commonplace, leaders will need to be bolder, becoming highly skilled in transformation and embracing the mindset of experimentation and risk-taking that is required to survive and stay relevant. Leaders cannot afford to hold the outdated mindsets of 'don't fix what isn't broken' and 'it's okay for me to go with what's tried and tested'. Our skills, knowledge, and recipes for success have a much shorter shelf life now. Consequently, whilst there is value in taking advantage of what works, only relying on what worked in the past will quickly become detrimental to performance. Stability soon turns to stagnation.[10,11]

Bill Taylor, co-founder of Fast Company, articulated how C-suite executives and entrepreneurs typically face two different fears: 'sinking the boat' and 'missing the boat'.[12] For those in the C-suite, who have taken responsibility for (or painstakingly built up) a large and highly successful company, the big risk is that they will 'sink the boat'. They will take something successful, tweak the winning recipe too much, make a few costly decisions, and the whole business will begin to sink; dragging down profits as well as people's jobs and livelihoods. In contrast, entrepreneurs, who are not so shackled by scale and past winning formulas, typically fear that if they fail to make a bold move, they will 'miss the boat' that would have led to success.

In today's fast-evolving business environment, the risk of leaders 'sinking the boat' or 'missing the boat' has increased. However, rather than being driven by these fears, leaders should instead become highly skilled at leading in a responsibly daring way.

Embracing this paradoxical mindset will help leaders protect the core of their business, turn big ideas into tangible action, deliver valuable innovation, and drive meaningful change.

Shifting Expectations Towards Long-Term Value Creation

With our society facing challenges, such as the rising levels of inequality and Earth approaching and surpassing various climate tipping points, there is growing expectation on businesses to step up and positively contribute. It is not good enough for organisations to have a 'locust' approach,[13] striving to increase growth and profit as much as possible, whilst dissociating themselves from the impact the organisation has on the wider system.[14] As author of *Doughnut Economics*, Kate Raworth explains:[15]

> *For over 70 years economics has been fixated on GDP, or national output, as its primary measure of progress. That fixation has been used to justify extreme inequalities of*

> *income and wealth coupled with unprecedented destruction of the living world. For the twenty-first century a far bigger goal is needed: meeting the human rights of every person within the means of our life-giving planet.*

Awareness and momentum are growing around the need to move away from the world's current economic model, in which resources are pillaged and discarded, and towards a more circular 'doughnut' economy, in which waste is eliminated, practices are sustainable, and value is created for a wider range of stakeholders. Specifically, survey findings show how:[7]

- 91% of CEOs expect business models to increasingly incorporate circular economy dimensions over the next few years
- 87% of CEOs agree long-term value creation across stakeholders will be rewarded by the market
- 80% of CEOs agree there is likely to be a global standard for measuring and reporting long-term value creation.

The call for business leaders to take greater responsibility and operate in the best interest of employees, customers, investors, suppliers, future generations, the environment, and society is deafening. It cannot be ignored. Leaders that excel in this era of business will by no means dismiss the importance of profit, but it will not be their sole consideration. Responsible leaders will expand their focus to long-term value creation, ensuring day-to-day decision-making throughout their business equally considers the needs of a much broader set of stakeholders. Research has long shown that leaders adopting such an approach outperform by a factor of 10.[16] The question is therefore not whether to embrace this fundamental change, but how.

Leading Responsibly: Making a Difference and Safeguarding the Organisation

US President Harry Truman famously had a sign on his desk that read: 'the buck stops here'. This sign showed everyone that he accepted personal responsibility for the way the country was governed. No excuses. No attempts to pass on blame. For years, many C-suite leaders have accepted similar responsibility for the success and survival of their organisation but now that sphere of responsibility is expanding.

Today, business leaders are not only required to take responsibility for the performance of their company but for the part their organisation plays in either helping or aggravating the challenges faced by wider society and the environment. This mindset is about helping you, as a leader, embrace the full extent of your responsibility, maximising the opportunity you have to make a difference and carefully steward the business into the future.

Before delving into how to embrace that responsibility effectively, let us first get clear on what we mean by 'responsibility'. In the *Oxford Dictionary*, responsibility is defined as follows:[17]

> *having the job or duty of doing something or taking care of somebody/something, so that you may be blamed if something goes wrong*

First and foremost, responsibility is about the duty of care. As Aristotle pointed out, responsibility is not just about fulfilling the functional obligations of a role, it also has a moral component.[18] Leaders are decision makers who have a moral responsibility to be aware of the actions and consequences, taken within and caused by, the business. For example, not only do business leaders have the functional obligation to protect the business and create profits for shareholders, but also a moral obligation to protect the livelihoods and well-being of employees. Similarly, not only do leaders have a functional duty to secure efficient supply chain agreements, but also a moral obligation to ensure those supply chains are sustainable and ethical.

In the academic literature, moral responsibility also refers to a willingness to act free from external compulsion.[19] It is therefore not about business leaders waiting for governments to regulate their industries and force organisations to 'do what's right' and take responsible action. That forced action assumes the government is responsible. Leading responsibly is about business leaders stepping forward proactively to take responsibility and embrace the duty of care they have both for their business and the wider societal ecosystem their organisation is a part of.

The type of responsibility required from leaders today is therefore both internalised and forward-facing.

1. Internalised responsibility: the call for leaders to take responsibility (not blame)

Internalising responsibility for something is not about feeling guilty or determining who is to blame. It is about being able to see our problems as our problems, not necessarily our fault.[20] There is no single individual, or solitary organisation, entirely responsible for the world's problems, but we all should take responsibility for helping to solve them. As philosopher David Enoch pointed out, there is a distinction between being responsible and taking responsibility:[21] *'while I am not responsible for my country's actions, I am under a moral duty to take (some) responsibility for them'.*

Future-fit leaders understand that everyone is responsible for the world and society we live in. Everyone can make a difference. Each individual, in their everyday choices plays an important role in shaping the future of our political, social, economic, and environmental conditions.[22] However, as Swedish researcher Dr. Jessica Nihlén Fahlquist points out,[23] a greater share of the responsibility should be assigned to the leaders of governments and corporations because they have the power and resources to do more and make it easier and less costly for individuals to do what is right.

Individuals should therefore do what they can (for example, buy locally produced food, sustainably made clothing, use public transport, reduce the thermostat in their house) against the background of their particular situation. Meanwhile, those in leadership positions should make the most of their position of power; making decisions and influencing the systems that either have a direct impact or trigger a ripple effect of change.

2. Forward-facing responsibility: embracing control and being accountable to future generations

Forward-facing responsibility is about taking responsibility for what will happen in the future and seeing ourselves as accountable to future generations, future employees, and future leaders of the business. Embracing forward-facing responsibility is easily avoided because it is likely those who will most feel the consequences of our decisions today will not be able to hold us to account. For example, future generations will not be able to hold each of us personally accountable for our CO_2 emissions – we will no longer be around. So, why worry?

Forward-facing responsibility hinges on knowledge and awareness. For example, Leslie Robertson, the structural engineer who designed the Twin Towers in New York came under scrutiny after the towers were destroyed. In one media interview, he was asked if he felt guilty that the two towers did not stand for longer after they had been hit by the planes in the September 11 terrorist attack, he replied:[24]

> *The responsibility for arriving at the ultimate strength of the towers was mine. The fact that they did not stand longer could be laid at my feet. Do I feel guilty about the fact that they collapsed? The circumstances on September 11th were outside of what we considered in the design.... If I knew then what I know now they would have stood longer, of course.*

The images of that terrible day never left Robertson who was forever haunted by grief and a belief that he could have done better.[25] However, he designed the buildings within the parameters considered reasonable based on what was known and anticipated at the time. The Twin Towers stood long enough to allow thousands of people to escape. He acted based on the knowledge available at the time.

What gives us control over the future is knowledge and awareness of what is happening and what the consequences of our action, or inaction, may be. More and more we are seeing leaders being held to account and required to justify their inaction to protect people and the environment, because there is clear evidence of what is happening and indications of what the consequences will be. This is why embracing forward-facing responsibility is so crucial in today's business landscape.

Safeguarding the business and 'keeping the lights on'

Most of this discussion so far has been focused on the big challenges being faced by society and the role senior business leaders must step up and play. However, it is important not to overlook that this expanded responsibility sits alongside the age-old responsibility senior leaders have of just 'keeping the lights on' and keeping the business running successfully. This alone is no mean feat. As Professor Jayne Barnard conveys:[26]

> *To be the final decision maker in a multibillion-dollar business with hundreds of thousands of employees and pensioners relying on you is an awesome responsibility. The stresses placed on CEOs almost requires them to be superhuman and they are not always that well-prepared for the role.*

These two responsibilities are highly interconnected. Tackling the big challenges faced by society, taking care of people and the environment (as well as maintaining healthy profit), will keep your business successful and relevant in the years to come. However, it is easier said than done. Shaping the future and 'keeping the lights on' requires a complex cocktail of focus on today and tomorrow, on what is desirable and what is feasible, on harnessing what works and striving for change.

Now, let us explore how to do that.

Five key skills required to lead responsibly

The key skills required to lead responsibly include: developing an internal locus of control, learning to accept reality, protecting the core of your business, cultivating strategic patience, and committing to short-term trade-offs for long-term gain. Let us look at each of these in more detail.

Key skill	Why it is relevant	How to develop it
1. Internal locus of control: *the belief that outcomes depend on our actions*	Leaders with an internal locus of control believe they are masters of their own destiny; their behaviour determines what happens, their actions impact outcomes. In contrast, leaders with an external locus of control perceive that outcomes are determined by external forces, such as luck, chance, fate, or other powerful people's choices.[27] In today's business environment, it is easy to slip into an external locus of control, feeling things are 'done to' us and perceiving events to be 'out of our hands'. However, leaders with an internal locus of control understand that while you do not have complete control over what happens, you do have control over your effort, attitude, response, and ability to be proactive. Research shows how developing a strong internal locus of control is critical for this mindset because it is linked to demonstrating a pragmatic	Developing an internal locus of control can be difficult as an external locus of control can be deeply embedded into our psyche from childhood.[29] For those who grew up with more authoritarian parents or caregivers, or perhaps who were the youngest in a large family, obeying rules and relinquishing power to others could be an ingrained habit.[30] If so, taking responsibility, defending your own ideas, and sticking to your own decisions will feel more uncomfortable. Here are some top tips on how to boost your internal locus of control: • **Focus on what you can control and take action (however small)** Pandemics, elections, stock market crashes, crimes, natural disasters, all sorts of things can be happening 'out there', impacting your business in ways you cannot control. However, rather than focusing on what you cannot control, stay focused on what you do have control over and what you can influence. Reflect on your strengths and draw up a plan of positive action you can take (however small the

Key skill	Why it is relevant	How to develop it
Internal locus of control (*Continued*)	spirit, perseverance, and high sense of responsibility for achieving objectives.[28] Leaders with a strong internal locus of control are also more task-focused in their coping style; taking direct action to alter problematic situations, rather than simply reframing the situation so it has less emotional impact on them.	steps may seem). Then map out how you can best use your strengths to influence these steps. • **Do not see criticism as a dead-end but a detour to somewhere better** When something does not go as anticipated, or you receive criticism on something you have worked hard on, it can be easy to react defensively. However, to improve and innovate, it is important not to let these opportunities to learn from criticism slip by.[31] Fine-tune your ability to detach yourself from the criticism and honestly assess the root of specific feedback or causes of certain outcomes. Is it internal? Could you have done something differently or better? Or is it external? Is it simply a case of bad luck? Does this person really just have an unfounded grudge, or is there something to be learnt and gained from what they are saying? The more you can correctly attribute your successes and failures, the more control you will take of what you can influence and change. By seizing every opportunity to accurately absorb the lessons, you will adapt quicker and perform better.

(*Continued*)

Key skill	Why it is relevant	How to develop it
2. Accepting reality: *the ability to face the reality of a situation, as it is, not as you wish it to be*	Leaders who are skilled in accepting reality do not shy away or wrestle against the truth. As author and adviser Scott Edinger stated, 'leaders can waste a lot of time, effort, and energy fighting reality'.[32] Whether it is a quarterly forecast that is much lower than the anticipated or a new competitor who has come in and massively disrupted the market. The quicker leaders can accept the circumstances as they are, the quicker they can deal with them effectively. As Carl Jung once wrote, 'we cannot change anything until we accept it'.[33] In today's fast-changing, unpredictable business environment, leaders cannot afford to force others to distort reality or fail to act because the situation is not what they would like it to be – or the truth not what they want to hear. This reality resistance only gets in the way of progress.	Accepting reality is not the same as being resigned to it. In fact, acceptance is about freeing yourself to move forward and deal with the situation in the most effective way possible. In psychology, this skill is referred to as 'radical acceptance'. Here are some initial tips on how to develop it:[34] • **Notice your resisting self-talk** The opposite of acceptance is resistance. When our brain is resisting reality, it is likely you will hear yourself saying, or obsessively thinking, things like: 'I can't believe this is happening!' 'This isn't fair'. 'It isn't right'. 'This can't be true'. Whilst this is often a natural reaction, it is important not to get stuck in the swell of resistant thoughts and the negative emotions they stir up (such as anger and bitterness). Notice these thoughts as they appear, breathe, relax your body, and focus on what you know and what is currently going on. Intentionally, try to shift towards thoughts such as:

Key skill	Why it is relevant	How to develop it
	Accepting reality is a key skill for leaders who wish to lead responsibly, move fast, and take effective action where necessary.	'It is what it is'. 'I can't change what's happened'. • **Let go of judgement and redirect your energy** Accepting reality does not mean you have to like it, condone it, or agree with it. All it is, is an acceptance of what is true now; the reality you are facing at that point in time. Avoid wasting energy judging the situation and lamenting what could or should have been. Focus your attention and energy on what you can do from this point forward to have the most positive impact on the future.
3. Strategic patience: *the ability to accept that meaningful goals take time to accomplish, and actively pursue progress*	Big, worthwhile goals are not accomplished overnight. Progress will inevitably take longer than you want it to, and way longer than you believe it should. Leading responsibly therefore requires patience.	To achieve meaningful goals, you must be prepared to play the long game and overcome setbacks. When you encounter a roadblock, it will be tempting to get frustrated, lose faith, and give up. Cultivating strategic patience will help you persevere and succeed in the long term.

(*Continued*)

Key skill	Why it is relevant	How to develop it
	The idea of 'patience' probably makes you think of someone sitting and waiting for something to happen; however, leading responsibly is not about passivity. Making a difference requires an active 'strategic' form of patience.[35] A leader with strategic patience understands that things do take time and they stay proactive in persisting towards their goal.	Here are a few top tips to help you stay patient and proactive: • **Hold your goal tightly and your plan lightly** Responsible leaders hold tightly to their goal (i.e. where they want to get to), but keep flexible in their plan (i.e. how they get there). As Prussian military commander Helmuth von Moltke is often quoted to have said: no plan survives first contact with the enemy. See your initial plan as just a hypothesis of the road you will take; a loose plan you will closely monitor, review, and adapt. Like any long journey, there will inevitably be roadblocks you did not expect but there will also be alternative paths that get you to the same destination. • **Reflect on your personal triggers** Tune in to what situations and circumstances spark your annoyance or frustration.

Key skill	Why it is relevant	How to develop it
Strategic patience (*Continued*)		Become skilled at noticing the earliest stirrings of impatience in yourself and, like a curious scientist, step back and reflect on what has really triggered that response in you. Once you have identified your triggers, research suggests two self-regulation strategies are particularly effective:[36] **1.** *Recognising the choice* – once triggered, it may feel like your behaviour and response is out of your control, but it is not. Whilst you may not have a choice in the situation you face, take a second to remind yourself that everyone has a choice on how to react to situations. **2.** *Reframing the situation* – almost all annoying situations can be reframed positively with a little effort. For example, a meeting with disgruntled employees could be reframed as a brainstorm for organisational improvements. Or, someone arriving late for an appointment can be viewed as a gift of unscheduled time to accomplish a few other quick tasks.

(*Continued*)

Key skill	Why it is relevant	How to develop it
4. Making short-term trade-offs for long-term gain	For decades, short-termism has dominated Western business practice, but gradually, the tide is turning towards a focus on longer-term value creation. However, embracing this new long-term outlook in practice is not easy. Business leaders must be able to deliver enough short-term returns for the business to stay successful in the present, whilst making the necessary choices, changes, and investments for the business to thrive in the future.	Over the course of 12 months, the World Economic Forum interviewed several C-suite leaders and uncovered the following tips around how to successfully make short-term trade-offs when striving for long-term value creation:[37] Here are the top two tips: **1. Stay vigilant to the megatrends and take relevant action** To drive long-term value, CEOs need to stay vigilant to how the world around them is changing. What might impact us as a business? What are the big challenges that need tackling? Where does it make sense for this business to step up and take responsibility? Crucially, this is about looking for relevant ways a business can act responsibly and play to the strengths within its existing and long-term strategy. For example, challenges that 'made sense' for

Key skill	Why it is relevant	How to develop it
Making short-term trade-offs for long-term gain (*Continued*)	In essence, leading responsibly requires leaders to be extremely skilled at balancing short-term trade-offs for long-term gain.	PepsiCo were reducing plastic waste and pivoting towards health and wellness. **2. Keep your communication detailed, coherent, transparent, and consistent** Do not communicate your long-term strategy in vague terms. The return expectations and time horizon of investments must be clearly articulated; with details dug into around how the transformations will be achieved, how investment decisions will be different, and how failures along the way will be navigated. The narrative around the long-term journey cannot be fluffy idealism; it must be a solid, compelling, and qualified narrative that engages people's hearts and minds. Furthermore, communication must be totally transparent. There should be no distinction between what different investors are told.

(*Continued*)

Key skill	Why it is relevant	How to develop it
5. Protecting the core of your business: *the ability to safeguard what aspects of the company shouldn't change*	In a business environment defined by change and disruption, it is important leaders tune into, develop, and protect the core of their business. Whilst it may be tempting to feel a constant pressure to change and transform every aspect of the company, responsible leaders also know what is important to hold on to. In *Built to Last* Jim Collins, emphasised the importance of a 'strong core',[38] showing how 'enduringly great companies know who they are, what they stand for and why they exist'. Similarly, professor Alex Hill flagged how leaders of centennial organisations (which have led their field for over 100 years) work hard to stabilise their core and safeguard what they stand for.[39]	Protecting the core of your business is not about sticking rigidly to a winning recipe; it is about understanding the fundamental identity of your organisation. Here are a few top tips around how to protect the core of your business: • **Get clear on your core ideology** As Jim Collins explained,[38] a company's core ideology is '*the base of continuity around which a visionary company can evolve, experiment, and change*'. Take the time to really reflect and get clear on the following 'big questions': Why does your business exist? What difference is it trying to make? What value does it create for society? What core values guide all decision-making? What ideas does your organisation stand for?

Key skill	Why it is relevant	How to develop it
Protecting the core of your business (*Continued*)	In this new era of business, all organisations will need to continuously transform, but leaders must be skilled at knowing what to change and what to protect. In a sea of change, it is stewardship of the stable core that will help leaders make informed decisions and keep evolving the business to be the best version of itself.	Only by everyone fully understanding the simplicity of what business you are in, what your business is and is not at its core, will you create an organisation that evolves, experiments, and holds true to itself. • **Translate the core into tangible operating principles** Values and purpose should not be abstract, or simply referred to loosely during executive away days. The ideology needs to be translated into tangible day-to-day operating principles that drive progress and guide decision-making throughout the business. The organisation should be examined at the most detailed level, exploring how the values and purpose come to life and play out in every aspect of people's experience with, and of, the company.

The Responsible Leader Continuum: How to Stay on Track

There is no such thing as a responsible business – there is only ever responsible people and responsible leaders who take action to set up and run an organisation in a responsible way. Responsible decisions and actions can seem like obvious choices with the benefit of hindsight and objective perspective. But, in the moment, when you are bearing the accountability for the business and people's livelihoods, leading in a truly responsible manner is far from easy.

Let us look at the various ways you can fail to act or 'walk the talk' when it comes to leading responsibly and the ways the moral duty of care can become overwhelming (see Figure 7.1).

Denial. Leaders stuck in denial are unwilling to acknowledge and deal with reality. In some instances, this may involve a flat-out denial of facts, reality, or the consequences and implications of that reality. However, denial may not always be so stark. It may also involve a leader admitting something is true but minimising its importance or accepting reality, and the gravity of the situation, but denying their own responsibility and role in it (instead opting to blame other people or outside forces).[40] Stark or subtle, denial puts the business at risk as it means a leader may refuse to address critical problems or make necessary changes, even despite overwhelming evidence of the urgency to do so. In a fast-evolving business environment, this

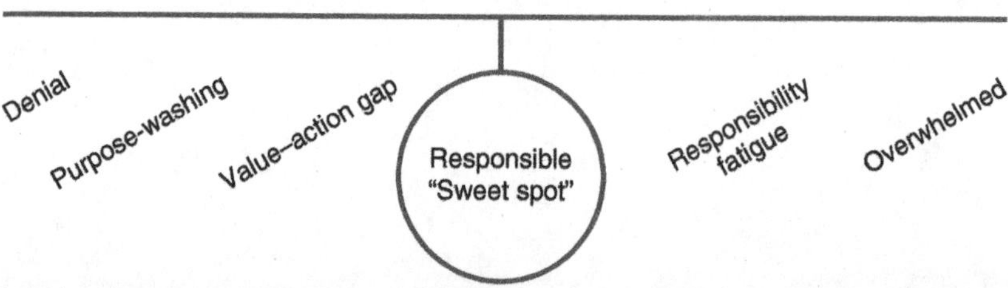

Figure 7.1 The responsible continuum.

is a particularly perilous trap and a common one for leaders of well-established organisations to fall into. After all, it is never pleasant to accept new realities, especially when the old realities seemed to work so well.

Staying future-fit top tips. The problem with denial is that you will not know you are trapped there. As author Richard Tedlow expressed, 'denial is not merely being wrong. Everybody makes mistakes. Denial is falling into a cognitive Bermuda Triangle. Everything is clear, yet you lose your bearings'.[41] Even the very best leaders can be in denial, as it is a common defence mechanism our brains use to shield us from external events and circumstances that would cause us distress and anxiety to acknowledge. As a senior leader, here are two ways you can avoid getting left behind in denial whilst the world moves on:

1. **Listen to middle managers.** As Andy Grove, Intel's former CEO, articulated in his book *Only the Paranoid Survive*:[42] 'when spring comes, snow melts first at the periphery, because that is where it is most exposed'. Consequently, whilst as a senior leader you may feel you have the best overall picture of what is occurring in and outside the business, do not be fooled. It is most likely the middle manager populations will first detect new realities and signs of change as they operate on the most exposed edges. It is therefore important to encourage those on the front-line to speak up honestly, preparing yourself to be receptive to uncomfortable news so you can keep connected to what is really going on.

2. **Be brutally realistic with yourself**. Sometimes senior leaders are required to accentuate the positives of a situation to keep morale and energy high in employees. However, this is only acceptable so long as you are confronting the full reality of the situation. Reflect on the part you are playing or could play

in exacerbating a situation; look at the data without overlaying any 'ifs', 'buts', or extenuating circumstances, and seek the opinions of those you do not necessarily like but respect. Talking to a skilful coach can also help shine a light on some of the realities you are avoiding, offering a safe space to identify and face what you fear most.

Purpose-washing. Doing the responsible thing, positively impacting society, and looking after the planet have never been so fashionable. The image of being a force for good is a compelling one, but it is also easily abused. 'Good-washing' or 'purpose-washing' is where leaders seize on this market change and opportunity by presenting their brand as if it serves a greater purpose and considers the triple bottom line (of people, planet, profit), when in reality it only operates to serve itself (i.e., to achieve growth and profit). In the 1960s, the Friedman doctrine outlined how the only responsibility a business has is to maximise returns for shareholders: a philosophy that is so pervasively ingrained in how companies operate, it is often hard for leaders to spot. For leaders who find themselves purpose-washing, responsibility remains narrowly focused on doing whatever it takes to 'keep the lights on', deliver results, and protect jobs. Responsibility, in the sense of tackling bigger societal issues and making a difference remains little more than a marketing tactic, a pretty shell of a strategy with very little substance to back it up.

Staying future-fit top tips. Most leaders do not set out to purpose-wash, they simply get swept up in the goodwill rhetoric and marketing opportunity. A narrative is created, an advertising campaign rolls out, perhaps even an innovative product, service, or CSR initiative is pushed . . . but it is all just jumping on the band wagon. Leaders need to avoid 'purpose' becoming a hollow buzzword to employees or marketing gimmick to clients; already 57% of consumers do not truly believe brands are living their stated purpose and it is only those businesses that truly transform their operating model who will continue to thrive and stay relevant.[43] To lead responsibly, make sure purpose does not start and end with the marketing department. Review the 'unglamorous' action the business needs to take, develop tangible goals, and pivot the entire way of doing things across the business so people–planet–profit becomes the lens through which innovation occurs and everyday decisions are made.

Value–action gap. Leaders just-off the sweet spot of responsible, know what they should do and what responsible actions are required from them. They get the importance of, and deeply value, responsible action that is good for the business and good for society. However, whilst they have the best intentions, their day-to-day leadership behaviours and crunch-point decisions fall short. This is known as the value–action gap: a phenomenon where people act in a way that contradicts or fails to support their values.[44] Leaders stuck here find themselves entrenched in old habits and routines. Despite plentiful knowledge and awareness of what changes are necessary, somehow, they find the short-term demands always take precedent. Ultimately, they fail to 'walk the talk' of change.

Staying future-fit top tips. All of us encounter the value–action gap in some area of our life, whether it is something small, like sticking to a new diet, or something big, like buying products that were manufactured in unethical working conditions. Years of research have proven knowledge and awareness are not enough to influence behaviour change for a variety of reasons.[45] 'Over-ruling', for example, is where our values conflict so that whilst we may hold certain long-term values, our specific actions often revolve around more immediate needs and values, such as comfort, money, and time. Similarly, there may be a lack of trust (e.g., not enough belief that certain changes will make a difference or protect the business in the long term). There is also the fact that we are often rewarded and praised just for announcing our intentions. Consequently, if announcing the positive intentions and worthy commitments alone is already enough to receive good publicity and attention, why do more? The goodwill benefits have been paid upfront. Here are two top tips to help you start closing the value–action gap:

1. **Demand and reward actions, not announcements.** Set a high standard for yourself and others in terms of what exactly is worthy of praise and recognition. Encourage and support commitments (that is a positive step in the right direction), but reserve rewards, compliments, and feelings of pride for actual accomplishments.

2. **Disrupt and unfreeze your habits.** The more we succumb to certain routines and ways of doing things, the deeper they embed. It is like you continue to grind a path for your future self, making the well-worn track ever deeper and easier to select. As psychologist Kurt Lewin once outlined, to change, we must overcome this inertia and unfreeze from our old behaviour.[46] One way to do this is to shock yourself: What are the real consequences of inaction? How much do I really care about those consequences? What risks am I taking by avoiding or delaying starting on this?

Responsibility fatigue. With more responsibilities resting on the shoulders of business leaders, there is an increased risk of moral distress and role conflict causing additional fatigue. Moral distress is when a leader knows an ethical dilemma is at stake, they know the right thing to do, but institutional constraints make it nearly impossible for them to pursue their desired course of action.[47] Over time, the frustration and anxiety caused by knowing what needs to be done but repeatedly feeling forced into incongruent actions can take its toll. Similarly, dealing with the constant tensions and the contradictory expectations that now accompany the duty of being a business leader can be exhausting. In many situations, the 'right answer' around what to do is not obvious, tough choices must be made in what feel like 'no-win' circumstances. The moral and ethical complexity here not only causes frustration but a nagging sense of self-doubt that, over time, eats away and adds to the sense of tiredness. In sum, embracing today's expansive level of responsibility can cause fatigue, both physically and mentally, resulting in anything from muscle soreness and headaches to increased illness and a more profound feeling of being completely burnt out and depleted.[48]

Stay future-fit top tips. People make different decisions when they are tired and leaders looking to have a meaningful, long-term impact will not achieve their goals on goodwill alone.[49] They need to be highly resilient, filling up their tank of resources, so they can keep taking positive action and making responsible decisions under pressure. Whilst it may seem basic, getting an adequate amount of sleep is a vital factor in leadership performance,[50] but one that is often casually dismissed. Business leaders are generally a sleep-deprived population, who struggle to detach themselves from work;[51] however, as the role of businesses in society ramps up and the pressure on leaders to create value for multiple stakeholders intensifies, detaching from work is only going to become harder. When it comes to sleep, being the sacrificial lamb will not help anyone. A lack of sleep makes it difficult to recall information, hard to pay attention to multiple tasks, lowers your emotional intelligence (i.e., making it harder for you to identify people's emotions, manage workplace conflicts, and avoid reacting in a 'knee-jerk' way, negatively and without thinking). It also makes it more likely your decision-making will be influenced by biases and prejudice.[52–54] It is therefore not the duty of a senior leader to learn to 'get by' on less sleep: starting at 6 a.m., working until late, worrying in the middle. It is the duty of a senior leader to maintain their performance by getting the sleep they really need. Do not fool yourself that five hours sleep each night is all you need. It is not. Make sleep a priority and develop healthy sleep habits, such as exercising in the afternoon, avoiding a large meal late in the evening, avoiding looking at screens one hour before you sleep, and, if necessary, keeping a notepad near so you can get those 'things you mustn't forget to do tomorrow' out from swirling around your head and onto paper.

Overwhelmed. The scale of the task being placed at a business leader's door is greater than ever. Constantly adapting and transforming the business to meet ever-changing market needs, delivering profit, looking after an array of different stakeholders, and positively contributing to societal-level challenges can feel like a seemingly insurmountable number of responsibilities. A job for a superhero. The demands have no doubt increased, but leaders often only have the same number of finite resources to draw upon (i.e., time, money, and energy). Consequently, the risk of senior leaders feeling overwhelmed is greater than ever, with survey findings showing how those in the C-suite are already 18% more likely to struggle with mental health issues than their employees.[55] At this end of the responsible spectrum, leaders feel stretched to their limits, like they have taken on more than they bargained for with the role and gone beyond what they can feasibly manage.

Stay future-fit top tips. Everyone feels overwhelmed from time to time, but as a senior leader in today's business context, the number and scale of challenges you are required to tackle may feel particularly daunting. Like the odds are stacked against your success. Luckily, there are a few ways you can avoid, or swim out of, that unhelpful whirlpool of despair and take back control:

1. **Remember you are a steward (not a saviour)** – as a senior leader, it can feel incumbent on you to solve all the organisation's issues, complete every major initiative that has started and deliver the organisation to its best possible 'ultimate end state' of being and performing. This is unrealistic. In your role, you are the temporary custodian of the business and have responsibility to both continue past progress and lay the foundations for future success. From this perspective, big, meaningful challenges will hopefully seem less daunting, and less optional. As stated by Rabbi Tarfon, 'It is not your duty to finish the work, but neither are you at liberty to neglect it'.[56]
2. **Remember you are not alone** – global climate change, coping with pandemics (and their knock-on consequences), tackling inequality. . . these are big challenges. But, you are not the only one grappling with them and trying to look for answers. More than ever, it is important to draw on your network and be part of mega-communities,[57] where leaders from governments, businesses, and non-profits come together and share ideas around possible solutions.
3. **Watch your narrative** – all too often our internal dialogue can talk us into feeling more overwhelmed than we are. Your inner voice starts saying things like 'it's too much' and 'I can't cope'. The more you tell yourself something, the more you believe it. Try to notice when the 'feeling overwhelmed' narrative starts to switch on in your head. Then gently challenge it. Thoughts and feelings are not always reality; would

someone looking objectively at your situation say you cannot cope? How true are those statements your mind keeps telling you when you look at the facts of what you have done and achieved?

Leading Daringly: Being Willing to Take Risks and Push Boundaries

In the *Oxford Dictionary* someone who is 'daring' is audaciously bold, they are:[58]

> *brave; willing to do dangerous or unusual things; involving danger or taking risks*

As the definition above highlights, leading in a daring way is about having the courage to push boundaries, to attempt what has not been done before, take risks, and carve out new territory. Becoming a daring leader is about embracing a highly entrepreneurial mindset, actively seeking out change and new opportunities, never being complacent, deeply believing anything is possible, and having the sheer stubborn tenacity to commit and accomplish it.

But can anyone truly *become* bold?

Throughout history and in various walks of life, we see examples of daring leaders. The documentary film *14 Peaks: Nothing Is Impossible*, for example, shows Nepali mountaineer Nirmal Purja lead his team to take on the quest to summit Earth's 14 highest mountains in just seven months. Purja's remarkable 'Project

Possible' was branded 'a unique statement in the history of mountaineering' by legendary alpinist Reinhold Messner; meanwhile his elder brother thought it so reckless they didn't speak for three months.[59] In the political arena there are also numerous examples of daring leaders in other forms. On 21 November 1985, for example, during what was dubbed 'the fireside summit', Secretary General Mikhail Gorbachev proposed to President Ronald Reagan that the Soviet Union and the United States collaborate on an initiative regarding nuclear fusion. A scientific project (later named ITER) proposed in the wake of the Cold War, which became the world's largest experiment to solve the world's energy problems and curb climate change by creating a machine that could literally 'bottle a star', reproducing on Earth the boundless energy that fuels the sun.

It is easy to read about the 'daring' leaders and see them as exceptions. Individuals who were simply born with astonishing levels of boldness and tenacity. However, while admittedly very few of us would take on climbing any of Earth's 8,000 meter summits (let alone all of them) or indeed dare to dream up the ITER project, leading in a daring way is not an innate gift granted to the few – it is a mindset and ability that can be cultivated.

Let us now explore what exactly it takes to become a daring leader...

The Five Ingredients of a Daring Mindset

Collectively, decades of research suggest there are five essential ingredients to a daring mindset:

Key ingredients	What	How
1. **Ability to set a clear, gut-grabbingly unreasonable goal**	Daring leaders set goals that are too difficult to achieve or, as Jim Collins, termed them 'Big Hairy Audacious Goals' (BHAGs).[38] These goals are very clear, do not require endless word-smithing, and fall just beyond the realm of reason, as Collins explains: *where prudence might say 'This is unreasonable', but the drive for progress says, 'we believe we can do it nonetheless'.* People do not get energised and fired up by grandiose, vague statements. In 1961, President Kennedy did not say, 'we're going to try to improve the space program'. People unite behind bold missions that are easy to grasp, time-bound, and challenge them to go beyond what is seemingly possible.	Look again at what you are asking your team, or workforce, to do; reflect on the big mission they have been set . . .ask yourself: • Could a five-year-old child understand this mission, with little or no explanation? • Does everyone agree it can be achieved? Or is its 'feasibility' hotly debated? • Does it have meaning and relevance for people in their day-to-day activities? • Is there a clear time frame committed to?
2. **High levels of optimism**	Research indicates that entrepreneurs are commonly high in optimism;[60] they tend to expect positive outcomes even when such expectations are not rationally justified.	Daring leaders are dissatisfied with the status quo and driven to deliver change, but their attitude is far from negative or grumbling.

Key ingredients	What	How
	While optimism is a double-edged sword (as we will explore later in the daring continuum), it is an essential ingredient of a daring mindset. To commit to and achieve an audacious goal, leaders need relentlessly high levels of optimism. They must stay positive and believe that the impossible can be made possible, inspiring people to push forward and tackle the challenges ahead. As Mary Barra, the Chairman and CEO of General Motors, stated, the power of optimism and belief should not be underestimated: *'if you think you can, you will'.*	To stay optimistic, focus on: • **Strengths (not deficits)** – do not spend time worrying about what is not there or you do not have yet. Focus your energy on the strengths, expertise, and assets you do currently have and how those can be wielded effectively. • **Solutions (not problems)** – reframe problems as inevitable puzzles to be worked through. Drill down into what exactly the key challenge is; review what has been tried before; explore new ideas, and figure out what partnerships and resources need to be in place to make the best solution happen. Pushing the boundaries of what has not been done before will require novel solutions to well-established issues. Keep building on each successive step.

(*Continued*)

Key ingredients	What	How
3. Willingness to fail	Doing something daring inherently requires an acceptance of risk and the chance of failure. But, as researchers Dr Fadil Çitaku and his colleagues assert:[61] *'very few people step-up to leadership without being frightened. We are by nature afraid of looking silly, of people not responding to our lead, of being wrong about where we are taking our organization; it's normal. Some aspiring leaders are never able to get over this'.* Consequently, whilst there is a lot written about the need to 'fail fast' and 'embrace failure', most of us remain petrified of it. Senior leaders may aim for an innovative culture that encourages failure and experimentation but still struggle to take risks themselves, in their role, with the business they are accountable for leading.	'Be willing to fail'. Easy to say, hard to do. Here are two things to remember to help you get comfortable with taking the chance on a bold dream: • **One of the biggest risks is standing still** – when committing to a daunting goal or pivoting your business model, it is easy to have doubts and imagine the worst-case scenario playing out. Thinking, 'What if I commit us to this and completely sink the business?' However, as Mark Zuckerberg, founder of Facebook, explained:[62] *In a world that is changing so quickly, the biggest risk you can take is not taking a risk...If you are stagnant and you don't make those changes, you are guaranteed to fail'.*

Key ingredients	What	How
	Daring leaders are not afraid to put their neck on the line and commit to something bold and meaningful. They are willing to take a chance, explore unchartered territory, make mistakes, and learn from those mistakes until their vision becomes reality. They are willing to go where others fear to tread.	• **Failure is rarely pervasive or permanent** (unless you are into skydiving) – the word 'failure' means to be unsuccessful in achieving one's goal. However, 'failing' is rarely as final or comprehensive as our minds like us to believe. In reality, 'failing' is often just a temporary state of adversity; a cycle of learning we need to go through in order to progress towards our goal. Rather than thinking 'am I prepared for this to fail?' reframe to 'am I prepared to try and learn?'
4. Decisiveness amidst ambiguity and doubt	Daring leaders have the courage to act where others may hesitate. They are willing to commit to a course of action, even when they only have partial information or lack 100% certainty.	Leading with conviction and committing to a decision is hard when the situation seems to be constantly evolving. There is always a temptation to delay; to wait just that bit longer for more information to emerge or total consensus to be reached. Here are some tips on how to stay daring and decisive:

(Continued)

Key ingredients	What	How
	Research shows that making a wrong decision is far better than making no decision and letting a lack of direction linger on. In fact, CEOs who make decisions earlier, faster, and with greater conviction (even amidst ambiguity and incomplete information) are 12 times more likely to be high performing.[63] As Theodore Roosevelt is quoted to have said: *'in any moment of decision, the best thing you can do is the right thing, the next best thing is the wrong thing, and the worst thing you can do is nothing'.* In a fast-changing landscape, the cost of making a wrong turn can seem huge; however, it is better to make a wrong turn than be frozen in the grips of indecision. To stay relevant and keep the business evolving, you must be willing to decide and commit. Moving with speed and conviction is better than making the perfect choice too late.	• **If you have 65% certainty on what the 'right' decision is – make the call.** Do not wait around for all the information to be nicely assembled so you can make the perfect choice. There will always be more information you could have, but as you wait for perfect conditions, the business drifts. Chances are you will miss the moment, deciding too little, too late. • **Do not seek consensus (give everyone a voice, not a vote).** It is very easy to get a unanimous vote to do nothing. People tend to be risk averse. Listen to others, hear people's views, but do not rely on decision-making by a committee. Daring decisions are inherently contentious. • **Once you have made the decision, commit (do not waffle or backtrack).** Nothing makes people lose faith in a bold challenge quicker than a leader who seems to waffle and backtrack once the goal has been announced. Do not

Key ingredients	What	How
		leave space for uncertainty to fester. Like a self-fulfilling prophecy, doubt will lead to failure. If people believe it is just 'pipe dreams', 'empty words', and 'never actually going to happen', they will not persevere when things get tough. They will give up at the first hurdle. Once you have committed, stay committed. Demonstrate that while 'the how' may have to flex, the ultimate goal will be achieved.
5. **Create a culture of experimentation**	Whilst it may take a lot of guts, sadly, it is not enough to 'throw down the gauntlet' and commit everyone to achieving a daring goal. Leaders also need to ensure they create an environment that gives that big goal the best chance of success. Pushing the boundaries of what is possible therefore requires far more than leaders simply repeating the phrase 'art of the possible' to people. They need to provide tangible resource and support and create an innovative environment, where fresh ideas and diverse thinking can flourish.	Review the culture within your organisation; explore whether it is an environment that supports people to achieve the 'seemingly impossible', and do industry-leading work, or, if it is a place where getting even the simplest task done is a painful process. Specifically, ask yourself, is this a culture where. . . • **. . .people are rewarded for trying out new ideas, testing possible solutions, taking risks, and failing?** (so long as their experimentation is purposeful, and they absorb the learnings)

(*Continued*)

Key ingredients	What	How
	As Theodore Levitt, professor at Harvard Business School, stated:[64] *'Organizations, by their very nature, are designed to promote order and routine; they are inhospitable environments for innovation'.* Daring leaders must overcome this inherent reality of big, established, successful organisations. They need to be great at removing the systemic blockers and bottlenecks, and work hard to create a culture where innovation and experimentation is enabled.	• . . .**cross-pollination of ideas and diverse thinking occurs?** (i.e., different perspectives, ideas, and concepts are encouraged and brought together, both within the organisation and from outside) • . . .**everyone has a clear understanding of the goals, objectives, and organisational context?** (with employees accessing the same level of information that owners receive, so they too can 'think like owners') • . . .**the resources for innovation are shielded from 'business-as-usual' logic and pressures?** (i.e., and resources are made available to innovation efforts, with efforts supported even though results may be uncertain. The organisation's performance engine, i.e., the structure that delivers predictable, short-term results for the business, does not prevent change by smothering the resources dedicated for innovation)

The Daring Leadership Continuum: How to Stay on Track

When you are at the helm of a large successful organisation, leading in the sweet spot of the daring mindset can be a real challenge. Most likely, you will slip towards risk aversion and caution; you will not want to be the one that sinks the ship that was sailing so well. The cautious path may feel safest, but ultimately, the dangers of stagnation are very real.

It is also important to acknowledge the perils of being too daring. In today's business environment, arguably being too daring is better than not being daring enough; however, over-optimism is more pervasive than you might think and can have a negative impact on your people and business. It is all about finding that sweet spot.

Let us look at how you can find yourself lured off course on the daring continuum (see Figure 7.2).

Thrill-seeking. Sensation seekers (or 'thrill seekers') crave new, complex, and intense experiences, and are willing to take on substantial risk for the sake of such experiences.[65] In the work setting, high sensation seekers can be both a blessing and a curse, especially when operating at senior leadership levels. On the plus side, leaders

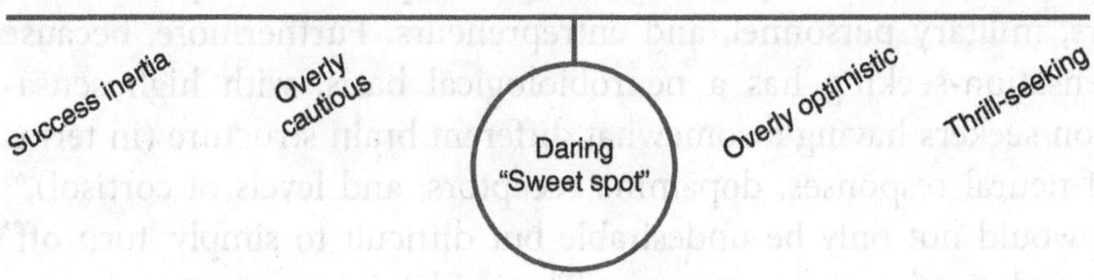

Figure 7.2 The daring leadership continuum.

with a high sensation-seeking personality type are often open to new ideas, unafraid to try new methods or products, are more creative, and generally boost innovation.[66] They thrive in environments that are ever-changing and unpredictable, actively 'shaking-things up' when things feel too mundane and repetitive within the business.

Whilst this may seem like the perfect personality type for today's fast-moving business context, there is a shadow side. Sensation-seeking senior leaders tend to have a casualness about control and rules, making them more likely to cut corners on compliance and other record-keeping functions, creating higher operational risk, which can harm the business and it's clients.[67] In times of high uncertainty and change, these leaders may also lack empathy for those in their workforce who are less sensation-seeking. They bull-doze through, inadvertently exacerbating the stress of those who have less tolerance for chaos, do not like surprises, and prefer to stick with what they know and are familiar with. Finally, at the most extreme end of this spectrum, leaders also inadvertently do damage to themselves, their career, their relationships, their business, and the livelihoods of others, in the addictive pursuit of new and ever-riskier thrills.[68]

Staying future-fit top tips. A high sensation-seeking personality is not necessarily a bad thing. Society relies on sensation seekers – they are often the first responders, firefighters, paramedics, police officers, military personnel, and entrepreneurs. Furthermore, because sensation-seeking has a neurobiological basis, with high sensation seekers having a somewhat different brain structure (in terms of neural responses, dopamine receptors, and levels of cortisol),[69] it would not only be undesirable but difficult to simply 'turn off' your desire for new experiences. That said, it is important to manage your sensation-seeking so it remains a positive rather than problematic. If you think you may be more towards the 'thrill-seeking' end of the daring continuum, here are three tips to help enhance your leadership performance:

1. **Curb your impulsiveness** – as a leader, avoid the temptation to get swept up into every new and exciting idea that comes along. Take a moment to pause, stop, think, and decide if the activity you are considering is worth the risk involved.

2. **Distinguish between novelty and risk** – typically, when we think of 'thrill-seeking' we think of risk, but the underlying drive behind sensation-seeking is for novelty, i.e. experience something new and different. Instead of assuming you always need to seek the next extreme 'high-risk high-reward' challenge, find ways to get your novelty fix without the risk attached. Seek diverse ways to try new things (i.e., new sports, new restaurants, different conferences, meet new people, form new partnerships) and add new elements to existing routines. Look for new opportunities at both a micro- and macro level; do not just default to more risky, extreme versions of your current activity.

3. **Increase your empathy** – do not assume everyone is like you or 'needs to be' to thrive in the current business environment. Be mindful that others have different personalities and preferences and that these too add value. Just as you might be good at driving change and innovation, low sensation seekers help keep the business operating by showing patience, being more inclined to take a long view, preserving what should be preserved, and protecting the business by remembering the rules. Get to know your team and their preferences. Appreciate the value difference brings. Remember that just as boredom and routine would stress you out, so too will chaos, novelty, and surprises cause anxiety for others.

Overly optimistic. Research suggests most people are highly optimistic most of the time.[70] We expect positive events in the future even when there is no evidence to support such expectations; for example, expecting to live longer than average and underestimating the likelihood of getting a divorce.[71] And, senior leaders are no exception. Research shows how typically our brains generate three positive illusions:[72] (i) 'above average' (we believe our skill set is above average and overestimate our positive traits), (ii) 'in control' (we believe our skill will determine the outcome of a plan and underestimate the role of chance and external factors), and (iii) 'good will come' (we believe we are more likely than other people to experience good outcomes and events, rather than bad ones).[73]

In moderation, these optimistic biases are healthy. Without them, nothing would probably ever get done. However, over-optimism can be perilous, causing leaders to severely underestimate the risks and a myriad of poor planning issues. In an organisational setting, these optimistic biases, alongside the usual business pressures, lead people to routinely overestimate how fast they can get things done, with many projects taking longer than planned and costing more than originally budgeted: a phenomenon known as the 'planning fallacy'.[74] Senior leaders also need to be particularly cautious of 'anchoring', where proposals that inevitably accentuate the positives to secure backing set the 'anchor', distorting all further analysis around those initial estimates. Of course, as a leader, you build in a certain level of contingency for overruns, but those contingencies are rarely enough because of where the initial anchor was placed. Over-optimism is therefore an easy trap for leaders to fall into and one that can be very damaging and costly to the business.

Staying future-fit top tip. Optimism has many benefits. It enables people to push boundaries, keeps employees motivated and focused, and helps teams stay resilient when confronting difficult situations.

However, when it comes to deciding whether or not to commit to a 'daring' goal, optimism needs to be balanced with a healthy dose of realism. One of the best ways to do this is to take an outside view.

- **Taking an outside view** – this process is about ignoring the details of the project at hand and examine the experiences of a class of similar projects. The challenge here is that many 'daring' projects by definition venture into unknown territory – they push the boundaries of what has been done before – so it is tempting for leaders to dismiss the value of taking an outside view, as the ambition feels so exceptional and alone in its class. However, no matter how unique the project may feel, examine the best comparisons out there. Take that time to look back and learn from the organisation's track record of similar initiatives; investigate how other companies carried out similar projects; search across industries to find those rough references. The comparison might not be perfect, but the exercise will provide useful insights and make your forecasts significantly more objective and reliable.

Overly cautious. In many organisations, heavily regulated industries, and government agencies, risk aversion is a positive. Caution keeps things operating safely and smoothly. As a leader in this setting, it is easy to justify overcautiousness as role modelling the 'safe', 'predictable', and 'responsible' approach required from everyone. Even in *Macmillan Dictionary*, caution is linked to the following synonyms: 'thorough', 'careful', 'systematic', and 'meticulous'. However, while undoubtedly, in some organisations, safe practice is and will always be paramount, overcaution can be a perilous mindset for senior leaders to find themselves stuck in.

Sticking with what has been proven to work, the time-tested solutions, and weighing up all the research and evidence available before deciding anything and, even then, only changing when there is an extremely compelling or unavoidable reason to do so is a dangerous default. It may feel like the 'safe bet' and safest way to lead, but in today's landscape, being so habitually risk averse is a major risk. By failing to act where required and continually seeking out more evidence to inform choices, leaders here not only risk missing out on key opportunities, but the lengthy delays will frustrate stakeholders and cause a dip in workforce confidence and enthusiasm.[75] What looks like the safest path, is a modern-day road to ruin.

Staying future-fit top tip. Overcaution is not a luxury leaders in today's business environment can afford. Often, it results in underinvestment in key strategic opportunities and sluggish responses to fast-changing markets and evolving customer needs.[76] Wariness and always waiting for someone else to leap first – the tempting 'fast second-mover' strategy – is itself a risky game to play. Instead of looking and waiting to make the perfect big move (or for someone else to), embrace a mindset of experimentation. As Jim Collins explains in his book *Great by Choice*: 'shoot bullets before cannonballs'.[77]

The ultimate vision and transformation may be big and bold, but the steps to get there can be small and experimental. Test out ideas, unproven processes, and new tools. Get people exploring whether a solution is viable. Keep the organisation moving forward towards its main mission by learning from a series of small, planned gambles. Do not get frozen by caution, thinking every step must be a big leap into the unknown.

Success inertia. When something has been very successful, it can be hard to find reasons to take risks and change it. After all, why mess with a winning formula? For leaders of large, well-established organisations, which have enjoyed decades of growth and profitability, this can be a real challenge. The momentum to just 'stick with what works' is huge; there is inertia to keep going in the same direction, with the same processes and ways of doing things. As T. Thomas, former chairman of Hindustan Unilever and Business Standard, once wrote:[78]

> *The inertia of success is a disease that companies have to be vigilant about, especially when they have a decade or more of sustained high performance.*

As organisations mature, bureaucracy and unnecessary policies and procedures slowly stifle innovation and entrepreneurial spirit. Once-living values and evolving methods of best practice harden into rigid rules and regulations. Processes shift from being a means to an end, to the ends in themselves, and they are followed not because they are effective and efficient but because they are well-known and comfortable – 'the way things are done'.[79] As senior leader, you can unwittingly find yourself part of the problem, holding on to past practices and worldviews that are no longer relevant. Alternatively, you might be very future focused, able to see the direction the organisation needs to take but struggling to get others on board.

Success inertia can also often masquerade in an active form, with management teams recognising changes need to be made early on, all being 'on board', and still finding that the flurry of initiatives fail to deliver meaningful transformation. What is happening is that old mindsets, well-established patterns of behaviour, the same tried-and-tested tactics are still being used. Consequently, rather than actions propelling the organisation forward in a new direction, leaders end up deepening the status quo, accelerating in an age-old direction.

Staying future-fit top tip. No matter how big or complex the company, it is the responsibility of both leaders and individuals throughout the organisation to maintain an entrepreneurial spirit; actively seeking change, evolving practices, questioning 'sacred cows', and driving innovation.

To help you counteract the pull of the past and overcome inertia to 'stay the same', here are five top tips:

1. **Challenge your strategic frames.** These 'frames' are the common assumptions and shared understandings people have of the business. In today's context, the pace of change means these frames will have to evolve more regularly. As a leadership team, do not be afraid to step back, check-in, and review 'the obvious': What business are we in? How do we create value? Who are our competitors? Which customers are vital? Which ones can we safely ignore?
2. **Hold your nerve.** When proposing something very bold to others in a well-established, highly successful organisation, be prepared for resistance and a massive amount of internal pressure to stay the same. Inevitably the proposal will feel 'too risky'. Withstand this pressure to fold or dilute your vision by staying connected to the evidence, the indisputable trends that are occurring, and the realities 'on-the-ground'. Hold your nerve by clearly and consistently communicating the rationale.
3. **Use propelling questions.** As Albert Einstein is quoted to have said: 'we cannot solve our problems with the same thinking we used when we created them'. Try igniting some fresh thinking and approaches by using some propelling questions. These questions pair bold ambitions with significant constraints to get teams thinking differently. For example, Scott Keogh, recalls how in 2006, Audi's chief engineer did not ask the team, 'How can we build a faster car?' but 'How could we win Le Mans if our car could go no faster that anyone else's?'[80] By adding constraints, you can often expand ideas.

4. **Just start.** When a grand vision or big goal has been dreamed up and put on the table, it is easy to find reasons to delay. You want to make it happen, but it is easy to wait for the perfect conditions: the right team, enough budget, a window when there is more time, or once another business-critical issue has been sorted. Begin today. Start removing obstacles. Set things in motion. Create some quick-win goals. Remember achieving big goals starts with small actions.
5. **Do not try to change everything at once.** You may think a complete overhaul of the business is needed, however, changing everything at once simply will not work. It will disorientate your people and your clients. Examine which processes and old formulas are most getting in the way of the transformation required and target them.

Notes

1. State of Green (2019). Denmark's green transition. *State Of Green Article.*
2. Christer Tryggestad (2020) Ørsted's renewable-energy transformation. *McKinsey Interview Article.*
3. Reguly, E. (2019). A tale of transformation: The Danish company that went from black to green energy. *Corporate Knights Article.*
4. Caldwell, C. and Hayes, L.A. (2010). Leadership, trustworthiness, and ethical stewardship. *Journal of Business Ethics* 96: 497–512.
5. Griffith, J., Connelly, S., Thiel, C., and Johnson, G. (2015). How outstanding leaders lead with affect: An examination of charismatic, ideological, and pragmatic leaders. *The Leadership Quarterly* 26: 502–517.
6. Rosing, K., Frese, M., and Bausch, A. (2011). Explaining the heterogeneity of the leadership-innovation relationship: Ambidextrous leadership. *The Leadership Quarterly* 22: 956–974.

7. Yonge, J. and Srinivasan, P. (2021). The CEO Imperative: How can today's leaders realize tomorrow's opportunities? *EY Article.*
8. Jay McCall (2020). COVID-19 Has Widespread, Overwhelming Impact on Digital Transformation. *Dev Pro Journal Article.*
9. Statistica (2020). Expected pace of digital transformation. *Survey Report.*
10. Buijs, J. (2012). The Delft Innovation Method a Design Thinker's Guide to Innovation. In *DS 71: Proceedings of NordDesign 2012, the 9th NordDesign Conference.* Denmark: Aarlborg University, 22–24.08. 2012.
11. Blandin, N.M. (2014). Leading at the Edge of Chaos. In *Transforming Public Leadership for the 21st Century* (pp. 152–167). Routledge.
12. Taylor, B. (2009). Recession Leadership: On Sinking the Boat, Missing the Boat, and Rocking the Boat. *Harvard Business Review.*
13. Avery, G.C. and Bergsteiner, H. (2012). *Sustainable Leadership: Honeybee and Locust Approaches.* Routledge.
14. Walters, A. (2019). The future of leadership; developing a new perspective. *EY White Paper.*
15. Raworth, K. (2017). *Doughnut Economics: Seven Ways to Think Like a 21st-Century Economist.* London, UK: Penguin Random House.
16. EY Global. (2018). Can a purpose, beyond profit, really drive results and long-term value? *EY Article.*
17. Hornby, A.S. and Cowie, A.P. (1995). *Oxford Advanced Learner's Dictionary (Vol. 1428).* Oxford: Oxford University Press.
18. Meyer, S. S. (2011). *Aristotle on moral responsibility: Character and cause.* Oxford, UK: Oxford University Press.
19. Bivins, T.H. (2006). Responsibility and accountability. *Ethics in Public Relations: Responsible Advocacy* 19–38.

20. Schmidtz, D. (1998), Taking responsibility. In David Schmidtz and Robert Goodin (eds.), *Social Welfare and Individual Responsibility: For and Against.* Cambridge, UK: Cambridge University Press.

21. Enoch D. (2012) Being Responsible, Taking Responsibility, and Penumbral Agency, in *Luck, Value, and Commitment: Themes From the Ethics of Bernard Williams,* Ulrike Heuer and Gerald Lang (eds.), Oxford, UK: Oxford University Press, 95–132.

22. Stolle, D. and Micheletti, M. (2013*). Political Consumerism: Global Responsibility in Action.* Cambridge, UK: Cambridge University Press.

23. Fahlquist, J.N. (2009). Moral responsibility for environmental problems—Individual or institutional? *Journal of Agricultural and Environmental Ethics* 22: 109–124.

24. Vincent, N.A., Van de Poel, I., and Van Den Hoven, J. (Eds.). (2011). *Moral responsibility: Beyond free will and determinism.* Berlin, Germany: Springer Science & Business Media.

25. Robertson, L. (2017). *Structure of Design, the: An Engineer's Extraordinary Life in Architecture.* New York, US: Monacelli Press.

26. Barnard, J.W. (2008). Narcissism, over-optimism, fear, anger, and depression: The interior lives of corporate leaders. *Univ. Cincinnati Law Rev* 77: 405.

27. Tyler, N., Heffernan, R., and Fortune, C.A. (2020). Reorienting Locus of Control in Individuals Who Have Offended Through Strengths-Based Interventions: Personal Agency and the Good Lives Model. *Frontiers in Psychology* 11: 2297.

28. Dumitriu, C., Timofti, I.C., Nechita, E., and Dumitriu, G. (2014). The influence of the locus of control and decision-making capacity upon the leadership style. *Procedia-Social and Behavioral Sciences* 141: 494–499.

29. Hamedoğlu, M.A., Kantor, J., and Gülay, E. (2012). The Effect of Locus of Control and Culture on Leader Preferences. *International Online Journal of Educational Sciences 4.*

30. Peyton, R.B., and Miller, B.A. (1980). Developing an internal locus of control as a prerequisite to environmental action taking. *Curr. Issues VI* 400: 193.

31. Glaze, S. (2021). *Staying Coachable: A Story with 4 Questions to Help You Thrive in Change, Keep Climbing, and Enjoy Relentless Improvement.* Atlanta, US: Sean Glaze.

32. Edinger, S. (2021). Good Leaders Know You Can't Fight Reality. *Harvard Business Review.*

33. Jung, C.G. (2014). *Modern Man in Search of a Soul.* UK: Routledge.

34. Cornell, A.W. and McGavin, B. (2005). The radical acceptance of everything: Living a focusing life. *Focusing Resources.*

35. Dorie Clark (2021). *The Long Game: How to Be a Long-Term Thinker in a Short-Term World.* Boston, MA: Harvard Business Review Press.

36. Comer, D.R. and Sekerka, L.E. (2014). Taking time for patience in organizations. *Journal of Management Development* 33: 6–23.

37. World Economic Forum and Baker McKenzie (2019). The Modern Dilemma Balancing Short- and Long-Term Business Pressures. *White Paper.*

38. Collins, J.C., Porras, J.I., and Porras, J. (2005). *Built to Last: Successful Habits of Visionary Companies.* Random House.

39. Hill, A., Mellon, L., and Goddard, J. (2018). How Winning Organizations Last 100 Years. *Harvard Business Review.*

40. Malle, B.F., Guglielmo, S., and Monroe, A.E. (2014). A Theory of Blame. *Psychological Inquiry* 25: 147–186.

41. Tedlow, R.S. (2010). *Denial: Why Business Leaders Fail to Look Facts in the Face--and What to do About it.* London, UK: Penguin.

42. Grove, A. (1999) *Only the Paranoid Survive: How to Exploit the Crisis Points That Challenge Every Company.* New York, US: Broadway Business.

43. Razorfish and VICE Media Group (2021). The truths, myths and nuances behind purpose. *Survey Report.*

44. Blake, J. (1999). Overcoming the 'value-action gap' in environmental policy: Tensions between national policy and local experience. *Local Environment* 4: 257–278.

45. Kollmuss, A. and Agyeman, J. (2002). Mind the gap: Why do people act environmentally and what are the barriers to pro-environmental behavior? *Environmental Education Research* 8: 239–260.

46. Lewin, K. (1947). Group decision and social change. *Readings in Social Psychology* 3: 197–211.

47. Kalvemark, S., Hoglund, A.T., Hansson, M.G., et al. (2004). Living with conflicts-ethical dilemmas and moral distress in the health care system. *Social Science & Medicine* 58: 1075–1084.

48. DeTienne, K.B., Agle, B.R., Phillips, J.C., and Ingerson, M.C. (2012). The impact of moral stress compared to other stressors on employee fatigue, job satisfaction, and turnover: An empirical investigation. *Journal of Business Ethics* 110: 377–391.

49. Timmons, S. and Byrne, R.M. (2019). Moral fatigue: The effects of cognitive fatigue on moral reasoning. *Quarterly Journal of Experimental Psychology* 72: 943–954.

50. Nowack, K. (2017). Sleep, emotional intelligence, and interpersonal effectiveness: Natural bedfellows. *Consulting Psychology Journal: Practice and Research* 69: 66–79.

51. Svetieva, E., Clerkin, C., and Ruderman, M.N. (2017). Can't sleep, won't sleep: Exploring leaders' sleep patterns, problems, and attitudes. *Consulting Psychology Journal: Practice and Research* 69: 80–97.

52. Barnes, C.M. and Watson, N.F. (2019). Why healthy sleep is good for business. *Sleep Medicine Reviews* 47: 112–118.

53. Ghumman, S. and Barnes, C.M. (2013). Sleep and prejudice: A resource recovery approach. *Journal of Applied Social Psychology* 43: 166–178.

54. Gujar, N., McDonald, S.A., Nishida, M., and Walker, M.P. (2011). A role for REM sleep in recalibrating the sensitivity of the human brain to specific emotions. *Cerebral Cortex* 21: 115–123.

55. Oracle. (2021). Global Study: C-Suite Execs Experienced More Mental Health Challenges Than Their Employees in Wake of Global Pandemic. *Survey Report*.

56. Pirkei Avot (Ethics of our Fathers). *Rabbi Tarfon* Chapter 2:16.

57. Gerencser, M., Van Lee, R., Napolitano, F., and Kelly, C. (2008). *Megacommunities: How Leaders of Government, Business and Non-Profits can Tackle Today's Global Challenges Together*. St. Martin's Press.

58. Hornby, A.S. and Cowie, A.P. (1995). *Oxford Advanced Learner's Dictionary (Vol. 1428)*. Oxford: Oxford University Press.

59. Tom Robbins (2021). Mountaineer Nirmal Purja: 'I'm sick of people saying things are impossible'. *Financial Times Article*.

60. Hmieleski, K.M. and Baron, R.A. (2009). Entrepreneurs' optimism and new venture performance: A social cognitive perspective. *Academy of Management Journal* 52: 473–488.

61. Çitaku, F., Ramadani, H., Zillioux, D., et al. (2020). Leadership, risk-taking, decision-making: The newest outcomes from the Science of Leadership. *American Journal of Leadership and Governance* 5: 40–53.

62. D'Onfro, J. (2016). Mark Zuckerberg: CEOs should take risks. *World Economic Forum Article*.

63. Botelho, E.L., Powell, K.R., Kincaid, S., and Wang, D. (2017) What Sets Successful CEOs Apart. *Harvard Business Review*.

64. Theodore Levitt (2002). Creativity Is Not Enough. *Harvard Business Review Article*.

65. Zuckerman, M. (1994). *Behavioral Expressions and Biosocial Bases of Sensation Seeking*. Cambridge, UK: Cambridge University Press.

66. Sunder, J., Sunder, S.V., and Zhang, J. (2017). Pilot CEOs and corporate innovation. *Journal of Financial Economics* 123: 209–224.

67. Brown, S., Lu, Y., Ray, S., and Teo, M. (2018). Sensation seeking and hedge funds. *The Journal of Finance* 73: 2871–2914.

68. Zuckerman, M. (2007). Sensation Seeking and Risky Behavior. *American Psychological Association.*

69. Frenkel, M.O., Heck, R.B., and Plessner, H. (2018). Cortisol and behavioral reaction of low and high sensation seekers differ in responding to a sport-specific stressor. *Anxiety, Stress, & Coping* 31: 580–593.

70. Lovallo, D. and Kahneman, D. (2003). Delusions of success. *Harvard Business Review* 81: 56–63.

71. Sharot, T., Riccardi, A.M., Raio, C.M., and Phelps, E.A. (2007). Neural mechanisms mediating optimism bias. *Nature* 450: 102–105.

72. Baumeister, R.F. (2010). *The Self.* Oxford, UK: Oxford University Press.

73. Taylor, S.E. and Brown, J.D. (1988). Illusion and well-being: A social psychological perspective on mental health. *Psychological Bulletin* 103: 193–210

74. Buehler, R., Griffin, D., and Ross, M. (1994). Exploring the 'planning fallacy': Why people underestimate their task completion times. *Journal of Personality and Social Psychology* 67: 366.

75. Walters, A.C. and Ramiah, V. (2016). Is it possible to be too risk averse? Considerations for financial management in the public sector. *Applied Economics Letters* 23: 1210–1214.

76. Dunn, S.L. and Jensen, J.D. (2021). Risk in Leadership and Management: Risk-seeking vs. Risk Averse. *International Journal of Business Administration* 12: 64–75.

77. Collins, J. and Hansen, M.T. (2011). *Great by Choice: Uncertainty, Chaos and Luck-Why Some Thrive Despite them all.* New York, US: Random House.

78. Thomas, T. (2013). T Thomas: Inertia of success. *Business Standard Article.*

79. Sull, D. (1999). Why good companies go bad. *Harvard Business Review.*

80. Barden, M. and Morgan, A. (2015). *A Beautiful Constraint: How to Transform your Limitations into Advantages, and Why it's Everyone's Business.* New Jersey, US: John Wiley & Sons.

CHAPTER 8
DEVELOPING AND EXPANDING YOUR LEADERSHIP IDENTITY

What makes us unique is our ability to be plural. To be many things. Identity cannot be identified once and for all, because it's about a long creative process, which is a life-times work. Who am I? What am I? I'm a collection of several parts of myself. Some I've been given, others I've chosen, and all I've experienced so far and also what I'm in process of becoming. My personal identity is still a work in progress.

—*Oum El Ghaït Benessahraoui, singer-songwriter*

Why Identity Is Important in Relation to Paradoxical Mindsets

Throughout Chapters 3–7, we have explored how to embrace a whole suite of seemingly contradictory leadership mindsets and behaviours. However, how you think and what you do is tightly woven into your identity. Certain preferences will have seeped into 'who you are' and your perception of how you add value in your role. Embracing this set of paradoxical mindsets will therefore inevitably require some recalibration of deeply ingrained beliefs and habits. It will require identity-level work.

Whereas previous chapters zoomed in on how to embrace each mindset, this chapter zooms back out: exploring how to expand your identity to embrace a whole suite of paradoxical mindsets into your leadership approach. Specifically, here we investigate what identity is (and is not), why integration of multiple identities is so important, the power of narratives, and finally how to go about the ongoing task of unravelling and expanding your leadership identity to enhance performance.

What Identity Refers To

To clarify, mindsets and identities are interlinked but not the same thing.

Whereas your mindset refers to 'what' (your beliefs, attitudes, values), identity refers to 'who' (your understanding of who you are). The mindset you have will guide your choices and actions and form part of who you are, but your identity is far broader.

Your identity is made up of a unique cocktail of factors, some of which you can change or influence (such as your job role, hobbies, life experiences, religion, and parental or marital status) and some you cannot (such as your race or age).[1] Identity also exists in subcomponents, such as your identity as a leader, coach, friend, or parent.[2]

Defining Terms

- **Mindset** refers to the set of beliefs, attitudes, and values that guide your actions; how you think, feel, and behave in any given situation.
- **Identity** is your understanding of who you are.
- **Leader identity** is the subcomponent of one's identity that relates to being a leader or how one thinks of oneself as a leader.

It is important to understand that embracing certain mindsets will not automatically shift who you are. The elements making up your identity are far more complex and wide-ranging for that. Instead, embracing these five mindsets is more of a fine-tuning and expanding exercise. It is about tweaking certain aspects that specifically make up your leadership identity to become more effective.

The Troublesome Myth of 'True Self'

There is a popular and romanticised image of identity, fuelled by writers and film producers, that each of us has a 'true self' buried somewhere inside. That people can somehow 'find themselves'. That their one 'true' identity is there underneath all along just waiting to be discovered, like a chest in a treasure hunt.

Unfortunately, the idea that each of us has a single, core, integrated 'true self' (just waiting to be discovered) is a myth.

Identity is plural. People have many selves. They have many different ideas about who they are and many versions of themselves that can be triggered or 'spotlighted', depending on the situation. As American philosopher and social psychologist George Herbert Mead explained, each of us contains 'a parliament of selves';[3] an array of different and potentially contradictory identities that can be 'animated' and 'foregrounded'.

A key aim of leadership development is therefore not to develop 'the self' but integrate multiple selves into your approach. The identity task being less of a 'treasure hunt' and more an 'ongoing cabinet reshuffle', with leaders required to continuously reflect on which of their identities need to be held 'more lightly' (or even let go of) and how the 'parliament of selves' can be added to and enriched. In other words, how your identity repertoire can be expanded so there is more to draw on; more knowledge, more resources, more capabilities, more 'selves' that enable you to be adaptable and effective as a leader.

The Ability to Integrate Multiple Identities Is a Predictor of Leadership Success

Our 'selves' can be different and even contradictory in nature. The five paradoxical mindsets are an example of this – all are necessary components of effective leadership, all are possible to embrace, but they are seemingly contradictory in nature, which poses a challenge. You do not want to flick between mindsets, with people never sure which 'you' will enter the room or join the meeting.

Consequently, it is not only important to expand but to integrate. Like those images created of people's faces, made from a mosaic of many smaller photographs of faces, each 'self' must be woven into the bigger picture; each element adding to the general understanding of oneself. This work of incorporating new identities and perspectives into your existing identity is referred to as 'identity integration'.[4]

Is it worth the effort? Yes. Research shows that being able to integrate multiple identities is a predictor of leadership success.[5] Specifically, identity integration is a predictor of more adaptive decision-making,[6] greater well-being,[7] more successful adjustment after life changes,[8] and enhanced creative performance.[9] Furthermore, integration of multiple identities enables leaders to adapt effectively to changing environments.[5]

Expanding to embrace multiple, seemingly contradictory, identities is a fundamental part of modern-day leadership development. By increasing the components within your identity, by making yourself more multifaceted, you maximise your chances of success and make high performance (in all its forms) inevitable.

Identity Is Not Fixed, but Continuously Created, Shaped, and Spotlighted

So far in this chapter, we have discussed how:

1. your identity is not singular but plural

2. integrating multiple, seemingly contradictory, identities will enhance your leadership performance.

Before we dig into how to expand and integrate different leadership identities, let us first get clear on how our identities form and evolve.

Much like the 'true self' myth, it can be comforting to think of our identity as something solid and unchanging. However, our identity is not fixed like a rock but ever evolving and interacting with the conditions around us (perhaps more like an octopus). It is important to remember that 'the self' is both continually shaped (for example, by our interactions with other people) and continually spotlighted in a different way, depending on our environment and context (i.e., different situations will trigger a different version of the self to surface).

Research and Psychology: the 'Phenomenal Self' in the Spotlight

In psychology, the contextual nature of identity, the idea that different aspects of the self can be activated and 'spotlighted' in our awareness depending on the situation is referred to as 'the phenomenal self'.[10] It is something everyone has experienced in some form; for example, a boy in a room full of girls will be more constantly aware of being a boy than if he was in a crowd of boys, just like a Black Jamaican-born American female leader will be more constantly aware of her gender, race, and ethnicity if working in a team predominantly full of white American men.

Identity is highly contextual. It shifts and spotlights depending on the environment you are in. How you think, feel, and act, what you tap into from the vast store of beliefs and self-knowledge will all be adjusting, or feel highlighted, depending on the particular setting or situation you are in.

In terms of how our identity is shaped, social psychologist Roy Baumeister explains how your perception of 'selfhood' will continually be:[11]

- **shaped by what you 'know' of yourself.** This is sometimes termed 'reflexive consciousness' and refers to your self-awareness and the knowledge you build up and store about yourself
- **shaped by others.** Your identity and sense of self is in part socially constructed, based on the people you know and interact with. 'Who you are' will be continually influenced by 'who you know': the role models you absorb, the interactions and relationships you have with other people
- **shaped by our choices and what we do.** The choices you make and control you exert over your life will also be continually informing and shaping your identity. Choices and actions show 'the self at work' and add to your understanding of yourself. For example, how you react to unprecedented situations or whether you follow through on commitments.
- **shaped by the stories we tell.** As discussed in the next section, identity is also shaped by the stories we tell (both ourselves and others)

Figure 8.1 provides a comprehensive model of all these elements that shape how identity continuously evolves.

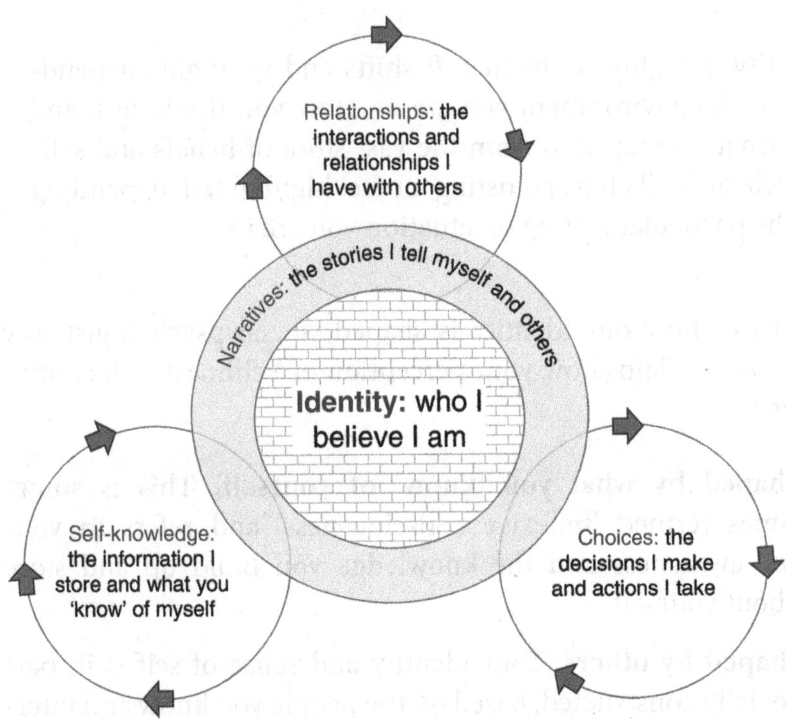

Figure 8.1 How identity continuously evolves.

Research and Psychology: 'The Barnum Effect' – Our Vulnerability to Accept Almost Any Personality Feedback

Worryingly, the multifaceted nature of identity mixed with our vast store of self-knowledge can leave us overly pliable in our self-views. Studies have shown people are willing to accept random feedback on their personality, if they believe the 'analysis' applies only to them, is conveyed by a perceived authority or expert, and if descriptions of themselves contain mainly positive traits.[11] For example, if a report tells you 'you have a tendency to be critical of yourself' or 'you prefer a certain amount of change and variety and become dissatisfied when hemmed in by restrictions and limitations' you may be willing to think this is correct, storing it as valuable insight about yourself. But in fact, the statement could apply to anyone.

In psychology, this willingness to accept random feedback relating to ourselves is known as the 'Barnum effect'.[12] But does it mean all personality feedback should be ignored?

Not quite. Some personality tests are scientifically validated and do help shine a light on certain preferences, but it is healthy to exercise caution. Any 'insight' into who you are should be viewed critically and held lightly. When reading personality feedback, step back and think: Is this statement really that specific or is it something vague that could apply to anyone? What is the level of rigour and expertise behind this 'test' or measure? Is this insight mainly feeding my need for approval by using mostly positive statements, with a few negative ones sprinkled in for credibility?

Insight reports into 'who you are' will also inevitably contain some form of presentation bias, as we answer in line with who we wish to be and how we want to be perceived by other people, based on our idealised self. It is also important to be aware that even the most rigorously validated personality tests only ever flag preferences, offering a guide of where you are most comfortable and what behaviours will feel most natural to you and require the least conscious effort. They do not set limits on what you can do or state that you can only operate in that way.

(*Continued*)

All this matters because a core tenet of paradoxical leadership is that to be effective as a leader, you cannot simply stay in the comfort zone of your preferences. To adapt and perform, you will need to embrace what is uncomfortable, even seemingly opposite, to your natural preferences.

The key takeaway message is therefore any feedback on who you are should be absorbed with caution and held lightly.

Narratives: How Identity Is Built Through the Stories We Tell

Our relationships, choices, self-knowledge, and current situation all continuously shape and influence our identity. But the most pervasive influence of all comes from the stories we tell ourselves. As author Patrick Rothfuss articulates:[13]

> *Everyone tells a story about themselves inside their own head. Always. All the time. That story makes you what you are. We build ourselves out of that story.*

The stories we tell ourselves are immensely powerful. They help us make sense of the world, of our own actions and emotions, of the events that happen to us. Storytelling is an intrinsic part of being human; it is the ongoing process by which we sculpt our understanding and identity. For example, you may tell private, personal stories to help a new romantic partner get to know you. Some of the narratives you choose to tell will be 'classics' (i.e. you have repeated in various forms throughout your life); for example, around where you grew up, where you have lived, key experiences you have had, or your career history. Whilst other stories will be woven in the moment or 'classics reworked' to portray a certain image, perhaps intentionally emphasising elements of your interests or values, or prompting a chapter of your life to be viewed in a specific way. Research has even shown that when people present themselves a particular way to strangers, their understanding of themselves shifts to be in line with that presentation.[14] In other words, providing the narrative is convincing, the individual's identity shifts to more closely resemble the version the other person had seen.[15]

Whilst it is tempting to think of these stories as factual points of reference about us, they morph all the time. The stories we tell ourselves (and others) are fluid and changeable. Problems come when we repeat certain narratives about ourselves so often that we begin to treat them as facts. For example, you might repeatedly tell yourself and others, 'I'm no good at public speaking', 'I don't do politics', 'I'm not here to be liked', or 'I'm no good at networking', excusing yourself from trying or expanding your approach and skill set based on 'facts' about who you are.

As discussed earlier, successful leadership requires the crafting and integration of multiple identity narratives. It is not enough to enact a fixed set play around who you are. Thriving in an unpredictable and changing world hinges on an ability to expand and adapt. It is therefore vitally important to pay attention to the stories you tell yourself every day and be aware of the ones that keep us fixed in the same patterns of thought and behaviour.

Leader to Leader

For an incredibly shy child, who always felt like an outsider looking in, Neil Basu has had an exceptional leadership career. Despite claiming his natural preferences to be 'the polar opposite of every senior police leader in history', Neil has stepped up to take on the toughest roles, leading at the highest level in the fields of anti-corruption, gangland violence, organised crime,

(*Continued*)

and, most recently, as the UK's Head of Counter-Terrorism. Over the years, Neil has learned to both embrace and expand his preferences, articulating how: 'your preferences are not you. You are capable of changing your preferences. All the best leaders have to be able to do it all, even if it feels incredibly uncomfortable'.

Personality assessments throughout his career have consistently flagged Neil as a 'mediator', indicating him as someone who is introverted, unassuming, and highly empathetic – always looking to understand, listen to, and support those around him. In his own words, a profile 'that would have made me a counsellor or a vicar not a command-and-control specialist who deals in critical incidents'. But, as Neil explains, to be an effective leader, you need to be able to adapt yourself and your mindset 'because the circumstance in front of you mean you can't just do what you'd normally do, which [for him] is sit everyone down and try to make them feel better about themselves'.

Just as Neil's strength as a leader has been his ability to always stand up and be counted for what he believes in, his Achilles' heel has been a tendency to give people 'third chances'. It was not until quite late in his career as a chief officer looking after a critical side of policing that a pivotal moment required Neil to kick the habit and expand his mindset and approach:

'I had two very senior, very highly paid people in my command chain who were warring, which makes it very difficult to achieve anything. I really liked them both. They both had massive strengths, but they were destroying each other. They were going to ruin each other's careers if they weren't careful'.

Given the seriousness of the situation and the gravity of the task, the special operations police perform in protecting the public from threats, Neil did not have time and could not afford to take the softly, softly approach. 'I sat the two people down and said "I'm going to fire one of you. You two decide which one of you is going to be fired. But, if you can't work together – I'm going to fire one of you, and it's that simple. Go away, sort your lives out and come back to me when you've made a decision collectively on who it's going to be"'.

What Neil wanted to do was try to make everyone feel good, throw his arms around them both, and help them work out their differences. But, as Neil described 'when you're under stress there's a difference between how you want to react and how you have to react'; this situation required him to expand his approach, embracing a tough strategy and brutal honesty. As he states, 'you can't be the lovely collaborator all the time, if you do that for every single problem it just won't work'.

In the end, the two officers 'worked it out, played nicely, and one got promoted'. But, looking back, Neil wishes he had expanded his approach sooner, stating: 'there had probably been other times in my career where my team had suffered, and our performance had suffered because of my tendency to wait and give people third chances. . .perhaps hindering performance in ways I'll never fully know'.

As Neil outlines, it is so important to hold personality assessments lightly: 'if you're fixed and you're never prepared to grow, and people keep giving you profile assessments and saying, "that's what you're like", you'll end up like that. You'll not adapt and lead effectively'. As Neil explains, leadership development does not stop when you get to a certain level of seniority, there is no point where it becomes more a case of simply putting existing knowledge and skills into practice:

(*Continued*)

'Your leadership journey is one of constant self-reflection, improving, and adapting yourself. And, if you're capable of doing that you're going to be a good leader. You'll be a good leader because you'll self-reflect, and you'll realise you are not a one trick pony. You are not what the psychologist is telling you, that's just your preference. You have the ability to change yourself and get the results you need'.

Quick Recap

Identity is a big topic and we have covered quite a lot in a short space of time (much like a tour bus driving past key landmarks at 90 miles and hour).

The four main things to take away about identity are:

1. **identity is plural** – like a kaleidoscope, your identity will have many different facets to it
2. **expanding your identity will help you succeed** – being able to expand your identity and integrate multiple, seemingly conflicting, 'selves' will boost your performance
3. **identity can and does change** – who you are is continuously being created and shaped
4. **narratives can trap you** – by telling and retelling the same stories about yourself, you can become trapped in the same limited patterns of thought and behaviour.

The question is therefore not 'Should I embrace all these paradoxical mindsets?' or 'Is it possible to?' but 'How do I make it happen?'

Let us find out. . .

Embracing All Five Mindsets: How to Develop and Expand Your Leadership Identity

The first thing to mention about how to embrace all five paradoxical mindsets into your leadership identity is this: do not try. It is too much. You simply cannot walk around with a big checklist of all the things you should be 'mastering' all at once.

Embracing these mindsets and expanding your identity is a gradual process, more like cooking a risotto than a stir fry. Pick one or two areas of focus that will have the most impact on your leadership performance, experiment with them, gradually work in some new habits. . . then, when balancing a certain paradox feels more natural, have a look at what else could use adding in. Just like a risotto, you will always need to keep tending the paradoxical mindsets you have already worked on, but over time, you can work on other elements and gradually feed more thinking and approaches in.

Alongside not attempting to develop all five mindsets at once, the second thing to mention is that you are not starting from scratch. As a senior leader, you will have already spent years cultivating your leadership approach and identity, very successfully. But, in an era where so much is required from leaders, much is put at risk when learning is considered done or no longer necessary. You will have certain leadership strengths, valuable habits, core values, certain preferences (a few inevitably being overplayed), and some development areas that have long been avoided or dismissed. This is not about building a 'new you' for a new era; it is a process of harnessing, fine-tuning, and adding to what already exists.

The final point to mention is that this will be uncomfortable.

When people talk about leadership development, they will often use words like 'growth' and 'progress'. But true development is not just about constructing, it also requires a level of uncomfortable 'unravelling'. It requires the discomfort of 'letting go', 'shaking up', and 'experimenting'. This is especially true when it comes to embracing the five mindsets and leadership development work that drills down into identity-level change. In psychology, this work is referred to as 'identity undoing'.[16] To be clear though, it is not about 'undoing' in the sense of destroying or ruining something, more an acceptance that to expand, you will need to open up, untie, and release your hold on certain aspects of yourself.

To help you get started, below are the next steps to take, as you begin your journey towards embracing all five paradoxical mindsets.

Step 1: Find a Coach: start building insight into your current narratives and 'possible selves'

Undoing and expanding your identity to embrace the paradoxical mindsets will be difficult and complex. It Is impossible to do this level of deep identity work alone – you will need support from a skilled coach to help you.

Having read through the mindset chapters, with your coach reflect on what stood out and really resonated with you: Is there a particular mindset you find harder to embrace? a continuum trap you fall into a lot? Alternatively, reverse-think it: Is there a challenge you are struggling with at the moment and a paradoxical mindset you could apply to the situation to broaden out your thinking and options around what to do?

Once you've sparked the discussion and started applying the mindsets to your own day-to-day world as a leader, a coach will be able to support you in surfacing the motivations and assumptions beneath your go-to leadership approach. Identifying, exploring, and unravelling the narratives that currently bind you, specifically helping you to:[5]

- **build awareness of your internal scripts** – shining a light on the narratives that currently shape your leadership identity, exploring deep-rooted beliefs and assumptions through the process of inquiry and mirroring
- **re-author your leadership narratives** – enabling you to step outside your experience, get a different perspective, and see your story in a more objective way; reflecting on which narratives are currently helping, or limiting, your performance
- **explore other 'possible selves'** – helping you to connect the dots between your existing identities and the other 'possible selves' you could embrace. Here you envision the leader you would like to become; opening up possibilities for your identity and surfacing the values you need to connect to in order to realise that vision.

It is important to remember that whilst a coach can support you, challenge you, stimulate reflection, and provide a container environment (where you can explore and face anxieties that arise), they cannot own anything for you. Identity undoing and expansion is difficult; so it will be tempting at times to just want 'the expert' to tell you what to do and give you a simple answer. But no one else can own this for you. You need to own it as a process. Only you can figure out who you are as a leader and who you need to be.

Step 2: Identity undoing: shake it up, let it go, experiment

Research in leadership development suggests that there are three key stages to identity undoing and expansion:[15]

1. shaking up
2. letting go
3. experimenting.

The narratives work you do with your coach should sit within this broader process. In the table below, each of the stages is explored in more detail with an outline of how to work through them.

Stage	What is it about?	What should I be doing?
1. Shaking up	This stage is about having your leadership identity disrupted and unsettled. Over time, with a track record of success, it will be comforting to think that you have your recipe for leadership nailed down. This part of the process is about 'shaking things up', taking an honest look at 'who you are as a leader', surfacing your behaviour patterns, habits, and blind spots.	Be open to your coach asking you agitating 'killer questions', such as: • I notice you take on *x* role or seem to embrace *x* mindset a lot as a leader; what does that give you? • What do you fear you will lose if you do not think and behave in the way you do currently? *(N.B.: Leadership identity roles such as 'the pacesetter', 'the knower', 'the diplomat' may be linked to specific areas of certain mindsets.)*

Stage	What is it about?	What should I be doing?
2. Letting go	'Letting go' suggests this stage is about discarding parts of your identity, but it is not quite that. When it comes to embracing paradox, it is less about discarding aspects of yourself and more about releasing your tight grip on certain identities in order to expand and embrace others. Referring back to the 'parliament of selves' idea, it is about no longer letting one approach or a narrow combination of identities constantly 'have the floor' and take up all the airtime.	One of the scariest aspects of the process is releasing and recalibrating parts of your leadership identity (parts that define you and have led to success). Here your coach should help you explore: • What elements of your leadership identity are you holding on too tightly to? • What impact do those overplayed preferences have on you and those around you? • What part of who you are, or what you value, needs to shift or expand? And how? • How else could effective leadership look?

(*Continued*)

Stage	What is it about?	What should I be doing?
3. Experimenting	Identity work is not about grand, dramatic gestures and massive shifts. This work is gradual and targeted. Having identified what might need to expand and adjust, this stage is about getting specific and experimenting: identifying a few key behaviours and committing to test them out. It is about playfully dipping your toe in the water of change.	The secret to successful change is starting small. Work with your coach to identify the following: • What other mindsets or roles, could you try on? • What experiments might you run? • What small actions could you take that would help you move in the direction you need? Once you have drilled down into the behaviours you would like to try out, commit to action. Do not be vague – think of a specific situation coming up and state when and where you are going to try those behaviours out.

Step 3: Repeat the Process

Identity undoing, through expansion and integration, is an ongoing process. It is not about shedding your identity and becoming something completely new. It is about expanding your identity, in an authentic and gradual way, to continually embrace new ways of thinking and operating.

This is therefore not a one-off exercise and there is no finished state. Evolving yourself and your self-narrative so that you can become a truly adaptable leader is a continuous and dynamic process. No matter how senior you are, there is always more to learn and subtle recalibrations to work on.

Your identity will either be evolving or entrenching in. This is a call to make that process more conscious.

Concluding Remarks: The Challenge of Being Adaptably Authentic

Embracing these five mindsets raises an overarching paradoxical challenge around how you can be, as authors Rob Goffee and Gareth Jones put it:[17] adaptably authentic.

Specifically, you are probably thinking:

- How can I be 'both/and' on all these elements whilst maintaining a sense of integrity and authenticity?
- How can I demonstrate consistency in who I am (helping others to know who their leader is and is not, who they are dealing with and working for), if my mindsets are so varied and complex?
- How can I be both 'true to myself' and so 'wide-ranging'?

As discussed in Chapter 2, no one wants a Jekyll and Hyde type leader – who flits between two elements of a mindset, dialling one up and the other down depending on the situation. Navigating paradoxes is not about flip-flopping between but embracing both elements in every moment. However, this question of authenticity runs deeper than the habit of adopting a 'both/and' approach. This is a fundamental question about how to be authentic and 'yourself' whilst being expansive and adaptable.

As this chapter has alluded to, the answer lies in the fact that leading authentically is about way more than simply 'being yourself' and following your natural preferences. For one thing, 'yourself' is multifaceted and, for another, authentic leadership is not about hooking on to a single unchanging style or persona that you subsequently roll out in every situation. As author and psychologist Dr. Karissa Thacker writes in her book *The Art of Authenticity*:[18]

> *We do well by being true to our multiple selves across the many contexts in which we live and work.*

Authentic leadership is therefore not about fixing yourself and your identity in stone. It is about embracing and expanding all elements of who you are and who you can be, with intention and care, so you can move beyond your natural preferences and skilfully respond to novel situations.

Notes

1. Gardenswartz, L., and Rowe, A. (2003). Diverse teams at work: Capitalizing on the power of diversity. *Alexandria, Va: Society for Human Resource Management*.
2. Day, D.V., and Harrison, M.H. 2007. A multilevel, identity-based approach to leadership development. *Human Resource Management Review* 17: 360–373.

3. Mead, G.H. (1934). *Mind, Self, and Society.* Chicago, IL: The University of Chicago Press.

4. Aron, A., and Aron, E.N. 1997. Self-expansion motivation and including other in the self. In S. Duck (Ed.), *Handbook of Personal Relationships: Theory, Research, and Interventions,* (2nd ed.): 251–270. Hoboken, NJ: John Wiley & Sons Inc.

5. Yip, J., Trainor, L.L., Black, H., et al. (2020). Coaching new leaders: A relational process of integrating multiple identities. *Academy of Management Learning & Education* 19: 503–520

6. Hannah, S.T., Balthazard, P.A., Waldman, D.A., et al. (2013). The psychological and neurological bases of leader self-complexity and effects on adaptive decision-making. *The Journal of Applied Psychology* 98: 393–411.

7. Thoits, P.A. 1983. Multiple identities and psychological wellbeing. A reformulation and test of the social isolation hypothesis. *American Sociological Review* 48: 174–187.

8. Iyer, A., Jetten, J., Tsivrikos, D., et al. (2009). The more (and the more compatible) the merrier: Multiple group memberships and identity compatibility as predictors of adjustment after life transitions. *British Journal of Social Psychology* 48: 707–733.

9. Steffens, N.K., Gocłowska, M.A., Cruwys, T., and Galinsky, A.D. 2016. How multiple social identities are related to creativity. *Personality and Social Psychology Bulletin* 42: 188–203.

10. Jones, E.E., and Gerard, H.B. (1967). *Foundations of Social Psychology.* New York, US: Wiley.

11. Baumeister, R.F. (2010). The self. In R.F. Baumeister and E.J. Finkel (Eds.), *Advanced Social Psychology: The State of the Science* (pp. 139–175). Oxford, UK: Oxford University Press.

12. Meehl, P. E. (1956). Wanted—a good cook-book. *American Psychologist,* 11, 263–272.

13. Rothfuss, P. (2010). *The Name of the Wind: The Kingkiller Chronicle: Book 1*. London, UK: Hachette UK.

14. Jones, E.E., Rhodewalt, F., Berglas, S., and Skelton, J.A. (1981). Effects of strategic self-presentation on subsequent self-esteem. *Journal of Personality and Social Psychology* 41: 407.

15. Schienker, B.R., Dlugolecki, D.W., and Doherty, K. (1994). The impact of self-presentations on self-appraisals and behavior: The power of public commitment. *Personality and Social Psychology Bulletin* 20: 20–33.

16. Nicholson, H., and Carroll, B. (2013). Identity undoing and power relations in leadership development. *Human Relations* 66: 1225–1248.

17. Goffee, R., and Jones, G. (2015). Why should anyone be led by you? With a new preface by the Authors: What it takes to be an authentic leader. *Harvard Business Review Press*.

18. Thacker, K. (2016). *The Art of Authenticity: Tools to Become an Authentic Leader and your Best Self*. New Jersey, US: John Wiley & Sons.

INDEX

Page numbers followed by *f* refer to figures and *t* refer to tables.